What people are saying about *With*

"It reads like an adventure story.

As has so often happened in the ᵖ

proved to have little to do with writing talent. Michelle Daly has a gripping story to tell, and she tells it simply. To say *With a Little Help From My Friends* is touching is an understatement. It was far from easy, but she makes the whole thing a story of excitement and triumph over the various odds that presented themselves with regularity."

~ Maeve Binchy

"I'm so glad that Michelle Daly wrote all of this down and told the truth about how raw and difficult it was. She is so brave and eloquent."

~ Bobbi Sheahan, columnist for *SI (Sensory Issues) Digest Magazine,* and regular contributor to *Autism Asperger's Digest*

"Congratulations, *With a Little Help From My Friends* is excellent and I thoroughly enjoyed reading it."

~ Anne Robinson

"*With a Little Help From My Friends* demonstrates what can be achieved if you have faith in the person, determination in your soul and love in your heart. This book is a must read for all learning disability nurses, and a source of inspiration for warrior mums and dads out there. Thank you for sharing your story with us."

~ Helen Laverty, Health Lecturer,
Nottingham University

"I have just finished Michelle Daly's wonderful book, *With a Little Help From My Friends* and I must say it was a terrific read from start to finish. It was informative, touching, a page-turner, inspirational, all anyone could want from a book. Michelle is an amazing woman, a real role model, a power to be reckoned with. You will want to be on her side and want her on your side."

~ Nicky Jones, counsellor and poet, North East UK

With a Little Help From My Friends

Other books by the author

Marie's Voice

I Love Charlotte Brontë

With a Little Help From My Friends

Michelle Daly

Michelle Daly • Liverpool

Front cover photo courtesy of *Woman's Own Magazine*, 1972.

Author photo by Melanie Seddon.

Book design and layout by MaryChris Bradley of The Book Team.

ISBN 978-0-9570487-3-7 (trade paperback)
978-0-9570487-4-4 (hardcover)
978-0-9570487-2-0 (ebook)

Contact the Author:
Email: michelleannedaly@yahoo.co.uk
Twitter: @MichelleDalyLiv
Facebook: facebook.com/michelleannedaly
Blog: michelledaly.blogspot.com

For Marie, Patrick, and Anna,
and to all those who believed in us.
Thank you.

Acknowledegements

- Dr Sheila Kidd, for all that she brought to the world of learning disability. Dr Prentice, Consultant psychiatrist, Matron and Sister Green at Sandhill Park Hospital, Taunton, Somerset. Dr Margaret Rogerson and Dr Arya, Consultant psychiatrists, at Olive Mount and Rathbone Hospital, Liverpool and Dr Garry, Consultant psychiatrist at Harmston Hall Hospital, Lincoln.

- Helen Laverty, Health Lecturer, School of Nursing, Midwifery & Physiotherapy, University of Nottingham.

- The nursing staff at Aras Attracta, Swinford, County Mayo, Ireland, for the love and care they gave to Marie.

- Rosa Monckton, for her tireless campaign for change and for affording 'special needs' parents a platform through her thought provoking, often heart-wrenching, documentaries.

- Jan Porteous, Social Worker, and Susan Cunningham, Operations Manager, Adult Health and Social Care–Liverpool.

- My dear friend, Erna Naughton, (Isle of Man) for the constant support and encouragement she has given me whilst writing this book and for always being there for me, and Anne Coyne, the famous Irish librarian featured in my books.

- The late, great, Maeve Binchy, may she rest in peace, and Anne Robinson for their help and advice.

- Jennifer Anderson, Indiana, USA. Jenn, you're one of my favourite people. Your son Johnny left this world too soon. You were a brilliant 'special needs' mum and I want you to know you're in my thoughts every day.

- Rosemary Gwaltney, Bobbie Sheahan, and Po Rippon.

- My Facebook and Twitter friends around the world, for your constant support, especially at three and four in the morning when you spurred me on through my writers block.

- And finally, I would like to thank MaryChris Bradley of The Book Team, for her patience, professionalism, and enthusiasm, and for being such a joy to work with.

Foreword by Dr Sheila Kidd

In my 30-odd years of working with learning disabled children, adults and their families, I have met some remarkable people; people who have lived with fortitude, devotion and love, embracing disappointment and exhaustion along the way.

Then one day, into my middle life, came a young woman who at the beginning of her life, chose to take along with her a vulnerable and highly dependent young girl with severe learning difficulties, mobility problems and epilepsy.

Michelle transformed this little girl's life and the two of them live happily together. So what is so extraordinary about all this? Michelle was herself only 19 years of age when, working as a cadet nurse in a large mental hospital, she made the decision to take Marie under her wing. She encountered blistering opposition from so many people in an earlier age when Community Care was still unheard of and not long after most learning disabled people were certified and compulsorily detained in hospitals. But Michelle has three strong characteristics, which sustained her then as now. In her fight for what she believes is right for Marie, she will not accept 'no', she will ask 'why' and she is not afraid of upsetting people. (Indeed experience has taught her to expect it!)

Success came eventually and Michelle became Marie's legal guardian. Marie was to enjoy a full family life in a loving home where she was totally accepted and loved and in which she was able to grow spiritually in the happy mix of rough and tumble, ups and downs, laughter and tears.

Thankfully, Michelle encountered various people along the way who saw her for what she is, encouraged her, and supported her efforts.

Michelle is now as then, lively and spirited, determined, courageous, loving and passionate, a visionary with that extra special ingredient—Liverpool humour. A force to be reckoned with indeed! Would that there were more Michelles on the side of those more vulnerable members of our society.

Michelle herself says that she wishes that she were more

conventional. I feel that if this were the case, there would not have been a story to be told-and Marie would have remained in her hospital setting.

With a Little Help From My Friends outlines so clearly what disabled relatives need—and illustrates that even now, almost everything their disabled relative needs has to be battled for by the family, most frequently the mother.

In the 1970s and 80s, there was enlightenment about the plight of the residents of the former long stay hospitals, who in those days were called mentally handicapped. Government money was made available to develop better services for them.

A typical pattern within the National Health Service would be that of a central unit which formed a hub from which services radiated out into the community. The unit itself could provide accommodation for fairly small numbers of people in small groups and with staff of several disciplines-nurses, doctors, psychologists, occupational therapists, physiotherapists, music therapists and, maybe social workers also. Community multidisciplinary teams from the staff supported families at home.

The team would work in close collaboration with other authorities in the area, principally education and social services. The residential accommodation would provide long or short term care (from an hour up to several weeks as needed) for moderately and severely mentally handicapped people of all ages. People with milder levels of handicap would be included in out-patient services, but any accommodation for them was provided by the social service department.

The aim was always to provide a comprehensive range of services which could respond to the needs of the family and try to give the mentally handicapped person a full and stimulating environment in which to achieve his or her full potential.

When it became clear that this could not be sustained within the Health Service, it was hoped that all the existing services and funding could be transferred to a new umbrella organization. It was felt that ideally this should be a new Government Department and the funding for the continuation of the service would therefore be ring-fenced for its original purpose.

Sadly, the opportunity was lost and the people and money were spread over a number of different organizations; thankfully, some of these are providing very much better lives for many people who were transferred into the community when the old hospitals were run down and eventually closed. But large gaps and deficiencies exist in the present system and families again feel isolated and left to go it alone.

Michelle and Marie's story is an extraordinary one and one which will be an inspiration and encouragement to many people, especially those who find themselves in the wilderness of disability. It would be encouraging too if it could give some pointers, to a more complete service for learning disabled people who cannot speak for themselves. It would be as well to consider these famous words— "You can judge a society by the way in which it looks after its most vulnerable members."

Dr. Kidd is a retired consultant psychiatrist in Learning Disabilities.

Part One

1

A World Without Love

It was April 10th 1970, just before my 17th birthday, when I arrived at Nazareth House children's home in Bristol, in the west of England.

Feeling tired and a little apprehensive, I lifted my heavy blue suitcase off the ground where the taxi driver had just deposited it, and walked towards the main entrance. I had heard so much about this former monastery from a nun in my previous job. She used to be in charge of the nursery, and it was one of her favourite places. Birds chirped noisily in the background, as if to spread the news that a stranger had arrived. I pressed the bell and waited nervously on the step.

The door was opened by a small, rather timid looking nun, dressed entirely in black. She shook my hand warmly, and after enquiring about my long train journey from Liverpool, showed me into the parlour while she went to find someone to take charge of me.

It's just as I imagined, I thought, looking through the window at the landscape. The grounds were enormous. I could see a nun stooping to pull the weeds here and there, as she tended the flowerbeds. There is no place in a convent for an idle nun.

The minutes ticked slowly by. The convent seemed so quiet I thought the nuns must have been in chapel. Then I heard the unmistakable swish of a long gown, together with the familiar sound of soft leather shoes on a wooden floor. I looked towards the door expectantly.

"Are you ready?" a little Irish nun asked me, popping her head inside the room. She shook my hand and introduced herself as Sister Alfred. I slung my bag over my shoulder, picked up my suitcase and followed her.

"You're a long way from Liverpool," she said opening a door that led onto a corridor. "Won't you get homesick?" We walked past the chapel and up a spiral staircase.

"Not really Sister," I told her as I tried to absorb the beauty of the architecture. "My sister is at Art College here."

We seemed to go up one staircase after another. The higher we climbed, the heavier my suitcase became.

"You've got your own bathroom," Sister Alfred smiled when we arrived onto a tiny landing at the top of the house. "Will you mind being up here on your own?" She turned the handle and opened the bedroom door.

I put down my luggage and strolled across the bedroom to stand by the window before replying.

"Oh no Sister, I'm the third eldest of seven children so it will be quite a change having some space around me." There had been eight of us, but Michael, the first born, died in infancy.

I was given an hour to unpack and folded my clothes away in an old-fashioned dressing table, on top of which I placed a picture of my mother. I was suddenly overwhelmed with guilt. I had spent the previous summer in this vibrant city with my sister Cathy, who was five years older than I was. However, my mother didn't know that Cathy was going away to India for the summer; she'd have been frantic.

"The Result Surprises Me"

I was the happy-go-lucky (troublesome) one, both in and out of school. That's why my mother worried about my future, especially after my headmaster gave me a reference stating, 'Michelle thinks life is one big joke!' He claimed I was a bad influence on the class and disrupted the lessons. But being difficult at school in my day is not the same as being difficult today. Being difficult in my day was looking at a teacher sideways, talking during a lesson when silence was demanded, or 'forgetting' my PE kit. And none of my classmates swore. It wasn't woven into our vocabulary as it is today.

I was useless at every subject, except maths. I came 2nd in the entire year, despite being in a B class. "The result surprises me!" was the sarcastic remark written on my test paper by the maths teacher.

There were too many distractions in the classroom I considered far more important than lessons. I sat beside a girl who lived in an abusive foster home. Some evenings after school, with the dinner money we saved, my friend and I would get the bus to the Social Services office in the city centre, to complain about her home life. Unfortunately, my friend's Social Worker was not in the least sympathetic. He would look up to heaven when he came out of his office and saw us sitting there waiting for him. "Just go back and try again." He would say in exasperation. "Just try again."

My friend was eventually placed in a different foster home, but the foster father was abusive. With only six months left 'in care', my aunty Terry, my mother's sister, offered, and was accepted as my friend's foster mother.

So I finished school the previous year, not thinking there would be any career openings. I was 15, and drifted into office work, undecided about my future.

One of the office girls told me her sister had recently left a job in a children's home because the work was too hard and the pay too low. The home was attached to a convent and was run by the Poor Sisters of Nazareth.

"Oh hey, I'd love a job working with children," I told her. "But I haven't got any qualifications."

"You don't need any!" she said to my surprise, "And they're always looking for staff."

Nazareth House, in Birkenhead, is across the River Mersey. It was too far to travel on a daily basis, which meant I would have to live-in. Four weeks later, much to my parents' horror, I moved into the convent and I loved it.

I worked with the toddlers, never dreaming anything could be so rewarding as I tucked them into bed at night. I was aware that these children had experienced tragedy at some time in their lives, yet they were happy, noisy little souls. On my days off I took two of the children on the ferry, across the Mersey, to visit my family in Liverpool. I couldn't believe I had a job I enjoyed so much.

One day, the sister in charge of our nursery ran off with one of our children's fathers and Sister Henry came to replace her. She was a tall Welsh nun, with a very pale complexion, and wore thin, gold rimmed specs. Sister Henry was a woman of few words, and hardly ever smiled.

The day after Sister Henry arrived, two sisters aged three and four were brought in to our toddler unit. They were crying and kept asking for their mummy. Their Mummy, was a lady of the night, and frequently left the children at home alone. A neighbour, not for the first time, called Social Services, and the two sisters were removed from their home by social workers and brought into us.

When I attempted to remove the girls' coats, Sister Henry advised me to leave them on. "You'll know when they are ready to take them off." She told me. The sisters sat through lunch and tea with their coats on. Then, after tea, when I looked over at the girls, the older sister was removing her coat before turning to the younger girl to remove hers.

When I took a dish from the cupboard to give cereal to one of the children, I could feel Sister Henry's eyes on me.

"Would you eat from that dish, Michelle?" She asked me. I looked down at the old faded Tupperware style bowl and shook my head. "Well then," she said, "never give a child food in something you would not eat out of yourself."

Sister Henry taught me a lot. Sadly, after a few months, we both went our separate ways. Sister Henry became ill, and went away to convalescence, and I was invited to go to the Bristol convent, which was one of the few convents that did the 'Nursery Nurse Course.'

I folded the last of my clothes away in the drawer, just as Sister Alfred arrived to collect me. Together, we walked through the convent, which not only housed the nuns, it provided residential quarters for childcare and domestic staff. Then we went out across the manicured lawns towards the nursery.

I could see children playing outside in the garden. The sound of their laughter reached my ears. I put a spring in my step and went to meet them.

I was aware of the traumatic world these children came from; a world, in most cases, where grownups had badly let them down. Yet, cocooned in the safety of the convent, they put their trust in anybody.

The gates into the nursery yard creaked, immediately attracting the children's attention. I watched the excited tots struggle to clamber off their battered old toys and come running over to greet us.

"What's the Matter with Her Head, Sister?"

The Home accommodated children up to five-years-old. The children slept on the top floor, where the sister-in-charge also slept, and used the ground floor during the day where their kitchen, dining-room and playroom were located.

The nursery floor, where I was to work, was on the middle floor.

Sister Alfred explained that she had overall responsibility for children and staff.

We went up the marble staircase and through a door that led onto a large square hallway, adorned with fresh flowers and holy statues. On we walked, passing the bedrooms, to the kitchen at the opposite end of the hall. Two nursery nurses were sitting down at the table and seemed engrossed in conversation. Sister Alfred took me into the kitchen to meet them.

"This is Michelle and she's come to help us look after the babies." They both nodded with an air of indifference before continuing their conversation.

We moved on to the immaculately clean bedrooms with sunny yellow walls and flowered curtains. Tiny babies lay on cots like balls of fluff. They were from six-days-old to nine months, with the exception of a little girl called Marie. Marie was just turned five, and Sister Alfred told me she was brain damaged and had lived at the Home since she was six weeks old. They were waiting for a hospital bed for Marie because the older she got the more difficult her behaviour was to manage, and the staff didn't know how much longer they could cope with her.

Marie had cropped hair, and the most beautiful blue eyes. She was extremely thin and I noticed a large lump on her forehead.

"What's the matter with her head, Sister?" It looked so sore, it made me cringe.

"Poor little thing," Sister replied. "She screams and screams—sometimes for hours on end—and bangs her head on the floor, or on the side of her cot. "Look!" She pointed to a rope around the pipe attaching itself to Marie's cot. "This is to stop her from tipping herself over."

I looked at the child's pale face; her eyes were like glass. I thought how strange it was that we stood so close and she didn't reach out to be picked up—as though she was used to being looked at, but not touched.

As we walked across the room, I watched her sad little eyes follow us.

In at the Deep End

Sister Alfred woke me at seven the next morning. I've always been an earlybird, so I was up and ready to start my new job. I opened my bedroom curtains to the beautiful view across Bristol. Cathy was leaving for India that morning and I hoped she'd have a safe journey, and I wouldn't miss her too much.

Linda and Jackie mumbled a 'Hello' to me when I went into the kitchen. The babies were guzzling on their bottles and Sister Alfred came into the kitchen to wish me a good morning, again. Then Linda put her baby into the bouncer beside her and went out into the first bedroom. I waited expectantly for her to bring me a tiny baby to feed. When she emerged from the room, she was carrying Marie.

"Will you feed this one, please?" she asked me. Marie was lowered into a high chair that had sawn off legs. The child seemed too big for it, but I suppose she was easier to manage in the chair.

I looked at Marie as she sat grinding her teeth. "Will she take her food from me?" I asked. "I mean, she doesn't really know me, does she?"

"Well, she'll just have to get used to you then, won't she?" came the reply. I pulled up a chair and was handed a small plastic bowl, into which Linda dropped a tablet.

"What's that for?" I enquired. I sat down preparing to feed Marie.

"It's Librium to calm her down. She has one three times a day; just stir the tablet in with her food and she won't notice it," she instructed, lifting one of the babies from its bouncing chair, coo cooing in that baby language we're all so good at.

It's hard to imagine in this day and age that any doctor would prescribe Librium three times a day for a five year-old child, but 40 years ago, it seemed to be the norm.

I stirred the cereal and attempted to give Marie her first mouthful —no problem. Her face was expressionless when she opened her mouth and swallowed. The second and third spoonful went down well, too, and then, without warning, when I looked down to dip the spoon into the bowl, Marie reached out with both hands and grabbed my hair and she wouldn't let go.

Linda and Jackie came to my rescue; as one tickled Marie the other tried to undo her fists.

"I forgot to tell you to watch your hair," Linda said. "She does it all the time." With that bit of late advice, I sat down to try again. This time Marie didn't get my hair because I didn't take my eyes from her. I found this difficult at times because the lump on her forehead kept turning my stomach. I had not been so close to a disabled child before; I didn't know how to react as she sat grinding her teeth in between mouthfuls of food.

I scraped the last of the cereal out of the bowl. She still seemed hungry. "Is this all Marie has for breakfast?" I asked.

"She can't chew and has cereal most of the time." Linda replied as she patted her baby on the back trying to bring up its wind. Even though Marie had not had sufficient to eat, she didn't look for any more food.

After breakfast, I was asked to take Marie into the bathroom to change her nappy and dress her (Talk about being thrown in at the deep end). I sat her on the changing locker and began to remove her nightclothes, but my thick wavy hair was too tempting, and, much to my horror, she grabbed it with both hands, again. And again, she wouldn't let go.

In desperation, I lifted her off the locker, thinking she would be distracted and loosen her hands, but she wasn't distracted and she didn't let go, and her weight took us both to the floor.

This time Sister Alfred came hurrying to my rescue, shouting, "You're a little devil; let go you naughty girl!" whilst trying to unclench Marie's fists. When this was finally achieved, Sister Alfred sat Marie up on the locker.

"You'll have to keep your eyes on her all the time, Michelle," she warned, as I felt to make sure my hair was still there; "or she'll grab you quickly when you're not looking."

I had only been on duty for half-an-hour and I'd been attacked— twice—by a five year-old.

Marie sat like a floppy doll, making no attempt to help Sister Alfred put her clothes on.

"Can't she walk, Sister?" I asked.

"No," Sister Alfred answered firmly, "she's spastic, but she can stand." Sister lifted Marie off the locker and stood her up to demonstrate, but the little imp plonked onto the floor, and there she sat, refusing to impress me.

"Goodness me, look at the time," Sister Alfred exclaimed. "There're not enough hours in the day!" She hurried out of the bathroom, leaving me standing there with Marie at my feet. I tried very hard to sound cross when I spoke.

"You're naughty!" I said, stooping to lift her up. "If you pull my hair again," I threatened, "I'm going to pull yours." I carried her to the kitchen.

The bottles were just being cleared away and the babies were lying on their cots contentedly. I stood in the doorway awaiting my instructions.

"Will you put Marie in that room at the end of the hallway?" Linda said. "If you put her on the floor she'll play in there, but make sure the veranda door is closed."

I carried this strange little girl towards the room Linda indicated. *They can't mean in here*, I said to myself as I stood in the doorway. I went back to the kitchen.

"Did you mean that room at the end?" I asked Linda. "The one with those big old fashioned baby prams lined along the walls?"

"Yes!" she snapped. "Just sit her on the floor, close the door and she'll play on her own."

I laughed nervously. "What? Just leave her there?"

She glared at me and said, "Yes!"

I did as I was told. When I sat Marie on the floor she immediately crashed her head down onto it. When she looked back up at me, I was shocked to see she had knocked the top off her sore, and a trickle of blood ran down her forehead. I didn't know what to do. I tried consoling her but it made no difference. I don't suppose she understood anything I was saying. To my relief, Sister Alfred appeared in the doorway.

"Come away Michelle," she said with a sense of urgency. "Marie will be all right in a while; she'll probably have a sleep on the floor."

How awful that we came away and closed the door after us, leaving her all alone. I bit my lip as I listened to the screams in the background.

"Why do you put Marie in that room, Sister?"

"Because there are things to do Michelle," she replied tying her apron over her habit. "We have the floors to polish each morning and if Marie is allowed out she'll drag her feet all over them. Besides," she added irritably, "Rev. Mother gets angry and expects the Nursery to be spotless for when she's bringing visitors around."

"How long does she have to stay in there?" I asked, not quite believing my ears.

"She can come out for dinner," she told me as if she were kindness itself! "And don't look so worried." She handed me a tin of polish and told me to start polishing the bedroom floors. But I wasn't worried—I was disgusted.

Marie's screams followed me from room to room as I spread the polish over the already polished floors. The staff laughed and chatted and went about their duties as though it was an everyday occurrence.

At lunch time when I saw Jackie wheeling the trolley full of bottles and dinners into the kitchen I went to fetch Marie. My eyes stung when I looked across the room at her; she was curled up in a ball fast asleep on the floor.

"Hello, Marie," I said gently. She immediately awoke and shuffled across the floor on her bottom. By the time she reached my feet she was giggling, arms outstretched for me to pick her up, which I gladly did. I carried her to the dining room and sat her in her big baby chair.

"We didn't want her yet," Jackie moaned; "we usually do her last."

"Never mind," I said, cheerfully. "She's here now so she can watch us, can't she?"

When I was younger there was always a baby to hold, feed, change or push in a pram, but I never was a fluffy baby person; I've always preferred toddlers. Now I had forgotten those baby skills that had come so naturally, yet here in the convent there was no time to learn things step by step; I was thrown in at the deep end and would have at least five or six babies to feed each meal time.

Because we worked such long hours, we were allowed two hours off during the day, either in the morning or afternoon. Whoever was left on duty in the afternoon did the laundry which was downstairs on the toddler's floor, leaving the nursery floor unattended for an hour or two. At three o'clock, babies were undressed, given their teas and put on their cots for the night. Marie was included in this routine.

On Sundays and Feast days the nuns expected me to go to church but I didn't mind because unlike my parents, who insisted we went to Mass every Sunday, in hail-rain-sleet-or-snow, the nuns went to Mass, too. Still, I used any excuse to get out of it and would hang back with the chores and promise to follow, maybe slipping into Mass at the end.

A Little Bit of Freedom

When I passed Marie's bedroom at half-seven each morning, she would be sitting on her cot looking through the bars.

I think she knew I was sticking up for her because she laughed excitedly when she saw me. I lifted her out of the cot and sat her in her *specially broken* high chair where she waited for the babies to be fed because she was always 'done' last.

I thought it was sad that cleaning took priority over the children's needs. Gradually I was given a certain amount of freedom with Marie, though there were times I had to do something important (like polishing a cupboard) and Sister Alfred told me to put her in the pram room. This used to make me so angry. I would unclench Marie's hands from around my neck with a lump in my throat. She would cry, knowing I was about to leave her on her own. I soon found myself taking Marie with me on my two hours off each day to avoid her being shut up alone.

There were days I took her into the garden and pushed her on the swing or let her sit in the sandpit with the toddlers. She didn't communicate much with the children and seemed happier amongst adults.

If it was raining I would sneak her into my room. I appreciated sleeping at the top of the house, because once there, I was unlikely to be discovered. The problem was getting to my room. People heard Marie before they saw her and children were not allowed into staff bedrooms. The nuns were usually in chapel and unlikely to see us, but I gently put my hand over Marie's mouth until we reached my room, just in case she started to screech and gave the game away.

There was a long mirror on the pram room wall and I imagined once the door was closed, and Marie was alone, many hours were spent watching her reflection. In my room, she would sit on the floor in front of the mirror moving different parts of her body. It seemed without the mirror she didn't know she was there. Her head would bob up and down; she would lean quite close to the glass and open her mouth trying to see inside. If I moved to another part of the room Marie would change positions on her bottom, shuffling about until she could see me—through the mirror. Her only demand was to be close by.

She also loved me to sing nursery rhymes to her and would watch my mouth as she clapped, head turned to one side trying to work out where the sound came from. 'Baa Baa Black Sheep' was a favourite; she would repeat 'Baa Baa', but that was as far as we got. I was rather pleased with this little attempt on her part and wondered how much potential she had.

We developed a game where I pretended to cry and then took her hand and put it on my head to stroke my hair; then I would put my hands over her face and she would moan as if she was crying, so that I could comfort her. I was pleased to see little bits of her personality slowly emerging.

Nothing to Call Her Own

Marie was born premature in a mother and baby home. She stopped breathing when she was five minutes old and was given mouth-to-mouth resuscitation. When she was six weeks-old she was admitted to Nazareth House to be put up for adoption, however, with the question of brain damage hanging over her, the adoption never happened. When she was 11 months, she was only able to sit propped with pillows and at two and a half, was able to stand, if supported.

I also discovered there had been a nurse who'd taken a great interest in Marie, but left a few years ago and had not been back to visit her. Marie had obviously known better times.

Even though Marie had lived at Nazareth House for five years, she didn't appear to have any identity or possess anything personal. Instead of having pretty clothes hanging in the wardrobe, all she had was a pile of bitty tights and jumpers folded on a shelf in the bathroom.

Marie wasn't even allowed a relationship with the children from downstairs, unless she went out into the garden. Whenever they would try to come to visit her, as soon as they put their noses around the landing door on our floor, Sister Alfred would shoo them away; she didn't want them spoiling *her* nursery floor. Had Sister Alfred encouraged the children, it would have been of enormous benefit to Marie, who was loved by all the toddlers and was looked on as the 'big baby.'

We were so busy it was almost impossible to look after the babies properly, let alone a disabled child. My conscience had been bothering me for a while over the risks Sister Alfred took with the infants. If we were having visitors—perhaps a couple coming to see a baby for adoption, Sister would be in a flap, going around the babies as they lay on their cots putting their bottles propped up with teddies in their mouths. The job she gave me while the babies lay sucking usually prevented me from watching them. After what seemed like an eternity Sister would collect the bottles. My job then was to lay the babies on the floor on their tummies where they brought up their own wind. I reluctantly followed her orders because she was in charge, but common sense told me what she was doing was wrong.

There were three bedrooms with five or six babies in each one. Had our visitors come early they'd have been quite shocked as they slowly passed each room to see five infants lying in their own vomit, having brought back their bottles with stomachs full of wind.

Sister Alfred was obviously under a lot of pressure from Rev. Mother whose idea of a children's home was a doll's house with spotless babies lying on their cots. The only time Rev. Mother saw the children was when she brought a visitor around, and looked on with pride as people remarked how beautiful our nursery was, but she never told the visitors it was at the expense of the childcare.

Marie screeched if I went out of the room and she was sitting in her chair, which prevented her from following me. When I returned, she was quietened down. Undoubtedly she irritated the staff.

"I think she's better on her cot," Linda said one day as she went to lift Marie out of her chair. I was in a difficult position; she was 'trained' I wasn't, but I didn't take my orders from her. I took them from Sister, who had never objected to the interest I took in Marie as long as it didn't affect my work. "Marie's ok where she is," I told her. "She's got a right to be here just like all the other children." I could tell by the way Linda banged about that I'd upset her. I wasn't bothered, although it did create an atmosphere between us at times.

One afternoon when I was doing the laundry, I looked to the ceiling as Marie's head thudded on the floor above. I stood folding piles of nappies and baby-grows as the noise continued. The nuns were in chapel; nobody else was about, so I sneaked upstairs to the pram room. As I opened the door Marie was sitting behind it crying.

"Come on!" I said, picking her up. "You'll get me shot!" I ran back down the stairs with her. She laughed; glad to be rescued. I sat her on the table in the empty laundry basket while I emptied the drier. For a bit of fun I put the hot nappies over her and she laughed again; she loved to get attention which was rare in those days. I turned my back on her to fill the washing machine and when I looked around again she was fast asleep; her little face still wet from crying.

2

A Breath of Fresh Air

I had been at the convent for eight weeks when Sister Alfred was moved to another convent and who came to take her place but Sister Henry. I was pleased she had recovered from her illness. I was also aware of how strict Sister Henry was, and wondered what kind of changes she would make to the Nursery.

But thanks to Sister Henry, the babies were never fed on their cots again and Marie was never put back in the pram room. Instead of crawling after me, Marie was soon walking by my side, encouraged to stay on her feet from the noise her shoes made.

She still plonked on the floor and would panic if she was left alone for a minute, banging her head onto the floor, though not as frequently. The quality of Marie's life improved so much that I hoped Sister Henry was going to stay for a long time.

There were lots of subtle changes in our nursery; one of them being that we opened the door to the toddlers, which gave us enormous pleasure as children popped in to see us throughout the day. One of them was a little boy called Morgan who took a great interest in Marie. She didn't take the slightest bit of notice of him except to grab his hair if he got in the way of her reflection in the mirror. He usually managed to jump out of the way but if he wasn't quick enough Marie would grab his hair.

I took her out almost every day, even if it was only to collect prescriptions from the chemist. I sat her in the big old fashioned baby pram, and off we'd go to the shops. She was walking much better, but was still unsteady on her feet, and couldn't walk very far. She enjoyed our short trips, still not responding to people except to screech if they approached her. I would leave the prescription in at the chemist's and while it was being prepared, I'd take Marie to the shop next door for our supply of chocolate. If I stood her beside me she became nervous and started screeching, so I quickly lifted her back into the pram. On the way home she sat contentedly in the safety of her pram sucking her chocolate as it slowly dribbled out of her mouth.

I went home to Liverpool for a few days and my 15 year-old sister, Trish, returned to the convent with me, where she helped out for the rest of her school holidays. Trish worked with the toddlers. When the weather was nice, she would take them to the pond at the back of the convent. I was so pleased when Trish came up to the nursery to fetch Marie to go with them.

At last we had a happy home. Although we didn't stop for a minute and lived on stale bread (sent in free from the bakery) and tinned baby food, I loved my job. Invariably, when I was going off duty for my two hour break, I'd plan to have a sleep. I said goodbye to the staff but when I reached the landing door Marie would plonk in the middle of the corridor and look at me sadly.

"See you later!" I would say. She didn't move. In the end I would take her with me.

"What's Going to Happen to All the Children?"

One sunny afternoon, my lovely sister Cathy came strolling into the convent; she had returned from India. We sat in the kitchen wide-eyed as she told of the places she visited and cringed in horror at her tales of crummy youth hostels and bed bugs. I laughed at the contrast in our lives. I'd probably made as many bottles and changed as many nappies as the miles Cathy travelled across the earth. I was happy to see her again!

I remember the following morning Sister Henry returned from chapel looking troubled. I didn't approach her, sensing she wanted to be left alone. I'd seen Sister Henry like this before on the odd occasion I found her rocking one of the babies to sleep. Sometimes, when I was changing a baby on the locker in the bathroom, I'd glance out of the window to see her returning to the convent, walking slowly as though her legs pained her. At these times I disappeared from view, realising I'd caught Sister in an unguarded moment.

That morning, however, she informed us that due to the recent Home Office inspection, the house had been condemned and the Home Office was closing us down. There had been rumours that it might close, which is why the Nursery Nurse Course had been put on hold, but we never thought it would happen and were shocked at the news.

"Where will everybody go?" I asked Sister sadly. "What's going to happen to the children?"

"That has yet to be decided Michelle," she told me quietly.

The social workers started buzzing in and out; getting children fostered or adopted or even placed in other children's homes. Nobody came to see Marie. I worried more and more about her future. Quite a few of the children were going to live in Nazareth House in Wales, with two of the staff. Even though their surroundings would be new, they would still be with familiar faces. Still there was no mention of Marie.

There was a ray of hope one day when I discovered Marie's annual appointment with the paediatrician was due.

"Would you like to take her, Michelle?" Sister asked me. I was delighted.

"Maybe if I tell the paediatrician how much Marie's improved she'll be able to go to a residential school."

"She might Michelle, but don't build your hopes too high," she told me kindly.

That afternoon I took Marie into the garden. I bought her some new clothes when I was in Liverpool, and it was lovely seeing her in pretty colours. I sat on the grass watching the birds fly by and envied their independence. I realised how vulnerable Marie was. After seeing the way Sister Alfred treated her and then Sister Henry's kindness, I knew the pendulum could swing either way depending on what people saw as they looked at her; some seeing Marie, others seeing nothing.

During the two weeks building up to Marie's appointment I was planning her debut with the doctor down to the finest detail.

"Which dress do you think is the nicest, Sister?" I asked, holding up three of Marie's dresses, as if one colour would make Marie look less disabled than the other. Sister Henry listened to my constant talk without a flicker of impatience, though I must have driven her mad.

Morgan sat on the chair in the bathroom, a tall boy for his seven years, looking at me from under his fringe.

"Where are you going?" he asked. He was such a friendly outgoing child, he missed nothing.

"I'm taking Marie to see the doctor at the hospital," I told him. He frowned. "She's coming back," I added quickly.

"Can I come with you?" he asked excitedly, making my poor baby jump as she lay in the bath with my hand supporting her head.

"You'll have to ask Sister." I told him but I knew she would let him come with us.

"Her Name is Marie."

At long last our appointment day arrived. I sat Marie on the bathroom locker and stood in front of her so she wouldn't fall off, whilst I watched for the ambulance through the window. Morgan stood with his nose pressed to the pane.

When the children in Nazareth House reached eighteen months, potential adoptive parents showed little interest in them or their future. Most couples were looking for a tiny baby. For Morgan, a trip to the hospital was like a day out.

The ambulance was 15 minutes late, so Sister Henry went over to the convent to ring the hospital, and a receptionist said she would send a taxi to collect us immediately.

My stomach was in knots. I was so nervous, knowing that this child's future could be decided in the next hour. I prayed I could convince the doctor to send Marie to a special school instead of a hospital, especially when she saw Marie was able to learn little things.

I lifted Marie off the locker and took Morgan by the hand. When we went out through the nursery gate the taxi was pulling up. I thought we were late for our appointment but we arrived at the hospital just in time.

I never had much experience with hospitals, apart from being in isolation for six weeks with dysentery when I was three years-old—too young to remember much, except that lingering smell of disinfectant.

We were sitting in the waiting room for a few minutes when a nurse called Marie's name. We followed her to a room off the corridor where I was asked to strip Marie to her underclothes to be weighed. When she saw the large weighing machine she began to screech so I took her hands in mine and eased her up onto the metal contraption. She was frightened of so many things; so insecure in strange places.

I then left Morgan in the waiting room and carried Marie in to Dr. Glover's office.

Dr. Glover, the paediatrician, was much older than I expected. She sat behind her desk without a flicker of warmth, as her cold, clinical eyes, looked over at me. A young woman in a white coat stood beside her.

My little friend sat silently on my knee. There was a loud unnerving silence in the room as Dr. Glover wrote in some notes in what I presume was Marie's file. The minutes ticked slowly by and Dr. Glover continued to ignore us both.

Today, I would not put up with such ignorant behaviour from anybody. However, at the age of 17, I was hardly equipped or articulate enough to deal with condescending professionals, for had I been, the following incident may not have occurred.

"Is she at school?" the Dr. Glover asked, still writing in the file.

"No," I answered. She looked up at her assistant with a slight raise of her eyebrow before turning to me.

"What about her diet?" She said resting her pen on the desk and giving me her full attention. "Does she eat meat and fruit?"

I shifted uneasily in my chair. "No," I whispered, "she can't chew properly." I wanted to explain about Marie choking on lumpy food, but she didn't give me the chance.

"This child has been neglected!" She roared. Then, turning to her colleague she said, "I think I'll keep her in for observation."

I thought I must have misunderstood until Dr. Glover asked her colleague to arrange for Marie to be admitted to the hospital.

"Wait outside," she said, dismissing me.

Marie and I sat in the corridor outside Dr. Glover's office. A nurse brought Morgan from the waiting room and he sat on the chair beside us. The young doctor in the white coat was asking me questions about Marie's family. I was too upset to speak and besides, I didn't know anything about Marie's family.

"She'll think we don't want her anymore," I said quietly. I kept my arms protectively around Marie wondering how I could prepare her for the distress she was about to encounter. I realised once again how desperately alone in the world she was. A nurse sat beside me and rested her hand on my shoulder.

"Would you like to bring the little girl down to the ward?" she asked.

"Her name is Marie," I said quietly. We followed the nurse down the corridor, Marie on my hip and Morgan by my side. The poor boy must have wondered what was happening.

"She hardly understands anything that's said to her," I told the nurse as we walked along. "She'll probably screech all the time." I was trying to pull myself together, to give them as much information as I could. No matter how much I told them, nothing would alleviate the fear and isolation Marie would feel.

The ward sister was waiting outside to greet us.

"Is this the little girl?" she asked cheerfully before opening the ward door for us to follow her.

I handed Marie over to her. I felt so helpless, standing there sobbing like a child.

"Come in with her if you want," Sister offered. I shook my head and walked away.

Morgan and I walked the two-and-a-half miles back to Nazareth House. It never occurred to me to catch a bus; I don't even remember the journey as I walked along unaware that I still held Marie's clothes in my hands.

When we arrived home I sent Morgan into the Nursery. I went to my room, unable to face anybody and sat down on my bed.

The truth was, Marie was neglected, and had been for years. Dr. Glover was right to be concerned, especially as I accompanied Marie to an important annual paediatric appointment instead of a more senior member of staff. But did she have to take such drastic steps?

"What's happened Michelle?" Sister Henry said, rushing into my room. "Morgan said they've taken Marie off you."

I began to relate the awful incident.

"Wait here," she said, "I'll go and see Rev. Mother."

Of course, I thought, wiping my eyes, *Rev. Mother will lend Sister Henry the car so we can bring Marie home.* I stood up and straightened Marie's crumpled clothes out on the bed. Before long I could hear Sister's heavy footsteps on the stairs again. She didn't speak when she came into my room; she just looked at me sadly.

"What did Rev. Mother say?" I asked miserably. I could tell from her expression it hadn't been good.

"Mother said maybe they will find Marie somewhere else to live," she answered quietly.

I was so overwhelmed with pity for Marie. After five-and-a-half years she was just another name to cross off the list. Rev Mother was proving Dr. Glover to be right; she was glad to see the back of her.

Continuity

Our Home was unusually quiet. Marie's demands had been modest, but she had always been there; it was a different nursery without her. I couldn't help glancing at her cot when I passed the bedroom door; her face no longer looking through the bars. As day turned to night I looked sadly at Marie's nightdress still folded on the bathroom shelf. I realised she was never coming back.

That night I lay in bed and wondered how many other children there were like Marie; in the hands of nobody, with nobody responsible for them but heartless officials. I didn't know which was worse; the fact that the doctor had removed Marie from the Home or that she hadn't been represented by the nuns in her hour of need.

When I rang and spoke to the staff nurse on Marie's ward the next morning, she told me Marie had cried for most of the night and would not sit on the pot.

"Can I visit her some time?" I asked, half expecting her to say no.

"Just come in whenever you want," she answered.

An hour later, as soon as the babies were fed, winded and changed, I grabbed my coat and ran for the bus.

We lived in a very posh part of Bristol, just the other side of the Clifton Downs. The bus ride was a familiar one. When I passed the University and approached St. Michael's Hill, I jumped down as the bus slowed and hurried on to the top of the steep hill. When I arrived at the hospital I climbed the steps two at a time. My mind had gone blank and I couldn't remember which ward Marie was on. I stopped to look in every window, scouring the children's faces and then I saw her. She was sitting on the floor on her own.

"Hello, Marie!" I said, walking into the ward. She began to laugh loudly, and shuffled over to me on her bottom. I stooped down to pick her up. She looked so happy to see me. I tickled her and she wriggled excitedly. "Have you been a good girl?" I asked teasingly, but of course, she couldn't answer me.

I found a cot with her name on; a big ugly thing, which looked like it had been slept in by a thousand children. I sat on the bedside chair and lifted Marie onto my knee. We spent a long time watching the other children playing on the ward and singing our nursery rhymes. She gently took my hand for 'Round and Round the Garden' staring at my face, dribbling as she tried to concentrate. Perhaps, in a way, my visit brought a little understanding to her; seeing a familiar face from her past could only help.

When I was leaving, I waved to Marie from the ward door, but she was already slipping into her old habits; banging her head on the bars of her cot, thinking I'd already gone. I longed to walk out of the hospital with her and take her back to Nazareth House, but I knew Rev. Mother would probably refuse to let her stay.

I slowly walked out of the hospital and down the steps towards the bus stop.

I visited again the next morning and Marie was sitting on her cot with blood down the front of her nightdress and on her face. The nurse said Marie had spent most of the night screaming and banging her head on the side of the cot. I was angry as I lifted her out, wondering once again what on earth she was doing in a hospital for sick children. I laughed to myself as I wondered whether she could be removed from the hospital because she was 'neglected.'

When I dressed her in the bathroom she never took her eyes off me. I knew my visits were important to her; I was the only link from the past. She needed that contact every day, at least until another home was found for her.

Better to Have a Little Love

I liked the nurses on Marie's ward. I watched them go about their duties and marvelled at their cheerful manner as they nursed children with cancer. I could never have done that kind of job; I'd have spent the whole time crying.

I visited every day on my two hours off, either in the morning or afternoon. One day after I left the ward I realised I'd forgotten my bag. I hurried back to collect it and hesitated at the door when I saw Marie through the window. She was curled up in a ball on her cot and she was crying. I signalled to the nurse for my bag to avoid upsetting her any further.

I couldn't blame the nurses for the situation. Hospitals are for sick children. Marie wasn't sick; she had nowhere else to go. Allowing Marie to roam around the ward unattended was like letting a 12 month-old baby crawl around, a baby with no sense of danger that needed to be watched constantly. The nurses were so busy it would have been impossible.

I began to wonder whether Marie might be better off if I stopped visiting her, thinking at least she wouldn't get upset when I left.

When the opportunity arose I spoke to Sister Henry about it.

"Do you think I'm selfish going to see Marie every day, Sister?" I asked.

She looked puzzled.

"I don't understand what you mean, Michelle."

I told her of my reservations.

"You mustn't look at it like that. Marie needs you; it's better to have a little love than no love at all."

"Even if it hurts?" I asked her.

"It isn't always possible for children in care to be loved by other people, and whenever it is it should never be discouraged, even if parting comes after it. No matter how it seems to you now, Michelle, she can only benefit from it."

And so I continued to visit my friend.

Then two weeks after Marie was admitted to the hospital, I was allowed to bring her home on Sunday afternoons! I took Morgan with me to collect her. I wanted to erase his memory of that awful day the doctor took her off us. I gave him my camera to play with, and he had lots of fun photographing anything and everything. When the three of us left the hospital he took a photo of me standing outside holding Marie.

When I took Marie back to the hospital that evening we seemed to be waiting ages for the bus. I held her in my arms to protect her from the cold wind when a blue car suddenly pulled up. The driver wound down the window asking if he and his wife could give us a lift. Such timing! I was grateful to be dropped off with Marie at the entrance to the Children's Hospital.

The couple, like many other people, had been surprised when I told them I worked at Nazareth House. They thought I looked too young to have such responsibility. Most of the parents on Marie's ward had thought I was one of the children from the Home and hadn't realised I worked there.

Throughout my life, especially after I left home, most people I met thought I was from Ireland. I think that was the reason most of the nuns took me under their wings.

~ 3 ~

Goodbye to Nazareth House

Nazareth House was slowly emptying as children were placed elsewhere and the babies were adopted. Instead of a newborn filling the cot, the bedding was stripped and the cots stayed bare.

Marie's final visit to the Home was a few days before it closed down. It was a cold, but sunny day. When I arrived at the hospital the nurse said Marie had a high temperature and couldn't go out. I understood but couldn't help feeling disappointed. I'd so much wanted her to see the remaining children before they left, and most of all I wanted her to see Sister Henry without whom my visits to the hospital would not have been possible.

The Staff-nurse took Marie's temperature on the hour. By the third attempt it gone down. It was 3 pm.

"Hurry up if you're going," she said, smiling at me. I breathed a sigh of relief, threw Marie's coat on, picked her up and ran for the bus. We crossed the Clifton Downs and soon arrived at the stop near the convent. I always felt happy when we reached this spot; it meant we were going home. However, that afternoon, as I carried Marie up the drive to the convent, I knew it would be for the last time; in a few days none of us would be living there. It would be standing empty.

The Home looked poverty stricken. Most of the children had gone, leaving just a few babies on our floor. The furniture was stacked in the corners of each room; empty prams and cots with a forlorn looking teddy hanging here and there, sad for the children who'd left them behind.

Marie clung to my hand as we walked across the landing towards the noisy kitchen.

"Hi everybody, come and look who's here." I shouted, bringing immediate cries of delight as the staff came running out to greet her. Sister Henry scooped her up and gave her a big hug. I felt so sad. Six months ago we were all strangers and now we were like family. Even Linda and Jackie outgrew their 'cliquishness', and accepted me into the fold.

Being at the nursery with Marie was far more relaxing than being at the hospital, where I had to constantly watch her in case she hurt one of the children. On this particular day, however, she must have sensed things were different because she never left my knee as she sat twiddling the material on the end of her dress.

"Have they sorted out anywhere for her yet, Michelle?" Sister Henry asked as she buttered the bread for sandwiches.

"Not yet Sister," I told her. "At least nobody has mentioned it to me. They're such a nice bunch I'm sure they'd have let me know."

"At least you will be in touch with her after we've all gone," she said. I was going to live with Cathy for a while until Marie was settled in a new home. There was plenty of job offers in various convents, but I had not made any firm decisions about my future.

"I wish we could turn the clock back," I whispered. "Just to give us all a little more time together." Our ties were being severed and my little friend had no place to live.

When we were about to leave, Sister Henry gave me a bag of clothes and some soft toys for Marie to keep. It was hard not to cry.

Everybody waved as we went out into the chilly October night. I carried Marie down the drive towards the bus stop, her little possessions in two carrier bags, the remains of her five and a half years at the Home.

One Last Chance

By the end of the week Nazareth House was closed down and my friends had gone. I only lived 10 minutes from the hospital, which enabled me to spend most of my time there, careful not to get under the nurses' feet. In all honesty, I think the nurses were glad I spent so much time on the ward – they had enough to do.

The ward sister let me take Marie home every afternoon and sometimes Cathy came to the hospital to collect her with me. One of the first things Marie did when we arrived back at Cathy's was to inspect herself in the mirror. She would sit and smile as though she'd forgotten what she looked like, and was pleased with what she saw. She had a plastic name tag on her wrist, which had to be worn on the ward. This kept reminding me that Marie had to go back, like a library book with a stamp on it.

When we returned to the children's hospital, it was through the back streets to avoid noisy traffic on the main road. Marie had spent so little time outside the convent—there was much she had to get used to.

The young doctor I met with Dr. Glover came into the ward each day. I asked her one day about the possibility of Marie getting a place in a residential school instead of going to live in a hospital for the mentally handicapped. She looked doubtful.

Marie's recent IQ test was 20-25 and her language was assessed as 8-months. I think the general feeling was Marie was too brain damaged to benefit from any schooling.

I had one last try when this particular doctor invited me to go along with herself and Marie to see Dr. Glover, the paediatrician.

"Oh, you must be joking," I told her. "She frightens me to death."

The doctor laughed and took Marie by the hand, walking towards the door. A minute later I heard a scream and realised what a coward I'd been. The doctor reappeared with Marie.

"Can't do a thing with her," she groaned.

I took hold of Marie's hand and all three of us left the ward. When we entered Dr. Glover's office, I couldn't blame Marie for screeching; it was full of medical students. I sat down and sat Marie on my lap.

"This is the nurse to whom the child is attached," Dr. Glover said, addressing the students. She looked at me and asked, "Now, dear, is she able to do anything?"

"Oh yes!" I answered, grabbing the opportunity to demonstrate Marie's intelligence; "she copies simple things."

"Like what?"

"Sometimes I pretend to cry and she comforts me," I answered, hoping she wouldn't ask for any more examples because there weren't any.

"Do you think you could get her to show us?" she asked, to my horror. I felt embarrassed when I looked at the students around the room—then, looking at Marie, I knew I had no choice. I lowered my head, and covering my face with my hands I pretended to cry. Marie gently stroked my hair. The doctor then started to speak but Marie silenced her as she covered her own face with her hands and started to moan quite dramatically as she waited for me to comfort her. I was very pleased with Marie's performance, thinking it would have made a great difference to the doctor.

"Is she toilet trained?" she asked. My leg suddenly felt hot. I looked down at the pool that was forming at my feet. Everybody was giggling. Dr. Glover grinned. "Obviously not," she said. I returned to the ward with the young doctor. I didn't know whether to laugh or cry. My last attempt had failed.

I was changing Marie in the bathroom one day when someone behind me said, "Hello, are you Michelle?" I turned around to see a middle-aged lady standing in the doorway. I nodded.

"I'm Marie's Social Worker," she said to my astonishment and looking over at Marie she said; "Hasn't she grown?"

"Well she would have, wouldn't she?" I said surprised at her sudden appearance. "Why didn't you visit her while I was at the convent?" I asked her, feeling the anger rising within me. "I didn't even know she had a social worker."

"I did visit her at Nazareth House," she said apologetically, "and Rev. Mother always told me she was fine."

I shook my head. "She wasn't fine and nobody bothered to help her," I answered, wondering why she was making this sudden appearance. I then went on to tell her how angry I was that everybody had washed their hands of Marie.

"She is removed from Nazareth House," I told her, "because the doctor thinks she is neglected. She is then placed in a far worse situation. God," I said, angrily, "people say don't get involved – it isn't fair on the child, I think it's unfair not to! Marie's in care," I said laughing sarcastically, "but whose care?"

Marie started getting impatient. I lifted her off the locker and the three of us returned to the ward.

"I have some good news," said the Social Worker. "We've got Marie a bed in a hospital." She smiled at me as though looking for some kind of approval. "She goes on Monday and because you know her so well, I wondered if you would like to go with her?"

"No, I wouldn't like to go with her," I said rudely, "and if I had my way she wouldn't be going either."

Ignoring my rudeness she went on to tell me about the hospital and how Marie would attend the hospital school.

With great reluctance I agreed to meet her on the ward the following Monday at 9 am.

I didn't go home that evening when I left the hospital; instead I walked around Bristol city centre looking in the shop windows. The lack of concern for Marie's welfare was beyond my comprehension; she seemed a burden to everybody, with a Social Worker who only appeared to sign exit and entrance forms – no doubt to allow Marie's whereabouts to be documented.

I dreaded Monday. I couldn't even explain to Marie what was happening; she was just being taken there and left. I would no longer be around to help her adjust to her new environment. The hospital was 30 miles away. I didn't think I'd be allowed to visit. She was being somersaulted back into loneliness.

4

A Hidden World

It rained as we left the children's hospital. Marie giggled with excitement as she sat snugly on my knee. She kept taking my hand to play 'Round and Round the Garden' and laughed when I tickled her.

"She's a sweet little thing, isn't she?" the Social Worker said; "if only she didn't screech so much." My blood started to boil.

"Maybe it's a good thing she does screech," I told her. "At least she knows how to object to things." I knew I was being very intolerant, yet I continued. "When you think of the awful life she's had it's hardly surprising is it?"

We didn't speak much after that; there didn't seem to be anything else to say.

Sandhill Park Hospital, in Bishop's Lydeard, Somerset, was built as a country house around 1720. It was later used as a prisoner of war camp, a home for handicapped children and later as a military and civilian hospital.

During World War 1, it was used as a prisoner of war camp for German and Austrian Officers. In 1919 it was converted by Somerset County Council into a home for handicapped children.

It was requisitioned by the military in August 1940 and became the 41st General Military Hospital, providing accommodation in tents and huts. From 1941 the hospital was leased to the Americans as a neurological hospital for over 1,000 patients in 32 new wards which were completed in 1942 serving as the 185th General Hospital. The hospital remained in military use until 1944. The psychiatric hospital reopened under the National Health Service in 1948 and further buildings were constructed. And, this was where Marie was going to live.

The hospital was just outside a small village and seemed bleak and isolated.

It was still raining heavy as we left the main road and turned onto a lane which ran through an expanse of green fields onto the 141 acres of land. A mansion stood out in the distance and as we got nearer, the institution came into view.

We crawled past rows of prefabricated wards/huts and drove up to an imposing square mansion, which stood in the centre of the grounds.

Matron came out to meet us. After the introductions, she walked on ahead with the Social Worker leaving Marie and I to follow. We went through the reception in the main hall and followed Matron into a large room on the left. An official looking man was sitting down at an enormous table with some forms for the Social Worker to sign. Marie began to screech.

"That's a good pair of lungs she's got," Matron said cheerfully.

"Yes, she can be quite a noisy child," the Social Worker commented as she smiled at me. I gave her a filthy look and turned away. At that moment I hated them all. We sat down at the table—Marie on my lap and let the formalities begin.

We were soon sitting in the car heading towards the ward which was to be Marie's new home. The rain danced on the windows; the windscreen wipers started the countdown.

As we drove to the ward, there was another member of staff waiting outside to greet us. This time it was the sister in charge whom I later learned was Sister Green. I lifted Marie out of the car.

"I'll wait here," the Social Worker said.

Today as I look back over the years, I wonder how she could have left me to go in alone.

Sister Green led the way. I had never been on a ward for mentally handicapped children before and didn't know what to expect.

Tears ran down my face as we made our way through what was known as the day-room. I stepped over the children who lay on the floor; so many children. Sounds rose to meet me but no words. Some of them were rocking or rolling over and others, staring into space. A young boy was groaning and punching the side of his red, swollen face. My eyes rested on a child who had the largest head I had ever seen.

We left the day-room and followed Sister Green through a hallway into her office. Marie was screeching, making any conversation difficult to hear. I wanted to screech too; I had no control over the awful things that happened to her.

We could see the dormitory through the office window. Sister Green was pointing to where Marie was going to sleep; "She'll be No 11," she stated, trying to give me some idea where her cot was in the large dormitory. In my oversensitive mood it was the straw that broke the camel's back. I handed Marie over to Sister Green and walked out of the office.

The Social Worker was sitting in her car reading the paper.

"Matron wants to see you," she said as I sat in beside her. "I'll take you there first, and then we can have some lunch." We drove back to the mansion. I went in alone. I didn't have a clue what Matron wanted, and I didn't really care. My mind was full of Marie. Last time she was taken, this time I gave her away; she was free to anybody that would have her because nobody wanted her – she was anybody's.

"Sit down," Matron offered kindly when I walked into her office.

"Have you got a job to go to?" she asked. I shrugged, too upset to speak.

"Would you like to work here?" she asked to my surprise. I looked at her, sitting behind her desk in her blue uniform, not quite believing what she had said. I finally managed to speak; "You mean work here in the hospital?"

She nodded. "Would you like to work with handicapped people?" she asked. It could have been a million pounds this kind lady was offering me. I never dreamt when I was being driven into the hospital half an hour earlier that I would be returning.

"Take these forms with you and think about it," she told me. I didn't have to think about it. I'd already made up my mind.

A short time later I was sitting in the staff dining room in the back of the mansion trying desperately to pull myself together. I was relieved that the build up of the past few months was over and saddened that Marie would never be able to understand how I had no choice but to leave her.

"Eat up, Michelle," the Social Worker said, trying to sound cheerful. My tears wouldn't stop. I sat with my head down and watched them dripping onto my dinner.

5

So Far Away From Home

I shook the snow from my coat as I boarded the train for Taunton. I hadn't seen Marie for six weeks; it seemed like six years. I had spent Christmas at home with my family and New Year with Cathy, in Bristol. It was now January 2nd 1971.

By late afternoon, I was cruising up the drive to Sandhill Park Hospital in a taxi. When we neared the wards, I glanced over to where Marie was living. I longed to stop the taxi to go and see her but knew I would have to tread carefully now that I was one of the staff.

I walked into the mansion and, finding nobody on reception, I put my case down by the desk and walked over to Matron's office, knocking gently on the door. It was almost dark outside. I assumed it was tea-time on the wards, but I hoped that Matron might suggest I visit Marie if I didn't stay too long. Some hope!

"Hello," I said stupidly when she opened the door. I was not yet aware of the formalities.

"Good evening," she said without a flicker of friendliness. "Would you wait over there and I'll get someone to show you where your room is." She closed the door again so I went and stood by my case. I looked at the room opposite with the door wide open revealing the long table where I sat when Marie was admitted.

When the nurse arrived I followed her through the door by the reception desk into the big hall. We walked up three flights of stairs to the nurse's home on the top floor.

"Are you hungry?" she asked, opening the landing door. I shook my head and explained how my health conscious sister, Cathy, had filled me with her macrobiotic food. I followed her into my tiny room and put my case on the bed. She quickly gave me lots of helpful information and advice before hurrying back on duty. Thanking her, I gently closed the door and walked towards my bedroom window. I sat on the ledge and looked out at the snow-covered wards still bright with decorations. My eyes rested on Marie's ward, too far to see inside; I longed for just a glimpse of her.

Life on a High Grade Ward

The next two hours were spent sitting in my room. Cathy had given me an enormous black trunk which I filled with books and other sentimental possessions I was unable to carry on the train. The trunk was arriving in a few days time.

I unpacked my case and put my clothes in the wardrobe.

At 7.30, when I heard lots of footsteps, I went along to the staff sitting room where some of the nurses had just come off duty.

"Are you the new girl?" a nurse in the far corner asked.

"Yes," I replied, feeling shy in a room full of strangers.

"Have you come to start your nurse's training?"

I shook my head.

"I'm a cadet nurse. I'm not old enough to do my training."

"How old are you then?" she asked me, lighting a cigarette.

"I'm 17." I replied. Changing the subject, and longing to know, I asked if anybody worked on the children's ward.

"Which one?" a nurse in a pink dress asked me.

"I'm not sure," I laughed nervously. "Do you know a little girl called Marie?"

"She means the screamer," said a nurse in a white coat.

"Why do you call her that?"

"Because that's all she does" she replied.

"Isn't she on the high-grade ward?" the nurse in the pink dress asked.

It sounded awful, so I asked them what they were talking about. Apparently there were two wards for each age group—low-grade and high-grade. That's the way it was in those days, when handicapped children were graded like vegetables.

"Why are you so interested in her anyway? Are you a relative?"

"No," I replied. "I used to look after her and I'm hoping that I can still visit and take her out."

"If you've come to work here you'll not be allowed to visit her," I was warned. "Staff are not allowed personal relationships with the patients."

I finally made an excuse to return to my room where I sat on my bed, hoping what they had told me wasn't true.

I lay awake for most of the night. For the first time since I left home I felt lonely. I wondered what was in store for me and how Marie was coping with her new life on a 'high-grade' ward.

Next morning I reported to Matron's office and was promptly collected by a young nurse I was to be working with. She took me to the laundry where I was given my white coat—then on to the sewing room where I collected my cape. Stepping outside in the cold morning air we walked carefully across the paths, trying not to slip on the snow. I folded my cape around me appreciatively.

The wards were in rows of two, with one entrance in the middle of the building where one ward was to the left and the other to the right. I was in the row above Marie's, which meant I was directly opposite, separated by a garden. It was still dark outside, and even though the lights were on in Marie's ward, I couldn't see very much.

I thanked the nurse for taking me under her wing as we hurried into the warmth of my new ward. Sister introduced me to the staff.

I smiled recognising some of the nurses from the previous evening. I was on the high-grade ward for teenagers. When I was taken into the dormitory to be introduced to the rest of the staff and patients, I was grateful that the curtains were still closed preventing me from looking over to Marie's ward, enabling me to concentrate on the job I had come to do.

Most of the patients were in the bathroom. Glancing along the dormitory, I took in two rows of beds separated by dressing tables, with personal items placed on top—photographs and dainty ornaments. There was a unit which ran the length of the end wall where most of the patients kept their dresses and coats with small cubicles at the bottom for underclothes and nightwear. One by one, the patients returned from the bathroom. I was surprised at how friendly they were and how easily they accepted someone new to look after them. A young girl named Debra came and showed me a photo of her mother.

"What's your name, nurse?" she asked.

"My name is Michelle."

"We're not allowed to be called by our first names," a nurse chipped in.

"Then my name is Nurse Shearon," I replied.

We spent the next half hour folding nightclothes, straightening beds, brushing hair and generally being available if anybody needed help. I was finding it difficult to concentrate since our curtains were now open. Just a little peep at her would have been enough; I needed to see if she was all right.

An Early Social Call

I followed the nurse out of the ward and looked over to where Marie was living. "Are you coming to breakfast?" she asked me, handing me my cape. I knew I couldn't wait any longer.

"Actually I'm not very hungry," I told her, hoping I didn't seem unfriendly. "I'll come over to the dining room in ten minutes and have a cup of tea." We parted to go our different ways; she must have wondered where I was going.

Off I walked down the drive to the next turning. When I reached the entrance I was scared to go in. I hadn't seen Marie for so long. After being used to virtually living with her, this was going to be a snatched ten minutes, if I was allowed to see her at all. My watch said 8.15. I quickly walked through the entrance and into the day-room. It was empty, except for a cleaner mopping the floor. I glanced down the ward through the window into Sister Green's office; she saw me and came out.

"Hello, Sister," I said cheerfully, trying to ignore her deadpan expression. "How is Marie?" My heart started thumping. I thought she would kick me off the ward for cheek with such an early social call.

"She's fine," was the icy reply. "We weren't given all the facts about her when she came to us," she went on, but I didn't understand what she meant. My legs felt like jelly as I stood there. Sister spoke again; "Her mother has been to see her. We didn't know she lived so near."

I didn't know what to say to her.

"I don't really know anything about Marie's history, Sister," I said cautiously. I looked down past Sister Green to see where the sudden noise was coming from; it was a porter. I cleared my throat.

"Can I go and see Marie, Sister—just for a minute?" My heart almost stopped as I waited for her to answer.

"She's in the bathroom," she finally replied. I followed her through the day room and she pointed to a door where there was lots of noise coming from. In I went.

The children were sitting on their pots on the floor. I greeted the nurse and was distracted by a squeal to the side of me that I'd have recognised anywhere. My eyes rested on my little friend in the corner. She sat clapping her hands with excitement, laughing loudly and looking in my direction.

"Hello, Marie," I said, crossing the bathroom and stooping down in front of her. Her hair had grown slightly and it bounced as she looked away from me and tried to hide. She wore an awful rust coloured dress on top of which she had a pink cardigan with no buttons, but she looked well and seemed a bit chubbier.

"Did you think I'd forgotten you?" I whispered, stroking her hair. I lifted her fringe and saw the lump on her forehead which told me of the hours she still spent banging her head. She laughed so loudly. Her eyes filled with tears. It must have been such a surprise to see a familiar face after being left with complete strangers (again).

"Doesn't she look happy?" the nurse shouted across the bathroom. She was busy washing one of the children's faces. "Did you used to know her?"

"Yes," I replied, looking at Marie tenderly. "I used to know her."

I wanted to take her off the pot and sit her on my knee but it was almost time for school. I remained crouched on the floor in front of her and she held onto my hand. The other children shuffled over to where we were sitting, pulling at my cape and beckoning for attention. Somehow they didn't seem as upsetting as they did the first time I saw them.

I sat for a while longer and then, looking at my watch, I realised it was time to go. I loosened Marie's hands and hesitated for a moment. I wish she could have understood that I was now living nearby, but she never would. I kissed her goodbye and left. I could hear her crying as I walked out through the day-room.

When I was outside there was a nurse walking ahead of me, and as I got nearer, I saw that it was Sister Green. *Shall I ask her?* I thought, and then suddenly ran to catch her up. I had to know one way or the other.

"Can I visit Marie again, Sister?"

"You can come between two and four Saturdays and Sundays," she replied to my great relief.

"Thanks, Sister," I said as I left her to run back to my ward before I was late.

6

Fun at the Disco

When I entered the day-room on my ward, the patients were sitting with their coats on ready to go to OT (Occupational Therapy).

"Are you coming to the disco tonight?" one of them asked.

"I don't know." I answered. "Is it in the hospital?"

"There's a staff Social Club and the patients have a disco down there every Monday night." The nurse sitting beside me said. "You'll see tonight when we take our patients down there."

My first day went slowly. After working in the convent and being Jack-of-all-trades, my only role on the ward was to attend to patients needs. Cleaning and cooking was no longer part of my job description and I felt quite useless at times, especially with the patients being at OT all day.

That evening, there was a buzz of excitement as the women took their dresses out of the wardrobe and laid them on their beds. The disco didn't start until half-seven, and there was hours to go, but the nurses encouraged the young women and were carried along with the patients' excitement.

We went out into the freezing cold and walked down the drive towards the Social Club. I listened to the patients talking about their boyfriends, and who they were going to dance with.

The disco lights were low, and some of the male patients started to cheer when our patients walked in. They giggled and went off to mingle. There was a bar in the corner where they bought refreshments. Although I was starting to realise how 'normal' these 'handicapped' women were, I wasn't too sure about the men; I was still a bit wary and felt out of my depth surrounded by so many people.

The door opened occasionally and groups of people came in shouting greetings across the room to their friends. It was all so different to what I imagined it would be. George Harrison's 'My Sweet Lord' was belting out in the background. It was a privilege to be there.

"Would you like to dance?" someone asked, breaking in on my thoughts.

"No thanks," I replied feeling guilty but not yet having the confidence to dance with a patient. Later on I had a dance with one of the male nurses—or so I thought. It wasn't until we were getting ready to return to the ward that I realised I'd danced with a patient and refused the nurse. Served me right!

Walking in the Moonlight

"Why do they live here if there's hardly anything wrong with them?" I asked one of the nurses on the way home from the disco.

"Some of them have lived here all their lives," she told me, "and they're quite happy here."

"Do you like working here?" I couldn't help noticing how kind she was to the patients, as though she really enjoyed the job. She nodded. Together with the patients we strolled up the moonlit drive towards the wards. There was something quite beautiful about these people, something that hit me with great force; their naturalness and lack of pretence, their kindness, warmth and affection for each other. It was overwhelming.

My eyes filled up when we passed my little friend's dormitory. The curtains were closed. She was probably asleep. I was aware of our feet crunching in the snow and wondered if we might waken her.

"Are you from Liverpool?" the nurse asked me. I smiled and waited for another phoney imitation of my Liverpool accent. "You're a long way from home. What made you come this far?"

"It's a long story," I answered and briefly told her about Marie and how I came to be at the hospital by accident more than anything. "I only really came to see if she was all right."

She groaned sympathetically. "Have you met Sister Green yet? She's very strict with the nurses and I don't think she'll let you take your little girl out."

"She said it's all right for me to visit," I told her, feeling relieved as I reflected on the friendly warnings and sleepless night I had the previous evening.

That night I lay in bed going over the day's events and, for the first time in weeks, had a decent night's sleep.

Treated Like One of the Family

The week dragged! When Saturday arrived I wandered around the nurses' home waiting for Marie's visiting time. With ten minutes to go, I left the mansion and made my way to the ward. I waved to some of the nurses through the ward windows. I must have been a curious figure indeed.

"You can take her into the dormitory if you like," Sister Green kindly offered. I left the noisy day-room and carried Marie to a chair at the side of her cot. It was as though we'd never been apart. There was a mirror at the end of the dormitory, so I stood Marie in front of it. I knew on that day when I looked at her reflection that I would always visit her wherever she was. We were bonded friends for life.

I was grateful to Sister Green for the privacy of the dormitory. I liked her despite all I'd heard. I thought she was just a very direct person. During the afternoon she sent one of the nurses in with a cup of tea for me. Sister Green hardly spoke to me, but in her own way she'd made me welcome. I was so grateful to her.

I visited Marie on Sunday too, cementing our weekend routine. After a while, whenever I visited, I would stop and peep through the day-room window and Marie would be sitting on the floor in her good clothes, ready to go out. When the weather got warmer we walked hand in hand around the hospital grounds.

When I was on duty I often shared a dining table with Sister Green, but neither of us mentioned Marie. We would simply greet each other. Matron and I passed each other during the week with a formal, "Good morning," or "Good afternoon," but at weekends I was treated like a visitor. They stopped to chat, and were always friendly and kind.

There was a recreation hall opposite the mansion which visitors used at weekends and where we could buy refreshments. I used to take Marie there on a Sunday. I had come to know quite a few of the patients so it was very interesting for me to be able to meet their families.

It was through talking to parents I had a better understanding of why it isn't always possible for the patients to live at home. I thought they lived in hospital because they had been rejected by their families but that was not the case. I began to realise how difficult it must be for parents when they visit their son or daughter, and understood why many of the parents did not bother.

I liked my work on the wards although I missed the homeliness of the convent. I was used to having one person in charge and working alongside her for most of the day. On the ward there were two shifts with a different person in charge, and, because of the different ideas they had, it was sometimes rather confusing.

If another ward was short-staffed I would be sent to cover for the day. I learnt quite a bit about various disabilities and the awful labels like "Mongol" and "Gargoyle" the children were given. There was an autistic girl who stood against the wall near Sister's office all day looking down at the floor. The sad thing was that she understood everything and would point to specific people when I asked her where they were.

Special Treatment

I am lucky in that I have always been a good mixer. I am also a lazy person. If I like someone, I love them; if I don't I find it very hard to make an effort and pretend. I liked most of the nurses and made some good friends. Most of them accepted my relationship with Marie; some were a little resentful that I was allowed to take her out. I remember an incident in the nurse's sitting room when one of the staff said how unfair it was that I was allowed to take one of the patients out and she couldn't. On and on she went; "You're not being very fair to her are you? She must think you're her mother."

I tried to explain that I wasn't picked out for any special treatment, that I had looked after Marie before working at the hospital, but still she went on.

"What happens to her when you leave? She's so attached to you and you're just playing with her emotions."

I told her if she had any qualms about my 'special treatment,' she was better taking her complaints higher up.

On the other hand, I didn't talk about Marie very much. I knew I was privileged and didn't want to rub salt in the wounds of other nurses, but also I was very aware that the nurses were off duty, and it wasn't fair on them.

One day I took the patients from my ward into the garden. I always stayed away from Marie's ward for fear of being a nuisance, so I took the group of girls up to the top part away from her day-room. We were playing ball when one of the girls shouted.

"Somebody wants you, nurse." When I turned around Sister Green was calling me to the window; she's seen me out in the garden and fetched Marie for me to see. I ran towards the window and was delighted to see she had stood Marie on the ledge. This was a special treat for me. I waved to Marie and blew her a kiss and sadly, returned to my patients.

I don't think Marie was aware that I was in the hospital all the time. When I took her back to the ward on a Sunday, I probably wouldn't see her until the following weekend when I was off duty. There were occasions when I saw her going for a walk but I used to hide. I knew if she saw me she would get upset and have to be pulled off me. It wasn't fair on her, so I would just follow her with my eyes until she was out of sight.

After I'd been at Sandhill a couple of months, I asked Sister Green if I could take Marie into Taunton to buy her some shoes.

"I don't see why not," she answered, "I'll have a word with Matron."

The next Saturday, with Matron's blessing, I collected Marie to take her out for the day. She was steadier on her feet, but her cerebral palsy meant she would always walk with a gait. I didn't mind carrying her but every so often I held her hand and encouraged her to walk.

We had chips and ice cream in British Home Stores café and when Marie finished eating she kept herself occupied by looking at people's noisy shoes. She had hardly altered since I met her at Nazareth House, except for the effort she was making to feed herself. There was still no sign of any speech.

When I took her for new shoes, she screamed in the shop and went stiff with fear at the foot measurer but the sales assistant persevered and Marie finally left the shop wearing a little pair of blue Clarke's shoes.

We walked around the town, which was still strange to me. I discovered a park full of rose gardens and paths and sat on the bench while Marie plodded up and down making as much noise as her little feet could. I never dreamt whilst sitting on that bench that Marie's grandmother lived just around the corner.

I returned to the ward, gave my little friend her tea, and then it was time for me to disappear. When Marie realised I was leaving her, she plonked herself down on the floor with her legs splayed out, and started crying. Sister Green would not allow any of the staff to comfort her as she crashed her head onto the floor. Perhaps Sister Green thought Marie would eventually outgrow the self-injurious behaviour, but she never did. I just wished they would sit her on a chair so she wouldn't hurt herself so much. I knew she had to learn not to screech, but we'd had such a wonderful day it seemed sad that it finished with her being upset.

It was at times like this I wondered whether I was doing her more harm than good.

When I arrived back at the mansion I was glad of the nurses company. Laura, one of the orderlies who slept in the room next to mine was a graduate and was working at Sandhill until she saved enough money to go abroad for a year. We worked on different wards but would spend hours talking in each other's room at night. She often went home on a Saturday night and returned to the hospital the next day and after much coaxing, I went with her. Laura's brother had Down's syndrome and was adored by all the family. Her mother was a member of the Hospital Board and always asked after Marie. I told her once that my biggest fear was being stopped from visiting Marie, but she told me emphatically that that would never happen.

The Quality of Their Day Depends on Who is in Charge

On occasions when I went to visit Marie and Sister Meaney, the deputy ward sister, was on duty, my visit wasn't so pleasant. Marie was always sitting on her cot alone in the empty dormitory, crying. She had been put there so she wouldn't dirty her 'going out' clothes, but it was a cruel thing to do to a child with such limited understanding. Marie was hysterical when I carried her off the ward, since she'd been so frightened to be left on her own. I used to feel so angry, but I wouldn't dare complain to her. At the flick of a switch Sister Meaney could stop my visits.

One of the nurses told me that Sister Meaney didn't like either Marie or myself and didn't agree with the freedom I was given with her. She thought Marie was a spiteful child because she pulled hair.

It was at times like this I realised how vulnerable the patients were and how the quality of their day depended on who was running the ward. Even on my own ward, despite having a very kind and competent ward sister, something happened one day which shook my whole confidence in the establishment.

It was Sister's day off. An S.E.N. (State Enrolled Nurse) had been left in charge for the day with a student nurse. It was disco night. As usual, the patients came running in from Occupational Therapy as though they had ten minutes to get ready instead of three hours. We laughed and encouraged them when they collected their dresses from the wardrobes. Denise, one of the patients, was walking over to her bed when the student nurse snatched her dress from her and threw it to the nurse in charge, who then childishly threw it back. Poor Denise began to cry. The nurses continued throwing the dress and Denise's effort to recover it failed miserably. She began to scream and cry uncontrollably, and out of pure frustration, threw herself on the floor. Within minutes, specks of blood appeared on her face as she flicked it with her nails. The nurses didn't like what they saw. They had carried the joke too far and it backfired on them. One of the nurses started shouting at Denise, and instead of leaving her to calm down, both the nurses dragged her up off the floor. Denise broke free from their grip and flung her glasses, smashing them, as both the nurses pushed and shoved her up the ward.

Poor Denise was sent to bed and missed the disco. Her 'outburst' was written in the diary but the nurses didn't add that they'd played a joke on somebody who wasn't emotionally mature enough to take it, and who had responded in the only way her mental age allowed. I was in such a dilemma! I wanted to report the nurses but I knew I'd have to keep my mouth shut if I wanted to see Marie every weekend. I'd learnt when a nurse complains about things she's seen as an upstart.

A few days later, my ward sister was making out a list of patients to see the doctor.

"I don't know what to do about Denise," she said, looking puzzled. "It's not like her at all to behave like that." She went on to say that her sedation might not be strong enough. Unable to contain my anger any longer I told her what had happened. I also added that if Denise was given more sedation because of the incident, then I would report the two nurses. Sister knew something was wrong because she knew her patients well. Denise didn't see the doctor and her drugs weren't changed. I felt that the lack of concern by the medical staff about Denise's 'rebellious' behaviour left an obvious question about the nurse's ability in looking after her. Although the incident had been extremely upsetting for Denise, all the nurses had done was draw attention to each other. However, this ward was Marie's next stop; I'd seen too much to ignore it. I started to think of ways to get her out of the hospital but I thought unless I was a relative it couldn't be done.

One evening something quite strange happened. I went home with one of the nurses and picked up the local paper to read as I sat idly waiting for my friend to make some coffee. I opened the obituary page and to this day I don't know what made me do it. I looked down the column to see if either of Marie's grandparent's was there. I was astonished to see Marie's grandfather had been buried that day. I felt quite shocked I thought it was possible and there it was in black and white. The fact that Marie's grandparents' address was there made me wonder at the coincidence. I cut out the clipping and when I returned to my room at the nurse's home I put it away in my letter box. I sat on my bed for a long while after wondering at the strange occurrence.

Then the thing I dreaded most happened; I was moved to the ward next to Marie's. This meant the same door was used for both wards on entering the building, but instead of going left into Marie's ward I turned right into my own. This really did make things very difficult. Every morning the children from both wards travelled to school on the same bus; the problem was that a member of staff had to take the children to meet the bus outside. I avoided this whenever possible because Marie got very upset when she saw me and had to be pulled off me and put on the bus for school. I knew it was a hopeless situation. I was trying to play the detached nurse and the loving mother at the same time. I couldn't do it. I began to think about leaving. My contract was coming up for renewal at the end of the month because I was almost eighteen and due to start my nurse's training which would have meant no more weekends off.

My mother must have been very disappointed though she never said anything. For the first time in my life I was doing something sensible. My family knew about Marie, but I don't think they realised how involved I was with her. To most people she was just a little girl I'd become fond of; to me she was like my own child. I now lived in a different world from that of my family—or so it seemed. We still kept in touch and wrote often. Leaving home so young and being so far away, I always had letters from them. They arrived in all shapes and sizes depending, of course, on who wrote them. I'd had pieces of toilet roll from Liz, full of news of Marathon the tortoise and Herbert the frog. I once received a letter from Maureen, written on a piece of Kleenex tissue. I remember the first letter I received from my mother, at the hospital. A five pound note had dropped out of the envelope. 'Put this money away for your train fare in case you want to leave.' I knew I had caused her a lot of worry as I drifted further and further away. Following destiny's path—or so I thought. Still rebelling against my Catholic upbringing, I had closed the door on God.

My final month was full of turmoil. Had I done the right thing? Would I still be able to visit Marie? All these questions played havoc with my sleep. Without realising, my relationship with Marie had turned me into a loner. I still liked being with people, and knew how to enjoy myself, but I needed to be alone for a certain amount of time each day. I needed to sit and think things through; things I refrained from discussing with the other nurses. My dilemma isolated me.

I had no trouble finding accommodation. My sister, Cathy, and most of her friends were leaving Bristol, so there was plenty of flats I could move into. My mother wanted me to return home, but I couldn't think about going so far away from the hospital—not yet anyway.

So once again, I was packing.

I Wonder Where We'll Go From Here, Marie.

On the Saturday before I left, I took Marie into Taunton with some friends. We took her to our usual haunts, and spent the rest of the afternoon at the park. Off she went along the paths, loving the freedom, stopping to check once in a while that we were still there. Later in the afternoon, when we arrived back at the hospital, we took it in turns to give Marie a piggy-back up the drive. Marie laughed uncontrollably when we raced with her. My friends kissed her goodbye and headed towards the nurses' home. I went on to Marie's ward.

Sister Green was sitting in the day room, with one of the children on her knee. I couldn't speak, so I smiled at her, and took Marie into the bathroom to undress her. I sat her on the locker and began to undo her shoes. She was watching me fold her clothes.

"I wonder where we'll go from here." I said sadly. Marie still had the big scab on her forehead, so I told her, "When I see you again, that's got to be better!" She laughed, not knowing what I was saying, but knowing from my tone I was having fun with her. I tried so hard not to cry, and now here I was with the tears running down my face. Sister Green came in. That made me worse. I thought of all the awful warnings I'd had about her, yet she'd been nothing but kind and supportive towards me.

"She'll miss you, won't she?" she asked, passing me Marie's nightdress. "You will come back and see her, won't you?" I was so relieved to hear those words; that I was still welcome.

"Of course I will, Sister. I'll come back whenever I can."

"I thought you liked working here?" she asked me, leaning on the locker top.

"I do, Sister, but I find it difficult trying to avoid Marie all the time and besides, if I continued to work at the hospital I wouldn't be able to see her at weekends anymore."

"I hadn't thought about that, and I suppose with her being at school throughout the week you'd hardly see her would you?" I shook my head.

I thanked her for always being so kind and making me welcome. Soon after, I kissed Marie goodbye and left. When I walked through the day room on my way out a little boy was sitting watching the television.

"Goodbye, nurse," he said softly.

"Goodbye," I replied. "See you soon." It was the little boy I'd seen with the large head when Marie had first been admitted to the ward. He had horrified me then; now I hardly noticed his disability. I had been the one with the handicap, not him.

7

Life is Full of Surprises

I was working in another hospital, which was so different to Sandhill Park.

Stoke Park Hospital, was a dreadful place, and described by the Hospital Advisory Service in 1971, as a slum. The wards were so overcrowded there was hardly any room to walk in between the patients beds. I must have been on the worst ward in the hospital because lots of staff refused to work on there.

My family were worried about me. I was no longer in a residential job and I lived in a flat on my own. My mother came to stay for a week.

I had caught scabies and head lice from the patients, and my poor mother was horrified. She bought me lotion from the chemist to douse on my skin after a scalding bath and each night she went through my hair with a tooth comb. She tried desperately to talk me into going home with her, but I wouldn't.

Cathy tried next, with her long letters about the wonders of London and how I would love living in the big city. Then my aunty Terry came to stay for a week. She almost talked me into going home to my family, but I told her I needed more time.

I had been back to visit Marie several times. I found it much easier not working at the hospital, yet I still wasn't happy about her living there.

It was six months later when I packed up my job and belongings and moved home to Liverpool. I regretted it almost immediately. How could I have moved so far away from my little friend? There was nobody to visit her at weekends anymore and take her out for the day.

People kept telling me to forget about Marie, that she'd be alright and was far too much responsibility for someone so young. I gave up arguing. How could I explain how close we were—how when I heard a cat cry during the night I thought about Marie lying in her cot with the dimmed dormitory light watching over her?

One evening I was talking to my younger sister, Liz. We were conspiring of ways to rescue Marie. I considered the possibility of Marie's mother adopting me, making me Marie's sister. That would give me the authority to have her discharged from the hospital. No, we decided, Marie's mother adopting me was too impractical. Then I had a brainwave!

"Hey, Liz, I wonder if it would be possible to have Marie transferred to a hospital in Liverpool?" That would have been too much to expect. Wouldn't it?

After thinking of nothing else for several days I finally sat down and wrote a letter to Dr. Bakker at Sandhill Park, telling him of my concern for Marie since I was so far away from Taunton, and wondering about the possibility of a transfer. I tried not to imagine how wonderful that would be.

A week later I received a reply. I was shaking as I opened the letter. I had to read it twice; I couldn't believe what he was telling me.

"What is he saying?" Liz asked as she came running down the stairs. I handed her the letter and watched her face as she read it. Looking at me with eyes that were about to pop, she said, "Oh Mish, they're looking into it for you!"

I was stunned.

Christmas came and went. While I was anxiously awaiting news from Sandhill, I was busy job hunting. I managed to get on a one year residential course in a residential school for physically disabled children.

In the meantime, I wrote to Dr. Bakker again and asked him if there were any developments regarding Marie's transfer. Almost immediately, I received a reply, from a Dr. Prentice, telling me that Dr. Bakker had left, and there was no trace of my previous letter. I had thought it was too good to be true. I expected the hospital staff to start ignoring me now that I lived so far away. They probably thought I would lose interest, but I wouldn't.

I wrote to Dr. Prentice explaining the situation and sending a copy of my previous letter to Dr. Bakker. I was delighted when I received a reply a week later saying he was looking into the possibilities of a transfer and was awaiting observations from Marie's parents.

Oh well, I thought, *at least he hasn't said no.*

Why Aren't There Doctors Like This Anymore?

Towards the middle of February, a letter arrived from the hospital. I had telephoned Sister Green, the previous week, enquiring after Marie. Dr. Prentice had written to say my telephone enquiry had been passed on to him, and he was still awaiting observations from the parents. How nice of him to let me know.

I was telling my friend Sue, at work about my plight. "I need to go to Somerset," I told her, "and I can't afford the train fare. Will you hitch with me?" I asked cautiously. I knew the route because I hitched up and down to Bristol with Cathy, but I would not hitch alone for obvious reasons.

"OK," Sue replied. "You arrange it with the hospital and then let me know when you want to go."

I didn't waste any time; a few days later, we left my mum's at five in the morning, having gone there from work the previous evening. It was March and Sue and I stood shivering in the thick fog as we tried to hitch a lift towards the M6 motorway. It wasn't long before a lorry pulled up.

"Where are you going?" the driver asked as we climbed up into the warm cab.

"We want to go to Taunton in Somerset," I told him.

"Well I'm only going as far as Birmingham so I'll drop you off and you can get another lift."

"Oh great!" I said, "We're hoping to get there for two o'clock because we have to be back in Liverpool tonight."

He looked at me like I'd suddenly grown two heads. "You're coming all the way back tonight?" he asked incredulously. We nodded. "You must be mad," he muttered, "you'll never do it."

"We will!" I whispered to Sue when I saw the worried look on her face.

"Don't Build Your Hopes Up Too Much"

The sun was shining when we reached Sandhill Park at almost two in the afternoon. Walking up the drive we waved to some of the patients and nurses I knew who were going for walks.

"Hello!" one of the nurses shouted cheerfully, "Have you come to see your little girl?"

"Yes," I answered, feeling excited as we neared the ward. The children were playing outside so we went through the day-room and out into the garden. My heart sank when I saw Sister Meaney, but I smiled and said "hello". Marie spotted us from the other side of the garden, stood up and came staggering over. I picked her up and gave her a hug. The look on her face told me she knew I would come back. I was shocked. I hadn't seen her for five months. I'd even wondered if she'd recognise me. How wrong I had been.

One of the children took Sue's hand, and was trying to pull her across the garden. I walked over to Sister Meaney and asked if it was all right to take Marie for a walk.

"Yes," she answered, "but under no circumstances is she to go out of the hospital grounds."

"What a strange thing to say," I whispered to Sue as we left the garden. "Something must be wrong. They know I'm only visiting for an hour, and why would I take Marie outside the hospital without asking them?"

We found a bench to sit on, and I lifted Marie onto my lap. I was upset. Marie's sad little face and the sore on her forehead, told me of the hours she spent banging her head onto the floor. What a life.

After a few minutes' rest, with Marie holding both our hands, we continued our walk. As we passed the next ward I could hear someone knocking. I turned to look and Sister Green was opening the window to speak to me. I was pleased to see her, but also surprised.

"Hello Sister." I said. "What are you doing on this ward?"

"I've been moved," she said sadly.

"That's a shame." I told her. "I bet all the children will miss you."

"They'll soon get used to somebody else," she said modestly, but as I left her my eyes stung. She loved those children. I knew they would miss her. She had looked after them so well.

We found a bench and sat down again. I studied Marie's appearance. I had never seen her look like this before. She wore brown leather spastic boots and had a horrible looking eczema on her scalp. I was frightened by what Sister Meaney said to me about taking Marie out and saddened by Sister Green's move. I felt very insecure as I realised that a nurse who objected to my relationship with Marie, was now in charge of her ward.

"I think I'll go and see Matron," I said to Sue. "I need to know where I stand." I wiped my eyes and blew my nose in an effort to compose myself. We walked over to the mansion. Sue waited in reception and I carried Marie into Matron's office. I told Matron what Sister Meaney said to me.

"You're not going to stop me having contact with Marie, are you?" I asked her. Matron smiled and assured me that was not the case, that Sister Meaney was just being cautious. I then told her of my plans to have Marie transferred.

"Don't build your hopes up too much," she told me gently, "in case her mother objects."

I was happier leaving Matron's office than I had been going in! When it was time, I said goodbye to my little friend and left her back on the ward. We walked down the drive for our long journey home.

We did make it back that same night—but only just.

Our Tour of Inspection

When Sue and I arrived back at the residential school where we worked, we were busy telling the staff what had happened.

"The hospital in Somerset will never agree to the transfer," one of the housemothers said. "Even if they do, what hospital up here would accept her? You're not even a relation. And what if you lose interest and don't visit?"

"I won't stop visiting her!" I said defensively, but I hadn't really given any thought to how the Liverpool hospital would react to my request to have Marie transferred.

"Anyway," she added, "you're not old enough."

I couldn't argue with that comment.

Because maturity was not on my side, I was wary about making a formal application to the hospital in Liverpool in case they refused. I started to wonder how I could get inside the wards without the hospital staff knowing the reason for my visit.

When I arrived home from work that weekend, my younger brothers and sister were sitting watching TV. I asked if they would come to look at a hospital with me. Their expressions told me it was not the kind of thing they normally did on a Saturday.

"The only thing is, I don't want the staff to know the reason for our visit," I told them.

"Why not?" Liz asked me.

"Because I don't know if I am old enough to apply to the hospital to have Marie transferred, and until I do, I need to keep a low profile. Will you go and sort your old toys out?" I asked them. "And then we can pretend we're visiting the patients, and taking toys for the children. When we arrive on the ward, I can have a look around at the conditions." I didn't want Marie moving to a place that was unsuitable, just for the sake of being near me.

Ten minutes later we were ready to go.

"Right then," I said looking gratefully at their offerings, "Don't forget you must look around the ward and remember everything you see, so that you can tell me after the visit."

We cut through the park at the back of our house to the bus stop. I looked at the three of them as they turned their backs to the wind, with their toys tucked under their arms. Liz was 14, John was 12, and Peter was 10.

The bus ride took twenty minutes and dropped us right outside the hospital, but we were unable to see over the high wall that enclosed it. I could see a man in uniform standing at the hospital lodge, so I signalled John, Liz and Peter to hurry along. With heads held high, the four of us strode through the gates and past the lodge as though we knew where we were going.

We walked towards the nearest ward. I pulled open the heavy door and we went inside. A nurse approached when we entered the day-room. I smiled and told her we'd brought some toys for the children. Before I could say anything else, one of the patients, a teenage boy, went up to Liz and put his arms around her. Liz looked panic stricken; it was her first time in this type of environment.

What did I expect? I should have thought about my reaction the first time I went onto a ward of this type.

The nurse thanked us and then diplomatically escorted us out of the ward to the dining room where we were given tea and biscuits.

What on earth was I thinking?

My two brothers laughed and teased Liz. She was still red with embarrassment. I thought the whole thing was hilarious; a complete waste of time. I wondered how I'd got us into this silly situation.

"Maybe we can try again next week, Mish," Peter said.

"I can bring my soldiers along," John added. They made me laugh.

"No, that's OK. I think it might look a little obvious if we start visiting every week to donate toys; besides, you'll have none left. I'll have to think of something else," I told them.

Not long after I returned from Taunton, I received a letter from Dr. Prentice. Judging from its contents I gathered Matron had spoken to him after my visit to Sandhill. In the letter he stated that Marie's mother's permission was required for a transfer, and he was still waiting to hear from her.

I was grateful to the doctor for keeping me informed. I had never met him and I thought he was very good to write to me as often as he did. Marie's mother had visited when Marie was admitted to Sandhill and had not been back since. I was concerned that she might never go to the hospital again. I could be waiting years for her to make a decision.

It wasn't long before I was plotting and scheming again. This time I was taking a very serious step. I took Marie's grandfather's obituary out of my letter box. 'Did I find this for a reason? Was I given it for a purpose?' That evening I went over to visit my sister, Maureen. It was almost Sara's bedtime and she sat snugly on my knee. She was a beautiful child, with jet black hair and huge blue eyes. I showed Maureen the newspaper cutting.

"Do you think I should write to Marie's grandmother?" I asked.

"It's up to you, isn't it?" she answered. "You have to do what you think is best."

"Well," I said wearily, "I'm fed up; I'm sick of watching my p's and q's and always being frightened of upsetting people in case they stop me from visiting Marie. It's such a strain because I'm so direct by nature and they could stop me from seeing her tomorrow."

"Yes," she agreed, "but the staff are good to you, aren't they? I thought you could just go in and see Marie any time."

"But it isn't just that!" I said. "Of course they're good to me; they always have been. But what happens if Matron leaves the hospital and somebody with different ideas and attitudes comes along? I'm not playing games, and there's no security in it for Marie or myself."

I decided to write to Marie's grandmother. I knew I could blow my chances with Marie, but felt I had no choice. It seemed awful to be opening up old wounds for the family and I hoped they would see that I was acting in Marie's interest. I had discovered the obituary in such a strange way that I felt it had to be for a reason.

When I wrote to Marie's grandmother, I explained how I'd looked after her granddaughter for some time, told her of the potential I thought Marie had and how I thought she would benefit from living near me. I also explained that Marie's mother's permission was needed for the transfer. I posted my letter that same evening, feeling very scared as I put it in the box. I walked back home in the rain.

Returning to work the following day I was glad to be distracted by a new arrival. The poor boy had been given the grand title of 'maladjusted'. After unpacking his few belongings, we both went for a walk along the beach. Sitting on the sand I watched him dance in and out of the water, forgetting his grievances with a world that did not want him. I thought about some of the other children at the school. There was Jonathan who, at six, was proudly showing me how he could change his colostomy bag himself and Peter who struggled every morning to put on his callipers. And Paul, who with the slightest knock his limbs, smiled bravely to hide the pain he was in when his blood failed to clot and slowly seeped into his joints until they were so swollen he needed be hospitalised. I thought about Marie living on her ward and all the other children in care. I longed to open my own children's home.

I walked into my mother's after work and as usual, my eyes flew to the mantelpiece to see if I had any mail. There was a letter for me. I looked closely at the blue envelope and gasped when I saw the Taunton postmark. My heart started to pound. I was scared to open it, yet I had to know. I picked up the envelope that held Marie's future inside, grabbed a knife from the kitchen and hurried upstairs to my room. I closed the door and sat down on my bed. "Please, God," I prayed, "Let everything be all right." I carefully slid the knife across the top of the envelope and pulled out the letter. The news was good! I went rushing back down the stairs calling for my mother. Everybody came out of the living room with faces full of fear.

"Look," I shouted, "It's from Marie's grandmother. She thinks Marie's mother would be grateful for Marie's transfer, and look," I yelled, waving the letter, "She's sent Marie's mother's address."

I was so relieved. No more sneaking around.

"Where are you going?" my mother asked as I put my coat on.

"I'm going to tell Maureen!" I ran out of the house and danced through the park in the rain towards the bus stop.

8

A Selfless Kind of Love

"Gosh, it doesn't seem like we were here a month ago, does it?" Sue said as we left Marie's hospital. "Sister Meaney's not very friendly towards you, is she?"

I grinned. "She never has been," I told her, "but I couldn't care less. I just wouldn't give her room to complain about me. Thank God Sister Green was on that ward when Marie was admitted." I dreaded to think how different things would have been. Sister Meaney would never have encouraged weekend visits from me. Then Sue asked the dreaded question.

"Do you think Marie's mother will reply to your letter?"

"I don't know. I hear from Marie's grandmother that she's moved house since I wrote to her. Maybe Marie's mother is waiting for my letter to be sent on to her."

We crossed the busy main road to our familiar hitching spot. I reached into my bag for the remains of our sandwiches and melted chocolate. We were starving and beginning to feel tired.

"Is Marie always dressed that way?" Sue asked as she tucked into a sandwich. "I mean, what do they do with all the clothes you buy for her?"

"They go on hangers in the wardrobe. I could never understand this when I worked there. Some days the patients looked so tatty and it was unnecessary because they had some lovely clothes."

"You'd think they'd make an effort with Marie, wouldn't you?" she said with disgust.

"I think, like everything else, it depends on who's in charge of the ward," I said, thinking of the linen cupboard stacked to the ceiling with new clothes that were never worn.

Blessings

A week later I finally received a letter from Marie's mother. It is very difficult for me to put into words how I felt as I kept reading it. The letter finished with:

> 'From your letter I realise you love Marie very much
> and I know you'll give her all the love you possibly can.
> It seems strange for someone else to say they want your
> child, but under the circumstances you may be able
> to give something to Marie, which I may never have
> the chance to, and I would in no way wish to stop her
> chance of happiness.'

Marie's mother and I started writing to each other and arranged
to meet in Taunton on Whit Sunday. She had also authorised Marie's
transfer with the hospital

Dr. Prentice was away the weekend I went to Taunton. I was
nervous and spent six hours on the train from Liverpool with
nothing to do but worry. *What if they didn't like me? What if we just
can't get along?* I needn't have worried. When I met Marie's mother
and grandmother at Taunton station, we got on like a house on fire. I
was so comfortable with Marie's mother, I felt like I'd known her for
years. Exchanging letters helped.

It was strange being back in Taunton, passing familiar places
full of memories, and never realising we'd almost passed Marie's
grandmother's house on our Saturday trips to the park. Strange
again, to be walking side by side with Marie's mother, as if it were the
most natural thing in the world.

The next morning we travelled by bus to collect Marie for the day.
I thought Marie's mother was one brave lady to make that journey
with me; to put her own feelings aside, and support my plans, in
order to give her daughter a better life.

If only Marie had known when we went onto the ward, that it was
her mother standing beside me, but how could she?

Such Inconvenience

The school where I worked was closing down for two weeks in
the summer and I mentioned to Marie's mother that I would
like to have Marie for a holiday. She gave me her permission and
I wrote to Dr. Prentice with my request. It was eight weeks away. I
started counting the days, thinking how wonderful it would be to

tuck Marie up in bed at night.

A few days later, I realised when I received a letter from Dr. Prentice that I was getting ahead of myself.

"What's the matter?" my mother asked as I folded the letter into the envelope. "It's from Dr. Prentice," I answered quietly. "Marie can't be transferred unless I'm her legal guardian. It's never going to happen. I think I'm making headway and then something crops up and it seems so far away." My mother went downstairs to make a cup of tea and I followed her into the hall.

"What are you doing now?" she asked me when I picked up the telephone directory.

"I'm going to ring a solicitor," I told her. "I'm only asking if there is anything I can do," I added when I saw the worried look on her face. I randomly picked out a solicitor and was given an appointment for the next day. My mother continued to stand near the phone.

"Are you sure this is what you want to do?" she asked when I hung up.

"Of course it is!" I answered. "But whether I'll be allowed to is a different matter."

"I'll come with you then," she said. "There must be something he can do."

The solicitor was sympathetic and so helpful. I had to provide him with Marie's birth certificate, her mother's address and Dr. Prentice's. As soon as he'd consulted with the people concerned, a Deed of Guardianship would be drawn up and sent to be signed by Marie's mother and witnessed by two people.

That day I collected the signed, sealed, document from the solicitors, I paused at the realisation of how entwined my life was with Marie's. It would never have been possible without the help and support of so many people.

Dumped Into Care

Meanwhile, back at work, we had lectures every week. Our Social Worker would arrange for a group of us to visit a Home or hospital. One particular visit which sticks in my mind was to a general hospital where there was a long-stay ward for severely handicapped children. They lay like dolls on top of their cots and some of the children wriggled with excitement when we approached them.

"Why are they here?" one of the housemothers asked the ward sister who was showing our group around. "Don't their parents want them?"

"Some of the little mites have never known their mothers," Sister said gravely.

"It's cruel, isn't it?" one of the girls whispered to me. "If I had a child like that I would look after it myself," she told me indignantly.

"Look at that little girl's head," someone remarked. "Why is it so big?" Sister then went on to explain about Hydrocephalus. The little girl lying on her cot followed us with her eyes when we moved on until we were out of sight.

"Do you leave them on their cots all day?" I asked, and immediately realised I said the wrong thing. "I suppose they're too handicapped to do anything with, are they?" I asked her, knowing I was talking a load of rubbish but not wanting to sound too critical—which I often did. I slowly left the group and tried to imagine what life was like for those little children when they lay looking at the ceiling all day.

"God, it was awful, wasn't it?" one of our group complained when we left the building. "The way people just dump their children. They should be made to look after them," she stated looking around our group for approval.

"Children don't just go into care because their parents don't want them," I told her, unable to keep my mouth closed any longer. "Some parents just can't cope; you don't know all the circumstances." I thought of the mothers I met. "Maybe those who can cope have been made to feel that they can't and have been convinced that the child is better off in care." I knew I was too involved with it all because of Marie and took it all so seriously. Whenever possible I said nothing, but sometimes I found it difficult and must have sounded like a know-all. Maybe if the girls had known about my relationship with Marie they'd have made allowances for my intolerance, but I didn't really talk about her except to close friends.

The weeks went by and I was busy preparing for Marie's holiday. I had arranged with Matron to stay overnight in the Nurse's Home so we could have an early start the following day. However, when I arrived at the hospital to collect Marie, Matron was off and nobody knew anything about my plan to have her for a holiday. *Oh no*, I thought as I looked at the stranger in Matron's chair. *Not now. Not when we're nearly there.*

"Who gave you permission?" the stranger asked.

"Matron and Dr. Prentice," I told him.

"Are you certain?" he enquired.

"Actually, I think I have the doctor's letter on me," I answered, reaching in my bag.

"If I could just see it?" he said, and reached over the desk for me to hand it to him. Luckily for me I had taken it, though it hadn't been for any special purpose. In fact, it is a habit I never lost over the years. I keep everything I receive in the post, right down to the tatty old envelopes. Today, I have two filing cabinets bursting with my past.

Later that night, I was sitting in the Nurse's Home catching-up with some friends, when Wendy came off duty from Marie's ward.

"Sister Meaney is angry," she said with some amusement; "She didn't know anything about Marie's holiday and had to rush getting her things ready for tomorrow."

I could understand Sister Meaney's anger at the inconvenience, but I would have thought her enthusiasm for Marie having a holiday would have over-ridden all of that. However, her attitude did not surprise me. I was well aware that she objected to our relationship.

We stayed with my sister, Maureen, and had two glorious weeks. My family had heard so much about Marie and welcomed her with open arms. We both went on the bus to my mother's every day and spent hours in the park at the back of the house. We stayed for our tea and returned to Maureen's where Marie watched my niece Sara, playing for hours. No matter how contented Marie seemed, I was never far away in case she reached out to grab Sara's hair. She still screeched at bedtime, but settled down after a while.

One morning during the holiday, I received a letter from Dr. Prentice, in Taunton suggesting I contact Dr. Rogerson at the Liverpool hospital to see if she would like to assess Marie while she was staying with me. I didn't hesitate and wrote a quick letter to Dr. Rogerson, posting it immediately.

Meeting Dr Rogerson

Our holiday flew and much to my relief, Dr. Rogerson replied to my letter with an immediate appointment. The hospital was a mile from Maureen's, but it was easier to walk than to get on a bus.

It was a gloriously sunny morning. I sat Marie in Sara's pram and pushed her, with Liz accompanying me for moral support. Liz and I laughed when we approached the hospital, thinking of our last visit with the toys and how it had all gone wrong. We found our way to out-patients and I left Liz in the waiting room when I went in to see the Doctor.

I was still a little apprehensive about doctors after my experience a few years previously when Marie was taken from me in the children's hospital in Bristol. However, from the moment we went into her office, Dr. Rogerson gave Marie and I her full attention She had received information from Dr Prentice and checked a few details with me then turned her attention to setting out some tests for Marie, who was sitting quietly on my knee. The blocks she stacked on her desk immediately aroused Marie's interest. She slid off my knee and approached the desk. Marie was not interested in building anything. She spread the blocks across the table and banged them, enjoying the noise they made. Then Marie pretended to sneeze, something she had started to do on her holiday.

"Bless you!" I said cheerfully.

"Don't have her doing that, dear," Dr. Rogerson said to my surprise. She looked at me from behind her desk. "After all, you don't want her spitting on people, do you?" I cleared my throat.

"No," I answered quietly, not really understanding what she meant.

"Now, dear," she said, as our interview was obviously coming to an end, "There is a residential school opening soon. Would you like me to put her name down for it?" I nodded. "In the meantime I will put Marie's name on the waiting list for a bed here and let you know when there is a vacancy."

I was very pleased with the way our interview had gone and breathed a sigh of relief outside as I sat Marie in her pram and told Liz what had happened. "Just think," I said, "no more trips down to Taunton. She'll be living here soon and be able to come home every weekend."

The weather was scorching and I stooped down in front of Marie to remove her cardigan. She was so pretty, and if she hadn't been dribbling you wouldn't have known she had a disability. She had enjoyed her holiday so much—we all had—and she'd had so much attention and been fussed by all of my family. Her hair was going yellow in the sun and her skin, a lovely golden brown. The blue and white flowered cotton dress made such a change from the hospital crimplene I was used to seeing her in. As I folded Marie's cardigan into my bag, I wondered what Dr. Rogerson meant about not encouraging Marie to sneeze and it slowly dawned on me. In my ignorance I thought Marie imitating anything was positive but what good did it do her if she sneezed on people? None at all! I was grateful to Dr. Rogerson for pointing this out to me.

Rising Above it All

I didn't feel so bad taking Marie back on the train. After meeting Dr. Rogerson, I knew the plans were set in motion to have her transferred to Liverpool.

Our train journey took most of my wages, so a taxi ride out to Sandhill was out of the question. Besides, the bus picked us up outside the station and dropped us off near the hospital. I had taken Sara's pram with us because the hospital drive was an awful long way for me to carry Marie.

We left Taunton station and rode out into the countryside. When we arrived at the stop outside the hospital, I stepped down with Marie in my arms and lowered her into the pram. Off we went; one hand pushing the pram, and the other carrying Marie's case. However, it wasn't long before I was walking back down the drive again. Sister Meaney met us at the ward door. No smile—no words—nothing. I lifted Marie out of the pram and Sister Meaney took hold of Marie's hand and her case, and said "Goodbye" to me. She walked Marie across the day-room, making it obvious I wasn't welcome.

Ten minutes later, she drove past me in her car as I walked down the drive carrying the folded up pram. I hadn't expected to spend the afternoon on the ward, but a cup of tea would have been welcome after the five-hour train journey I was about to repeat.

A Spoke in the Works

I soon got back into the swing of things at work, and was busily distracted looking after the boys. I was still writing to Marie's mother and the hospital regarding the transfer, and one day I had an unexpected surprise. It was a letter from Dr. Rogerson saying there was a vacancy at the Liverpool hospital on December 29th. That meant I could bring Marie home for Christmas! I couldn't believe it.

I was collecting clothes for Marie and bought her a little something each week so she would have plenty when she was admitted to her new hospital. Four weeks before Christmas, I received a letter from Marie's mother, which almost made my heart stop.

"I went to Sandhill last week to see Marie and am going again this coming week so I will find out her shoe size for you. When I went out last week they fetched her back from school to the ward. You would never think she had any nice clothes, the dress she had on was terrible, far too small, and the cardigan was fit for the dustbin. I was quite shocked. The Sister said they never put decent clothes on them for school, silly. No wonder you mentioned her clothes always looked new —she never gets the chance to wear them. I felt quite upset seeing her like that, Michelle. Makes you wonder, doesn't it?

They told me that she was going to Liverpool in January but they didn't know about you having her for Christmas. Haven't you mentioned it yet? Sister also said they had a very difficult time with her when you brought her back from Liverpool in August and she gets tantrums, throws her food down and was uncontrollable, if she didn't feed herself, her food was taken away. I thought she looked very thin. I don't think she's been eating, Michelle 'cause they won't feed her. She is walking much better but has made no headway with speech.

I hope she will improve when she gets to Liverpool, Michelle. You don't think the move will upset her do you? I know that Sister does not like the idea of her going. She kept saying, come out more often and get used to her. Anybody would think I didn't know how to look after her. Still, Michelle, Dr. Prentice never queried her being transferred did he?"

"You should report that Sister Meaney!" Sue said when she handed me back the letter. "Did they tell you Marie was upset when you phoned?"

"They never mentioned it," I said in amazement. I could hardly speak.

"Maybe Marie missed you when she went back to the hospital after her holiday," Sue said. "Did she eat her food for you?"

"She was as good as gold," I told her. "And when you think about it, Sue, Marie's only questioning her surroundings, isn't she?" Even though Marie's behaviour wasn't good, I thought it was understandable.

"I didn't know Sister Meaney didn't want Marie to come to Liverpool," Sue said, "but then, I suppose when you think of the reception we get when we go to the hospital, it doesn't really surprise me."

"True," I said, because it didn't surprise me either, "but it's a bit late for her to be voicing doubts. She should discuss it with Dr. Prentice, not Marie's mother. She's not being very fair." I wondered what was going to happen next. We stood up to go back on duty.

"Poor Marie," Sue said. "If you hadn't written to Marie's mother, you'd never have known how upset she was, would you?" I shook my head wearily and followed her out of the dining room.

"By the way, have you arranged when you're collecting her yet?" she asked me.

"Yes," I told her eagerly. "We finish on December 22nd and my train leaves for Taunton at midnight and arrives at eight the next morning."

"That's great!" She said sincerely.

"Providing there are no disasters and everything goes all right."

"Will you see Marie's mother when you go, because she's living back in Taunton isn't she?"

"She's collecting her with me."

"It's funny the way she's suddenly taken an interest isn't it?" Sue asked me cautiously.

"Not really," I told her, "it's nice that she's enjoying her daughter for a little while. There's no pressure on her, you see. I've taken over the responsibility and she knows Marie will be leaving the area soon."

Fingers Crossed

It was December; no news was good news! I gathered Sister Meaney had failed to change Marie's mother's mind. My training course was coming to an end, so once again I was busy packing. What a send off I had. I was overwhelmed when the staff handed me a watch and records as a leaving present, and they'd all bought Christmas gifts for Marie, piling them into my bag. I'd also bought Marie some brown leather boots. It was great to be alive.

Sad Goodbyes

I'd just been paid so when I arrived at Lime Street station I bought a return ticket for myself and would purchase Marie's the next afternoon, on the way home. Hers would be for a one way trip.

At five minutes past midnight the train left Liverpool. It was almost empty and I sat back to enjoy the peacefulness and looked out into the night. I was so thankful for the way things had turned out. I no longer believed destiny was responsible. There were too many coincidences in my life. I wondered if there really was a God. Everything seemed to fall into place as though there was something or someone guiding me.

At three in the morning I sat shivering in the waiting room at Cardiff in Wales, waiting for my connection. The ticket office was closed and there wasn't a soul to be seen. No sounds came from anywhere but I wasn't afraid. I was too preoccupied with my own thoughts as I kept trying to glimpse into the future. Marie would be fast asleep in her dormitory. If only she knew she would be going to start a new life when she woke up.

The train pulled into Taunton and I smiled and waved when I spotted Marie's mother standing on the platform. We hugged each other and went into Taunton for a coffee.

Later that morning, when the bus reached Sandhill Park, it was to be my last journey—and what a journey. I thought about that first day I arrived with the social worker in the teaming rain. It was like stepping into another world; a world where human beings were described as subnormal. What a shock it had been to see so many children living together—herded like cattle, simply because they were mentally handicapped, spending day-in and day-out on overcrowded wards, looking at the same view through the ward window, year in and year out, the only stimulation being the clatter of the food trolley, which called three times a day. But in the early 70s fostering or adoption was not a consideration for anybody with even a slight disability, and once they entered the hospital and became the responsibility of the NHS, they never left it.

However, my experience with the senior hospital staff had been a learning curve. They had bent over backwards to help me have Marie transferred, demonstrating they were all for progress.

Marie was ready when we went into the ward. She walked towards me with outstretched arms for me to lift her up.

"Hello!" I said. "Look who's come to see you." Marie's mother leaned over and kissed her daughter. Marie obviously thought I was her mother and Marie's mother accepted this without question, though no doubt it hurt. I was always conscious that this kind lady didn't feel left out.

Marie was doing peek-a-boo with her hands while we waited for Sister Meaney to fetch her clothes from the office.

She looked beautiful in her little light-blue coat with the navy blue velvet collar. Sister came into the ward with Marie's case. I thanked Sister Meaney as I took the case from her and walked towards the door with Marie and her mother. Sister Meaney didn't look our way. I was obviously taking Marie against her will.

Later that afternoon, Marie's mother stood on the platform waving to us sadly as the train left Taunton taking Marie to start her new life. I waved until she was out of sight. After that day, we only ever saw Marie's mother twice, and that was in the 70s.

"Come on, Marie," I said, "let's take your coat off." I rubbed her cold little hands trying to make her warm again before sitting her on my knee for the long journey ahead. The train was packed, since it was Christmas time. I tightened my arms protectively around her and kissed her cold cheek. She giggled and looked around the compartment. Perhaps people felt her eyes upon them as they glanced up and quickly looked away, feeling uncomfortable and not knowing how to react to her. I was singing inside; I felt so happy and there was nobody to tell. I wanted to say, "Please don't look away. She's been so hard to get; it's such a special day. She's one of thousands who live alone, surrounded by people in a place they call home…"

9

The Best Christmas Ever

By the time I carried Marie off the train at Crewe, night had fallen. I pulled her woolly hat over her ears to protect her from the cold. Walking along the platform, I noticed someone waving to us; it was my Aunty Terry! With Marie on one arm and the suitcase on the other I rushed forward to meet her. Over the years, Terry had heard so much about Marie and now she was finally about to see her. I had no doubts at all that Marie would steal her heart—a heart Terry gave so freely to everybody she met. I put my case down and waved to Terry's boys, Peter and Paul, who were heading towards us, weaving in and out of the crowd. They laughed shyly at Marie when they noticed the blue and white Everton hat Terry had knitted for her. Marie was grinding her teeth as she looked about her anxiously.

Terry approached us. Standing there in the bitter cold she kissed Marie and lifted her into her arms. Her eyes were full of tears as she gave her an affectionate squeeze and I could tell that she was just too choked to speak.

"Well?" I said expectantly, trying to cheer her up. "What do you think?"

"Suffering Jesus, Michelle, she's gorgeous," was her characteristic reply. "I mean…how could you not love a child like that?"

"She's been so good, Terry, she just sat on my knee all the way."

"That's because she knows you care about her, Michelle. She knows who's good to her and who isn't."

Marie held onto our hands when we walked out of the station, banging her feet on the ground, enjoying the sound of her new boots. Our train didn't stop at Winsford where Terry lived so we had to get off a stop earlier. And despite the fact that Terry, a widow, had been working all day, she'd gone home, collected the boys and brought a taxi to meet us.

I don't know who was more bewildered—Marie or I, as we drove through the snowy streets to where we were to spend our first Christmas together. At long last, a dream had become reality.

I sat on the sofa tired and happy with not a care in the world. The

Christmas toys I'd left stacked in the corner of Terry's living room for Marie had grown significantly higher. Terry filled the kettle in the kitchen then came in to sit with us. "Trish came up today," she said, "and she brought presents for Marie from all the family." I took Marie's hand and strolled to the corner of the room. My eye caught a beautifully coloured box and inside was a multi-coloured wooden train with three carriages that held different coloured shapes that Maureen had sent. On top of the box a big grey donkey smiled at me from the back of the pile; it was from Trish. I lifted it out for Marie to see.

"Look, Marie!" I said, holding the donkey by its ears and pretending to take it for a walk. She followed me around the room but when I offered it to her she wouldn't hold it herself; she liked to be entertained rather than to entertain.

Terry couldn't take her eyes off Marie and looked on sadly as she struggled to feed herself. Terry loved the bones of her and thoroughly spoilt her. Marie cried when I put her to bed. I brought her downstairs and then took her back up again. Being alone in a room must have been so strange for Marie after sleeping in a dormitory with other children close by. We knew it was natural for her to be upset but she looked so afraid and kept staring at the pink flowered wallpaper in Terry's bedroom.

"Don't you like them, love?" Terry asked her. "They're horrible, aren't they? I never did like this paper," she said to me as she reached for the top of the strip and started to pull it away from the wall. My horrified protests at the inconvenience we were causing were soon silenced as Terry said, "Oh for Jesus' sake, it's only wallpaper!"

After a few days, Marie was walking her donkey around the house, making a clicking noise like a horse as she held it by its ears.

When Christmas was over and it was almost time for her to go to her new hospital, I took her home to my mum's for a couple of days. Of course, everybody was over the moon to see her. I was surprised that Marie remembered them all from her visit in the summer. She clapped her hands noisily as they greeted her with kisses. And then it was time for her to go.

Our Short-Lived Happiness

It was snowing when we finally left for the hospital, and unfortunately we arrived there fifteen minutes late because of the effect of the bad weather had on public transport. Trudging through the hospital gates in the snow, I felt incredibly sad. I shouldn't have, I know. There were so many plusses to Marie's move. It was what I'd always wanted—I just wished I could have looked after her myself. Case in one hand and Marie on the other, I headed towards C Ward.

"You're late," Sister said when we entered the ward. She was down at the other end feeding one of the children.

"Sorry," I said as I undid Marie's coat, "the buses were running slow." I tried to sound cheerful. "Look at the children playing, Marie," I remarked, thinking what a lousy welcome we had received so far. Nobody came over to us.

"Where shall I put Marie's case, Sister?" I asked walking down the ward towards her.

"On the bed, dear," she replied. "Just leave it there and a nurse will see to it." I sat Marie on the chair by her bed and started taking off her boots which were wet with melted snow.

"Nurse will see to her, dear," Sister shouted over to me. "And don't visit for a few weeks will you, dear, because we want to give her time to settle in."

There must be something wrong with me, I thought as I left the ward. This is supposed to be a wonderful day and I feel dreadful. Joining the long queue outside the hospital gates, I waited for the bus home. I fought off the doom and gloom. If only I'd known then that within five months Marie would be living with me.

"You were quick," Liz said when I walked into my mum's. "I thought they'd have to kick you off the ward tonight."

"Gosh, Liz," I said after a while, "I hope Marie's going to be okay. They weren't very friendly but then maybe they were just busy."

"What was it like?" Liz asked.

"I didn't really notice, Liz. I was too nervous, believe it or not. I was almost tempted to tell the ward sister how ignorant I thought she was, but that wouldn't have helped Marie, would it?" I said, shrugging my shoulders.

Mother of the House

Life, of course, went on, and with Marie being left to settle in her new environment I started my new job with my old friend Sue, as a housemother. Ironically, I returned to the Nazareth House where I first worked when I left school. Sue and I were in charge of about thirty toddlers along with a young helper and a nun. I didn't see Sue very often because we were on opposite shifts and met maybe once a week. Our interview had been very promising, with great emphasis on the nun's part of the need for decent childcare. There had been many changes for the better during my absence and I was looking forward to working as one of a team of childcare staff. However, the changes were superficial and both Sue and I were treated like maids. I was worn out from the time I went on duty to when I finished. The nun in charge of our nursery was worn out too. She was very bad tempered and shouted and slammed doors all the time. She had no feelings whatsoever for the children and they flinched whenever she went near them in case they got a slap. We were all nervous wrecks.

Going on duty at 7.30 in the morning, I'd walk into a dining room to thirty silent children, struggling to eat a breakfast that had been cooked the evening before. Relieved to see a friendly face, they'd all start to speak to me at once. Most children found my name difficult to pronounce and I was usually called Shell, Shelf or Mishelf.

"Silence!" the nun would holler at them. "I am the mother of this house and always remember that!" The children would continue to eat their breakfast in a deafening silence. To make matters worse, we were not allowed to have the lights on after 7.30 in the morning to avoid wasting electricity. It was pretty bleak. After breakfast, we made the beds and bed-wetters were made to stand at the end of their beds to teach them a lesson. Another appalling cruelty, considering the oldest child in our nursery was five years-old.

Not as Easy as They Expected

I next saw Marie two weeks after she had been admitted to the hospital. She was sitting on the ward floor watching one of the children through its cot.

"Yoohoo!" I teased as I hid behind the door. She came shuffling over to investigate on her bottom and we laughed together and went back into the ward.

"We weren't given all the facts about her when she was admitted," Sister stated. I wondered where I'd heard that remark before and remembered Sister Green saying it on my first visit to Taunton. She went on, "We were told she was toilet trained and she isn't."

"I think they were going to start her with it, Sister," I began but she walked away before I could finish.

"Hiya, Marie," I whispered. I was glad that Sister hadn't moaned about anything else. "Do you like it here?" I asked as I inspected her for little signs of I don't know what. I was hungry to know how she was doing, but nobody seemed interested enough to talk to me.

"Had to move her cot next to the office window," Sister called back from her office door. "She's noisy at night, isn't she?"

"She always has been, Sister," I said in amusement but before I'd finished she's disappeared again. I didn't know how to cope with their obvious hostility. Once again I was concerned that if they didn't like me they'd take it out on Marie. I wondered if their reason for this was because Marie was quite active and most of the children were physically disabled. There was another hospital up the road where I'd first met Dr. Rogerson, but after seeing them both I preferred the smaller of the two, thinking that with fewer patients the standard of care would be better. Maybe the staff felt that Marie was hard work, but she was only there until a place was available in a residential school.

I decided to ignore them in the hope that they would eventually see I had Marie's interest at heart, but I did find this rather difficult at times. I always did the right thing—phoning before I visited and not going at meal times because they were usually busy and they didn't like visitors on the ward then, although it could have been quite a help to them if their attitude had been different.

Trying to Plan in Advance

I visited Marie every week, but on different days, because I worked shifts and didn't always have the same days off. This didn't create any problems with the school because the teachers encouraged relatives to visit and take the children out at any time, but Matron had this policy about visiting whereby parents had to put their request in writing two days before taking the child out. My friend Sue was very supportive and whenever possible would swap a day off with me, enabling me to plan well in advance. Sometimes I only just made it with my written request because I hadn't known until the last minute when I would be free. I was told the reason for such rigid rules was for the child to be passed fit to go out by the doctor.

When I went into the hospital school, Marie's teachers made me very welcome, and were always eager to speak to me. One day, when

I went into the big hall, the children were sitting on rubber mats and the teachers were singing to them. Marie stood up and walked towards me, so I sneaked to the back of the hall with her so as not to disturb the happy little group. Later, she was sitting on my knee while I was talking with one of the teaching staff. I got Marie an old doll out of the toy box and she immediately started to bang it on the back. The teacher frowned. "I've noticed her doing that often," she said; "she's obviously been hit on the back some time in her previous home."

"Oh no!" I said, grinning, "Look, she's getting the doll's wind up. She remembers this from living with babies for so many years." I gave Marie a hug. I was delighted to see her playing with the doll.

One day, we were standing at the window in my mum's watching the snow fall.

"Look, Marie," I said, pointing out of the window; "Look at the snow." To my astonishment she said "Look." I thought I hadn't heard her correctly when she repeated it.

Each time I took her Marie for the day, she would hold my hand and off we'd run through the hospital gates towards the bus stop. I always warned her when she reached the kerbs so her feet wouldn't get all twisted up and she'd step down carefully.

"Jump," I said to her as she laughed and squealed excitedly. She repeated that word too! Whenever I took her home, I always put on the records because we both loved music.

"Listen, Marie," I'd say. Her little face lit up and she clapped her hands; it wasn't long before she was saying, "Nisten."

The only explanation I could give for Marie's speech was the attention my family and I lavished on her. We talked to her as though she understood everything even though she hardly ever responded.

For some strange reason Marie started calling me "Mam." When I visited her on the ward the nurse would call out, "Here's your mam, Marie," which is where she must have picked up the word. It felt strange and moving to hear her address me as her mother. Another new word was "Gor gone," but only when people hid from her. She never asked for, or looked for toys that suddenly disappeared. Whenever we stopped singing she would say, "Again." She seemed to pick up words when she was stimulated.

She loved visiting my aunty Terry on the train. My kind-hearted aunt had become a new and welcome dimension in Marie's life. A bond had developed between them which lasted for the next twenty years.

Marie got on surprisingly well with Sara, Maureen's little girl, whom she'd met the previous year. Because of Marie's placid nature and Sara being a bossy three year-old, they complemented each other. She never interfered in Sara's play, and was happy to watch. Sara, on the other hand, tended to mother Marie, finding her toys to play with, and wiping her mouth with a tissue when she dribbled. We still had the problem of hair pulling but, more often than not, Marie couldn't help herself. Sometimes, Marie pulled Sara's hair if she was angry, but it was mostly for effect. I could tell from the way she watched Sara's mouth, as if fascinated, just as you'd push a button on a doll and it cried, Marie pulled Sara's hair and she screamed.

If it was a warm afternoon, I took Marie and Sara to the park. Sara would always cry to sit in the pram beside Marie.

"Move your feet over," I said to Marie and lifted Sara up into the pram, but because Marie didn't understand, I ended up doing for or with Marie, what I had asked her to do. It was the only way she could learn.

"Here's some bread for the ducks," Maureen would say, placing a loaf in Marie's lap.

"You'd better keep hold of it, hadn't you, Sara, or Marie will eat it before we get there." Off we'd go. The two girls in similar hats that Terry had knitted for them—Sara's was red and white for Liverpool and Marie's was blue and white for Everton. Reaching the park gates, I'd lift them out of the pram. Marie toddled off after Sara who ran like the clappers towards the lake. When they reached the lake, Sara excitedly fed the ducks as they quacked around her ankles, and Marie fed herself.

When Marie grew tired, she plonked on the floor with her legs splayed out. It didn't matter where—dog muck, bird muck, she never noticed.

"Come on, Marie," I'd say, in a sing-song voice, "up off the floor, please." I would stand her up, telling her how good she was, as though she stood up on her own. She spent most of her life indoors and had a lot to learn.

On one of our trips home from Stanley Park, Marie lost a shoe. I didn't notice until we reached the gates at the other side of the park, and, gazing back across the field, I didn't know where to start looking.

What if a dog had run off with it? I thought. The shoes were only a week old, and I didn't have the money to buy her another pair. Then there was the problem of telling Marie's ward sister that I'd lost a shoe. I pushed the pram back across the field and sighed with relief when I found it under a bench by the lake.

I didn't realise until this incident how uncomfortable I felt with the ward staff, how I was always careful not to upset them. I'd go to collect Marie and the nurse-in-charge would say she couldn't go out because of an illness on the ward. Nobody had bothered to telephone me; they just waited until I arrived.

Marie's hair was growing onto her shoulders and I started putting it into pigtails. One day when I went to collect her she came running up to me with her hair cropped short. I went to Sister's office.

"Who cut Marie's hair?" I asked her.

"Staff Nurse took her to town on her day off," she said casually, "and she took her into the hairdressers." What could I say? Staff Nurse wanted Marie's hair cut so she had it done. I wondered if other parents were treated like this and realised why I never saw any on the ward. I don't think the nursing staff had anything against me. I think they couldn't be bothered with visitors, mistaking any interest shown in ward routines as interference. I was beginning to understand what a skilled job nursing was, how it wasn't enough to care about the children—it involved other people too. I wondered how many parents didn't visit because they didn't feel welcome. How many nurses thought parents didn't visit because they didn't care.

I couldn't help noticing in the last few places I worked, how there was always friction between education, childcare and nursing staff. They never worked together. It seemed that one department always resented the other.

I remember the teachers in the hospital school wanted to take the children out in the snow, but when the ward sister's permission was sought, she refused to give it. So what did the teachers do? They got a large plastic sheet and took some snow in to the children! The teachers were eager to stimulate the children and let them experience as much as possible—the ward staff were concerned that illness would sweep through the wards because of it. I could see both their points, but sometimes the child in care is the child in the middle.

As time went on the nursing staff did their utmost to cold-shoulder me. Some days I felt really miserable when I was leaving Marie on the ward. What probably annoyed them was my tolerance of their ignorant behaviour. They pulled my strings: I was at their mercy. I couldn't afford to fall out with them. On the other hand, I was no fool. They knew I saw right through them, and wouldn't give them the satisfaction of complaining about me. On Marie's birthday, for example, Maureen and I went to collect her at half-eleven, as arranged so she could have a party at home. When Maureen and I arrived, we were told there was illness on the ward and Marie couldn't go out. I felt really sad. Marie's birthday cards and presents were at home. Maureen and I stayed until the trolley was brought in for lunch, then we left. Maureen was disgusted; "They should be ashamed of themselves," she said when we were outside. Poor Marie had followed us to the door and we could hear her crying at the other side of it.

"I can't leave her there," I told Maureen. "I'll find somewhere to live and look after her myself."

My New Career as a Skivvy

Things were growing increasingly difficult at work. The nuns were supposed to supply our meals but all we seemed to be offered was runny (and I mean runny) boiled eggs and stale bread. Yuk! Always a sufferer from tonsillitis, I was struck with it almost every other week. I couldn't go off sick because there was no staff cover. Sue was off sick with Laryngitis, and hadn't been replaced, making work conditions pretty grim. The Social Worker in charge of our residential social work course rang to see how Sue and I were getting on in our new 'careers'. She was outraged when we told her the conditions under which we worked. She complained to Rev. Mother and a week later, the nun in charge was moved and replaced with Sister Assumptor.

Sister Assumptor spent the last eighteen years working in the midlands with teenagers. She was given a day's notice before coming to work in our nursery. She was understandably hurt and did not know how she was going to cope with a bunch of tiny children. We laughed at the absurdity of it all.

Sister Assumptor, was great fun. Even the children started to relax and became noisy and mischievous! However, she didn't stay long.

She was sent to a new children's unit in the convent in Wales. After she left, I had a letter from her. She'd met some staff and children from the Bristol convent who remembered me. She also invited me to go to Wales, to run the new unit with her. I was flattered, but it was out of the question.

Tickencote

I'd recently returned from a week's holiday with Cathy. Cathy and her husband, Raynor, lived in an old schoolhouse in Tickencote, which was a tiny village in Rutland. They lived in London for most of the time. Cathy studied at the Royal College of Art, and Raynor, worked as a translator during the week, and returned home for weekends and holidays. Their house was close to the A1, which meant easy travelling back and forth to London.

We spent the day going for long walks and the nights, sitting around the log fire catching up on each other's lives. I was soon able to unwind and clear my head of all the worry and stress of the last few months. The night before I left, I was filling Cathy in about Marie's hospital; how she was waiting to go to residential school, and my plans for the future.

I was looking for a place to rent in Liverpool so I could bring Marie home to live with me. Cathy and Raynor listened with great interest. When I finished, Cathy said, "Listen! Why don't you bring Marie here to live instead?"

I couldn't believe my ears. It had never even occurred to me.

"You mean for me to live here—with Marie?" I asked incredulously. She nodded. I looked at the fire and watched the flames dancing around the logs.

"But wouldn't you mind?" I asked them quietly.

"Of course not," Raynor said. "In fact it will be nice to have someone living here while we're in London. Just so long as you remember that the roof leaks and we have no bath or inside toilet, but ahh!" he said grandly, "We do have a tin bath and one can get water from a tap in the back shed."

"Well," I said convinced, "what more can one ask for?"

Before I left I went into nearby Stamford, to the Town Hall, with Cathy. We met the Medical Officer of Health, the man who dealt with Special Schooling. I explained about Marie and my plans to move to the area. He very kindly gave me all of the info I needed along with his details for Dr. Rogerson to write to him.

I was very nervous when I went to tell Dr. Rogerson of my plans just in case she tried to stop me. I needn't have worried. She took down the Medical Officers details then smiled at me and told me I was a brick, which of course had a much nicer meaning then than it has today.

Marie left the hospital a month later on June 2nd 1972. Just before she left, her assessment by the Clinical Educational Psychologist showed as follows:

> Mental age: 20 months
> Hearing and speech: 17 months
> Locomotive: 21 months
> Hand/eye co-ordination: 20 months
> Performance: 21 months
>
> She was 8 ½ years old.

10

There's No Place like Home

My mother rang me one evening when I was on duty at Nazareth House. She told me a Sunday newspaper reporter had been making enquiries about me. He was interested in writing and article about Marie and me.

Cathy's husband had written to the editor after seeing Marie's photograph which they'd taken at the hospital to raise money for horse riding for disabled children. He (Cathy's husband) explained about my relationship with Marie and my hopes for her future. In the letter he asked if the newspaper could help in any way.

My feelings about this were mixed, the strongest one being that I didn't want to do the article. However, I kept an open mind and arranged a brief meeting after work one evening. He made me an offer I couldn't refuse. He said the newspaper would pay £300, for the article. My only thought was the fee and the possibilities it gave me. It would enable Marie and I to live off the money for a while when we moved to Tickencote.

In those early years, I had to get used to people asking "Why this particular child? Why not a normal one?" I was just turned 19, and people often said they could understand somebody old looking after Marie, but not someone young like me. This journalist was no exception.

I don't know why people expected me to be a mouse or social misfit because I took an interest in Marie, as though she could only be used to fill gaps in people's lives. I didn't think I was giving up my life to look after her, as some people suggested. Nor did I didn't think she was a bind. I loved her company and cared very much about her. I hoped I could give her a better life than she'd had so far because she was entitled to it. The interviewer wasn't convinced at first—typical journalist, never quite trusting anybody. We arranged to meet up at Tickencote, as soon as Marie and I were settled.

By now I was walking on air! My family and friends were very supportive and only a few people were doubtful. In a way, even they were quite helpful, because I was able to appreciate difficulties that might arise in the future. I wasn't a bit worried. I always felt things would work out all right. People's main concern seemed to be; "What will happen to Marie when she gets older?" I suppose I appeared cocky and arrogant, but on reflection, I couldn't have done it if I'd been any other way. I wasn't playing games with her. I was the best offer she had—the only offer, in fact. I wasn't offering a bed of roses. I was far from domesticated, hated cooking, cleaning and any other household chores. Maybe others could do better, but I promise you I will do the best I can, and how proud I feel to have been given the chance.

Settling In

Cathy was at the schoolhouse when we arrived, busily making beds and preparing food. I changed Marie's nappy, she had her lunch and toddled off outside into the schoolyard dragging her doll after her by the hair. Up and down, up and down she walked, listening intently to the noise her shoes made. We watched her through the kitchen window, although she wasn't aware of this and would frequently walk back into the house to check that we were still there.

"The reporter is coming to do the article next week," I told Cathy as I screwed up my face with dread.

"Oh it won't be all that bad," she laughed. "Besides, nobody knows you here."

"That's true," I told her, "but I hope it won't be too sentimental, you know, poor lonely woman" I giggled.

"They won't say that," she said, laughing again.

"I hope not," I told her, "because there are many other children like Marie who would benefit from living at home given the opportunity. So much depends upon how the article is presented, because, who knows, it may encourage other people to consider offering a home and love to a disabled child."

Marie was in her element. Two of Cathy's friends came to stay, so there were five adults to give her attention and within a few days she had us all peeling grapes, or nearly. That first evening, I put her to bed but after five minutes she was still screaming, so I told Cathy I would go to bed because Marie did not like being on her own. Her look said I was a dope! Her mouth said, "All right, but you can't be doing this every night. You're going to need a break from her."

"Oh well," I mumbled, "just tonight." When I walked into the bedroom, Marie stopped screeching and began to laugh. I got into bed and she snuggled under her covers and went to seep. The next night when Marie went to bed, she screeched loudly again. Fortunately Cathy wasn't around to question my hasty exit. This makes things easier, I told myself as I ran up the stairs to join Marie in her bedroom. When I reached the top, it was only to see Cathy sitting outside Marie's bedroom door.

"What are you doing?" I whispered, although there was no need to whisper for Marie was making so much noise you wouldn't have heard a bomb going off. "I'm waiting for you," Cathy said. She looked like a big rag doll sitting on the floor with her long dark curly hair falling about her shoulders. "Just leave Marie to cry for a while, she'll soon get tired."

I was shocked.

"Oh no! I can't do that. She's upset, and what if she should hurt herself?"

"Just try it," Cathy repeated.

I reluctantly agreed and joined Cathy on the floor, cringing each time Marie smacked her own face, longing to pick her up. I realised I would have to persevere as it was impractical to go to bed with her every night. After what seemed like hours (ten minutes!), the screaming began to fade and the silence somehow seemed louder. *Is she all right?* I thought. *What if she's knocked herself out,* but Marie broke my thoughts with another scream. The screams were less urgent now, the panic had disappeared and were a last weary attempt. When she was quiet, Cathy and I crept downstairs and went out into the garden.

I waited until Cathy was distracted (coward that I was) before I crept back up the stairs. I was worried in case Marie had knocked herself unconscious. I quietly turned the handle and slowly opened the door. That little devil immediately emerged from under her bed covers and started to scream again. "Oh no," I thought as she scrambled across her bed for me to pick her up. She *was* asleep, and I woke her. "I'll have to be firm," I kept telling myself as I gently put

Marie back into bed.

"Go to sleep, there's a good girl," I whispered. She started to scream again as I closed the door behind me. Five minutes later, there was silence. From then on Marie went to bed without any bother and went to sleep almost immediately. (Thanks, Cathy!)

~ 11 ~

The Sunday People

The journalist was James (Jim) Copeland, Deputy Editor of the *Sunday People* and author of recently published 'For the Love of Anne', a groundbreaking book about Anne Hodges, one of the first people to be diagnosed with autism. I read *For the Love of Anne*, the week I went to stay with Cathy, never imagining when I returned to Liverpool after that short holiday break at Tickencote that we would be meeting up.

Jim came to collect Marie and I at Cathy's, and drove us to Bristol for a couple of days to do some filming, for the newspaper TV commercial. The newspaper article was to be a two week double page spread in the Sunday People, and no expense was spared.

When we arrived in Bristol Jim booked the three of us into a rather grand hotel near the Clifton Suspension Bridge. Oh, the thrill of going from a house with a cold water tap and an outside toilet, to a luxurious suite with *a bath*.

It was July and the weather was beautiful. Marie had a lovely tan, but I was like a bottle of milk. The sun turned my fair skin a bright red, so I tended to stay out of it.

Jim and his team were good company and looked after us very well. I was so self-conscious during the filming and photo shoots. We went to a park a few miles away and no sooner had we arrived when a bread van pulled up, courtesy of the newspaper, and scattered twenty loaves of bread across the green. We had to wait ten minutes for the birds to gather, and just as they were getting stuck into their unusually fresh bread, someone set off some firecrackers. The film crew got the desired effect as the flock of birds abandoned the feast, and soared into the sky. What a beautiful scene, but not for the little girl terrified of noise.

We moved to another location near a waterfall, where I had to walk slowly, holding Marie's hand, and after counting to ten, pick her up and swing her around. Poor Marie screamed again. It was noisy and she was terrified as the director kept shouting 'cut' and I tried not to swear at them. What a cheeky sod I was.

The day before our article appeared in the newspaper, Marie and I watched the TV commercial with the elderly couple next door. I laughed when I saw it—it was over in a flash and took a day to film.

Cathy and Raynor were back at the schoolhouse for the summer. On the day the article appeared, Raynor went to London for the day.

"Did you enjoy yourself?" I asked him when he returned.

"I just couldn't get away from you," he exclaimed. "Everywhere I went, you were watching me."

"What do you mean?"

"There are posters of you on the newspaper placards, pictures of you and Marie. They're even on bill-boards outside the shops." I was astonished.

"What does it say on the poster?" I asked.

"This year's most moving love story," he said tentatively, looking across at Cathy. I felt so embarrassed.

After a few days, it began to dawn on me that the article hadn't been about children in care; it had been about my relationship with Marie. Was it that unusual at the time? I thought not. As I look back today, I see things quite differently. Then, I was described as the youngest single woman in Britain to obtain legal guardianship over someone else' child. I suppose it was news, but I was too young to process it.

There was such an outpour of love from the newspaper articles. I received so many cards and letters from all over the country and abroad. Some of the cards and letters were from parents with disabled children, saying how the story about Marie and I had given them hope. Others were from pensioners who wished us well, enclosing small amounts of money to buy a gift for Marie.

I was happy that our story brightened up so many lives. People rang my mother in Liverpool, and one caller told my mother she must feel like the Queen, having such a wonderful daughter. Hahaha, I didn't think so.

Before the newspaper excitement died down, a telegram arrived from *Woman's Own* magazine, telling me their feature writer would be coming from London the next day to write an article. This was to be the last interview. I refused *Woman* magazine and any more offers. I just wanted to be left alone to be Marie's mother.

When Cathy and Raynor came into the kitchen for breakfast, I told them about the impending journalist visit. I glanced around for the telegram, but couldn't find it. "Anyway," I said, "the journalists name is Iris something or other. I can't remember at the moment" Raynor shot me a look.

"Iris…?" he said. "Iris?"

"Yes, Iris!" I answered wondering at his reaction.

"It's not Iris Murdoch is it?" They both stared at me like a pair of deer caught in headlights. I hesitated for a few seconds trying to recall the name. Then I nodded.

"Yeah, that's her." I said nonchalantly. They both gasped. Cathy slid her chair back "Oh, my God!" she said, looking around the room "Just look at the state of the place. We'd better get cracking. Oh and we'll need shopping from town" Raynor quickly drank his coffee and looked at his watch. "Don't worry, I'll nip in. I've got five minutes to get the bus into Stamford." He shoved his chair back noisily and took his jacket off the back of the door.

"Hey, why all the panic?" I asked, I mean, nothing fazed these two; they were the coolest couple on this earth, and here they were faffing about because this lady was arriving in less than 24 hours. "The place looks lovely, honestly it does!"

"Oh, the place is filthy." Cathy said gravely. "We'll have to have it looking nice for her."

"It's not that bad!" I told her. "I mean you don't have to put yourselves to any trouble."

"It's no trouble at all." Raynor assured me with a big smile on his face.

"Oh, you'll need a list!" Cathy told him. They both had lists for everything. How I wished I was so organised.

"I haven't got time." He told her sticking the last bit of toast in his mouth.

"Okay, well then please don't forget the polish!" She called after him as he hurried out of the house, over the stile and across the field for the bus.

How could anybody forget Cathy's polish? I was always telling her she should have been a nun the way she waxed everything until we could see our faces in it.

Raynor got a lift off a neighbour and was back in an hour. Together, they emptied the contents of the schoolroom into the yard, and set too cleaning it. I made some tea and sandwiches for lunch, and Marie and I sat at the huge wooden table amidst tea chests, Persian rugs, and all their other treasures purchased in junk shops.

"Who is Iris Murdoch, anyway?" I asked them when they joined us at the table. They told me she was a famous writer, but with all the excitement, I thought she must have been someone *really* special.

"Who is she?" Raynor repeated. "Who is she?"

Cathy glared at him, clearly irritated, and turning to me she said, "She's more than just a writer she's."

"She's amazing, Michelle." Raynor chirped in. "You'll see for yourself when you meet her tomorrow."

"Oh, okay." I said.

I didn't find the telegram until much later when I was getting ready for bed. I put my hand in my dressing gown pocket and there it was. I read it again, and then I went to find my sister and her hubby. When I stuck my head around the door of the immaculately clean schoolroom, Cathy and Raynor were sitting in front of the log fire. "Found it!" I said waiving the telegram. "What was that woman's name again?"

"Iris Murdoch." Raynor said. I glanced at the message. "Oh no, it's not her." I told them. "It's a lady called Iris Brown." Cathy burst out laughing and Raynor began to chuckle. Soon they were laughing so hard they couldn't talk. I could still hear roars of laughter through the bedroom wall when I climbed into bed.

The feature writer arrived by taxi early the next morning. We spent a lovely day together before she hurried off at tea time to catch the train back to London. She wanted to be home in time to put her daughter to bed.

The BBC wrote to tell me I was to be presented with the *Charlie Chester Award*, for bringing sunshine to the news headlines. I was invited to the BBC award ceremony in London on New Year's Eve. I was flattered, but a trip to London on New Year's Eve? I wrote and thanked them for the invitation, but said I couldn't get a babysitter, and wouldn't be able to make it. They wrote to me again and suggested I listen to Radio 2 on New Year's Eve.

Silly me, I forgot all about the programme. However, a few of my neighbours were regular radio listeners and told me my name had been mentioned on the radio. The Beatles record, '*Michelle*' had been played in my honour. I thought that was very nice!

12

Settling Down

I loved being a mum. I found that, because of Marie's earlier insti-tutional life, she would wake up at the crack of dawn and climb across the bed to cuddle up with me. I was awake instantly never quite used to our situation and marvelled   that this little girl was now home with me. I talked to her all the time and she watched every move I made. Her eyes would follow me from the cooker to the cupboard, watching what I put where. It was as though she was seeing everything for the first time, and indeed she was in many in-stances. She still had her tantrums, but they weren't as frequent. If she started her screeching, I always sat her on a chair to prevent her from banging her head on the floor. She would resort to pulling her hair out or smacking her face, screeching as loudly as she could. She no longer wore nappies around the house, and on most occasions we were successful with the pot. This surprised me, as it seemed to happen so quickly, making me wonder why it had not been achieved sooner.

I always knew Marie would be much happier at home but I never thought she would improve so much. The scab on her forehead began to heal and her speech was progressing to simple words in order to make her needs understood. "No," was her favourite. She talked to her doll most of the time, pretending to feed it or change its nappy. She would always chatter after meals and imitate conversations in her own way. She was still fascinated with the mirrors, and was starting to be a little more adventurous in her play. She would sit trying to thread laces or simply look at the reflection of a picture in a book. Without the mirror, she was unable to stimulate this kind of play and would wait for me to amuse her instead. However, there were times when I had to put the mirror away. When people came into the room, instead of turning to look at them as they greeted her she would search for the person's reflection in the mirror and, once satisfied, she would continue her play.

We gradually established a daily routine. I had found our biggest problem was the hair pulling which she usually did for attention.

For example, if my friends came with their children, Marie would reach out quite unexpectedly and pull someone's hair. I found this quite difficult to handle and in other people's company spent most of my time watching over her or telling her off, which must have been quite boring for people. After a while I realised that even if I told her off she was still getting attention so I decided that the next time she did this I would put her in another room to see if it made any difference. I was careful to leave the door open because of her fear of being enclosed. It didn't work at first, but when she started to realise she got more attention when she didn't pull hair than when she did, her behaviour improved. There were times when she was so angry she couldn't help doing it and would pull her hand away quickly, regretting her impulsive action. At times like this I pretended not to notice because she really hadn't been able to help herself. Sometimes she'd put her hand out towards someone and suddenly stop when she touched their hair, then we all clapped and cheered and praised her. She'd laugh and clap her hands with pleasure.

What Did I Know

Two weeks before the summer holidays, Marie started her new day school. I felt it was a nice time for her to start because of the six weeks' holiday, and thought it would give her a little taste of what was to come. I would have preferred for her to have gone part time, and I knew that the teachers would have problems with her. The school was 10 miles away and Marie shared transport with 3 other children who were picked up at various points along the way.

Marie must have been very confused with this new routine. It was the first time in her life she'd gone to school away from where she lived.

When the headmaster said he wanted Marie to go to school full time, I told him I thought it was too long a day to be away from home. I asked if I could call in and see her at some time during the day, or go in to class with her for odd days. I thought the school and I needed to work closely together. But no; he wanted to do things his way without any help from me.

During Marie's first few days at school, when I rang to see how she was the headmaster told me she'd been screeching at lunch time and they had to feed her.

"Can't you just leave her?" I asked him, "Because she eats all right at home and when she sees you won't feed her, she'll probably attempt to feed herself."

"It's all right for you," he told me angrily. "What you've done is given her an ideal situation, but it's an unnatural one, and you've just made it difficult for everyone else."

I didn't pay too much attention to his criticism. If I took everything people said to me to heart, I'd have given up my interest in Marie years ago. If he was going to shut me out, problems were inevitable because Marie was unable to communicate. I was glad when the school holidays arrived and what fun we had.

Cathy took Marie for a walk one day and when I looked out of the schoolroom window across the field there was Marie, bobbing up and down on Cathy's shoulders. I went to meet them. It was at times like this the absurdity of the Headmaster's words sprang to mind. The cows had followed them from the bottom field (much to Marie's delight). We just had to watch Marie didn't sit in a cow pat. It was mid-afternoon and very hot, so we sat in the shade under a tree. Marie decided to show off in front of the cows and did a somersault, so I ran on ahead of her making sure the path was clear and she wouldn't land in any cow-muck. She was tossing over nonstop, flashing her bright pink knickers every time her bottom went into the air until she got tired. She relished being out in the open, going for walks or sometimes pushing her doll's pram around the field.

That evening when we were almost home I lifted Marie over the stile. She usually took off then, making her own way to the house as I walked behind her. She had her wellington boots on and I watched her little spastic legs as she tried to run across the field squealing with excitement. I thanked God she lived with us because it was obvious to me she just loved the air that she breathed.

Last in the Queue—First on the Bus

I was building up a nice circle of friends and lots of people recognised us from the newspaper article. Even Charlie, the bus driver, beeped his horn as he drove past us on the other side of the field.

Tuesday was our day in town; a bit of shopping, a cup of tea and some cake in the café, and then the bus back home. Marie really enjoyed this experience, but when we arrived at the bus station she screeched like mad if we had to wait for the bus. When it arrived, she screeched again as the queue slowly moved forward. More often than not, well-meaning people stood back to let her be first on the bus.

'You little monkey!' I used to whisper to her. She would giggle as she climbed the steps onto the bus, like royalty, going on ahead of everyone. After weeks of this anti-social behaviour I devised a plan. Marie and I waited in the bus shelter and when the bus arrived if she began to screech I told her she had to stop the noise or I would not take her on the bus. I knew it was difficult for her to understand, but she had to learn to be a little more civil. Wouldn't it make life easier for her in the long run? It was instinctive for her to react to situations in this way and took weeks for the penny to drop. So, instead of her screeching, she would stamp her foot and stick her neck out impatiently whilst at the same time giving me dirty looks. But – she was clever enough to know if she started screeching she would not be allowed on the bus.

Slovenly Mother

She had been at school for about nine months, but I did find the Headmaster's attitude somewhat peculiar. One day when Marie returned from school, the lady who escorted the children to school in the taxi handed me a letter. It was dated the previous day and went like this:

> *'Marie was sick (vomiting) at school today. I think from the smell of her clothing you had a cleaning up period before she left home this morning.'*

I was incredulous and wondered if he talked to all the parents like this. I was also very angry that he should think I would wipe vomit off Marie's clothes and send her to school. She only had to look tired and I kept her at home.

I'd had enough of him.

The next day I went to the Education Department and asked to speak with the Director. I never paid much attention to rank and always felt the quickest way to get a problem sorted is go to the top, after all, aren't they the ones who make the rules? The good man saw me right away and listened to what I had to say.

Firstly, I told him how concerned I was that the Headmaster's personal feelings about me being allowed to look after Marie were interfering with her welfare at school.

Secondly, I asked, what was the point in feeding Marie at school when she could feed herself at home?

Thirdly, what was the point of Marie attending school at all if the staff and I didn't work on her problems together?

He was very nice. He said he could see my point and would have a word with the Headmaster. Shortly after the meeting the Headmaster sent for me. He was very angry.

"You should have approached me first!" he said to my astonishment. I thought of all the times I asked if I could go into the school. "Just you remember this," he instructed, pointing his finger at me, "the only thing anybody can sack me for is sexual assault or physical abuse!" After he had his little say he told me I could go into the school two afternoons a week to see what they were doing with Marie in the classroom.

I don't know why he was so upset at the steps I took. Maybe he thought he was a law unto himself and was accountable to nobody and he'd had a short-sharp-shock. I don't know why he thought I was trying to get him sacked.

When I went into the school, the children had just eaten lunch and were playing in the hall without any adult supervision. There was a window at the end of the hall which looked into the staff room enabling staff to observe the children to a certain point. They couldn't see around corners and were unable to see a boy of about 12 giving a little boy of about six, a long lingering kiss as he sat on his knee. There were chairs stacked too high for safety along the walls and none of the children had anything to do.

I asked the Headmaster why the children were left alone.

Looking back, I suspect he must have been seething. I was only twenty years-old and not only had I been allowed to bring a severely disabled child out of hospital to live with me, I had complained to his boss about him. Now, I was standing in *his* school asking *him* to account for the way he ran it.

He told me that children felt too inhibited when staff were around all the time. I disagreed. I wasn't surprised that Marie spent her lunch time crying and banging her head if there were no adults in sight.

And there was I, getting all the blame because of the unstable life I was providing.

13

Dr. Kidd

Unfortunately, Marie started having epileptic fits when she went swimming and my GP recommended that I take her to see a specialist. Although I agreed to this, I was a little dubious about the meeting. I was unsure about her reaction to my taking Marie out of a hospital and expected to walk into a lecture on how selfish I had been. However, when I did meet the specialist, I realised that my fears had been unfounded. I liked her immediately. The first bolt for me was when she asked if it was okay to speak in front of Marie. It was so nice to meet someone who was sensitive to Marie's feelings and didn't claim to know all about her at a glance.

Dr. Sheila Kidd was a consultant psychiatrist at Peterborough District Hospital and later at Gloucester Centre, a purpose built residential complex for people with a learning disability.

I don't think the parents had ever met anybody like Dr. Kidd. I used to look forward to seeing her and discussing any issues that developed since our last appointment. If a problem arose with Marie in between appointments, I was able to ring Dr. Kidd at home to discuss the situation, although I rarely did because I didn't want to abuse that privilege. Nowadays we'd be lucky to see a psychiatrist, let alone ring one at home.

We managed to survive quite happily over the next few years. I have many happy memories and many sad ones. I took in lots of disabled children from the local area; some for an overnight or weekend stay and others whilst their family went on holiday. I loved having the children to stay, but I suppose while all this was happening my marriage was crumbling.

It lasted two years and broke up when Marie was twelve. He loved Marie so much, but in the end I think helping others took up so much of my time that it killed our relationship.

We had been honest with each other from the start. He told me that although he loved Marie and would give her most of his attention, he would never give him all of himself. I asked him never to make me choose between them because had I chosen him, I could not build happiness on someone else's misery.

Marie had been so jealous of my husband at first and would pinch him or pull his hair whenever he sat near her, but it wasn't long before she was holding his hand on a Saturday morning and going down to the snooker hall with him. She used to sit on the chair with a packet of crisps, fascinated with the coloured snooker balls.

"Hiya!" she'd greet when she arrived home and sometimes she'd have a bunch of daffodils in her hand that he'd given her outside the door. Sometimes, if he was going fishing he'd chase me around the house with a bowl of maggots and she'd run after him, screaming and laughing at the fun of it all.

The only serious problem we had with Marie was at mealtimes when she suddenly started throwing her food. It got so bad we dreaded sitting down to a meal with her because she just point blank refused to eat. I was baffled and thought she must be unhappy at home, especially when I rang the school and they weren't having any problems. She had changed schools by this time and I had a very good relationship with the staff. But Marie would no sooner be sat down at the table when she would chuck her plate anywhere; at the wall, on the floor, up at the ceiling and as much as we tried to ignore her, I would end up smacking her hand and sending her out of the room. If we didn't react to her, she would pick up handfuls of food and wipe them all over our arms or just squash them in her fingers. I was at my wits' end with her.

After weeks of putting up with these chaotic mealtimes, it was clear that smacking was not helping the situation, especially when she continued to be defiant, so we decided to ignore her completely. This was very difficult because I didn't even coax her with her food. I felt there had been too much importance attached to it, so we let her sling the plate, or do whatever she wanted with it, but she had to remain at the table and sit through the meal. It was so hard not to laugh. I remember one day sitting opposite my husband and we both had lumps of mashed potatoes on our heads. Another time after we'd eaten he got the ladder out to wipe the food off the ceiling.

When the meal was over and I began to clear the table, I would say quite casually; "Come on, Marie, clear up your mess." I handed her a little bin. My eyes stung as I watched her discreetly bending down, tutting to herself in disgust at the mess she'd made as if someone else had done it.

She soon became bored and realised it was more fun to sit at the table and join in the meal.

It was a year later that I learned Marie was being fed at school. If the teachers didn't feed her, she would shove her plate onto the floor and scream, creating a disturbance in the dining room. Naturally she had been confused when she had come home from school and tried the same thing with us and we'd reacted in a completely different way.

And now my marriage was over and I found it difficult living in a small town and bumping into my ex all the time, trying to move on with my life when everything was so depressing. Cathy came to see me. She thought I needed to get away and start afresh so she rang my mother and arranged for Marie and I to go back home and stay with my parents for a while. We actually stayed with them for five months and they were a great support. They made us so welcome and never interfered with our routine.

Marie and I had single beds in my old bedroom and she was in seventh heaven. Some mornings my mother woke us with tea and toast on a tray and I'd squeeze Marie into bed with me while she ate her toast, passing her drink now and again then resting it back on the tray. I think we were quite spoilt!

The problem started when we began to live on our own again. Within half an hour of Marie going to bed the screeching would start and she roared like a lion. Today I wonder why I didn't allow her to familiarise herself with the change. She could have continued to share a room with me and slowly been introduced to her own room, but I guess none of us are perfect and I made a big mistake expecting her to adjust to being alone again, when she hated it so much. She would scream and screech for hours and I mean hours. All the continuity with her bedtime routine had been wiped out. When I went to check on her the mattress would be half off her bed, and the curtains pulled down off the windows. Again, she would tutt as if someone else had done it.

I can't remember how long it went on for, but I realised it was too long after the neighbour knocked on the wall for me to shut her up.

On a scale of 1–10, the psychological effect of Marie's screams was a 2—the neighbour banging on the wall was a 20.

Our neighbour was actually very nice and apologised to me the next day, explaining she arrived home after a stressful day at work and snapped when she heard Marie.

My nerves became jarred. My neighbour only banged on the wall once, but once was enough to make me aware her peace was being shattered every night when the screeching began. I didn't know where to turn. Night after night I sat for hours listening to the screams, expecting the neighbour to knock at any time. I was twenty-five and trying to cope with a broken marriage, and being alone again. I lost so much weight I was down to eight-and-a-half stone. Marie was trying to cope with the change too. I didn't know what to do anymore.

In desperation, I wrote to Dr. Kidd at Gloucester Centre in Peterborough and asked if Marie and I could go and see her.

We were one 140 miles away and hardly Dr. Kidd's responsibility. Dr. Kidd could have replied suggesting I see my GP for a referral to a local specialist, but she didn't; she gave me an appointment to go and see her almost immediately.

It's strange that I don't remember how we got to the station that morning when we left the house, or the train journey down to Peterborough. I felt dead inside. In a way, I dreaded seeing Dr. Kidd. I couldn't cope any more. I was going to ask her to take Marie into Gloucester Centre.

I have a clear memory of being in Dr. Kidd's office and Marie going into one of her screaming bouts. I couldn't do anything with her. It was difficult to talk above her noise and I felt so useless and so drained and knew I brought the situation on myself.

On reflection, it was probably a good thing for Dr. Kidd to see Marie's unmanageable behaviour. Dr. Kidd explained Marie's system was pulling against her and suggested spreading her medication out more evenly instead of having a high dose at night. She said she would write to our GP to inform him of the changes. I asked Dr. Kidd about the possibility of Marie going to live at Gloucester Centre. I was filled with shame but it seemed the only way out.

Dr. Kidd was kind and concerned and I was sorry to have put her in such an impossible situation. She said she didn't think I would like myself very much if I took those steps. I knew she was right. I would hate myself if I let Marie go. She also said I put other people before my marriage. It was true. I knew she hadn't meant Marie. That was a big fault of mine. I went where I was needed and expected a marriage to work without any effort on my part. It was just the way I was and try as I might I would never change.

I DO remember the train journey home that evening. We didn't get into Liverpool until after eleven that night. I felt so much better. Sometimes it takes other people to remind us of who and what we are. I went to Peterborough that morning full of despair and returned feeling quite positive. The doubt and uncertainty began to melt away and I decided I was in it for the long haul. My mother often remarked at my resilience and used to say that whatever happened to me in life, I always bounced back. It was true.

The experience made me painfully aware of the difficulties parents of disabled children face. A child that does not sleep wears you down with the sheer endlessness of it all—night after night. I was fortunate to have found a solution and could not believe the difference in Marie when her medication was spread out. She was her old self again. The screaming bouts stopped and she gradually settled down at night. I'm not saying she didn't have her moments, but that was Marie. I was so thankful to Dr. Kidd. What would we have done without her?

14

Back on my Feet

"Don't you dare take on any more kids." My mother warned me a few months later when I told her I was going to foster a young disabled boy every other weekend.

"But Mum, his mum's not well." I told her.

"I mean it, Michelle!" she warned again but her words fell on deaf ears and the child was soon coming to us every other Saturday and Sunday. I couldn't help it. It was something I loved doing and besides, my mother soon came around to the idea.

I was back on my feet and began to look for work. I found a job in a hospital once again, but this time in the Physio department as an assistant. I was working in the hospital Marie was admitted to from Taunton five years earlier. Dr. Rogerson had retired but nothing much else had changed. I suppose that's the nature of an institution; it plods along with the same routine day after day after day. It was sad to see children still living on wards. There must have been families across the community that would offer these children a home but it was getting the powers-that-be to set the wheels in motion.

I loved working with disabled children. Our one-to-one morning session in the hydrotherapy pool was as close as they got to individual attention. They yelled and shouted playfully, stimulated by the water, enjoying the freedom their swimming aids provided for their normally immobile bodies. After lunch we collected the children from the wards and brought them to the physiotherapy unit where we did the appropriate exercises with them.

My job worked out well, particularly during Marie's school holidays. I would take her to work with me each morning where she'd either stay in the unit with me or go and play on the wards. I had no pangs about this: had Marie not approved of the arrangement, she'd have been the first to let everybody know. She enjoyed watching the nurses feed and change the less able children, following them around the ward. When I went to collect her after work, she'd come plodding over to me, dangling her monkey by its foot. On occasion she'd greet me with, 'Oh Mam, nauzy girl!' I'd have to pretend to be cross. She was so funny and would tut in disgust, imitating the nurse. Then there were days she'd be sitting on the chair in Sister's office swinging her legs. 'Bye now!' she'd say sliding off the chair and off we'd go hand in hand for the bus home.

Meeting Alison

We collected four children from the wards twice a day for a one-hour physio session. Our physiotherapist was based in the larger of the two hospitals which were half a mile apart. However, most of the time, myself and two other assistants, were left on our own after we were shown the individual exercises for the children. It was a joy having such a small group and after the exercises, they had orange juice and biscuits. The children responded more to the rustle of the biscuit packet than they did to any of our treatments, smiling gleefully, jerking their legs with excitement.

In my group there was a little girl called Alison; she was ten years old. Alison was blind and mentally retarded. She was unable to walk unless she held onto an adult's hand. She looked younger than her age with her curly fair hair and big blue eyes. The nurses were fond of Alison and agreed she was too bright to be on that particular ward and needed to be with more active children. They were also aware that Sister's priority for cleanliness left them hardly any time to play with the children, but they never complained. If ever they came over to the unit, they would prolong their stay enjoying the time spent with the children. We took advantage of this and picked their brains as we tried to find out more about the children's likes and dislikes. There was Richard, who apart from having a severe learning disability, had regular asthma attacks. He would sit on the floor wheezing, deriving great comfort from the towelling bib he took everywhere with him. Then there was Rachel in her wheelchair, who flinched every time a man went near her because of the beatings her father had given her when she was younger. We nicknamed her Giggler because that was all she did most of the time, as she sat beside Audrey, who giggled too in between her frequent *petit mal* fits.

The first time Alison came into our unit, she was accompanied by one of the nurses who hardly took her eyes off the child whilst she sat amongst the other children. I was soon to learn why when Alison reached out and grabbed one of the children by the hair. The nurse jumped up and quickly came to the rescue, telling Alison how naughty she was.

'Fuck off, you stupid Get!' Alison told the nurse, obviously resentful at being chastised. You could have heard a pin drop as we all looked at each other open-mouthed. I don't know where Alison picked up this language, but she used it quite appropriately.

Alison never smiled: whether she was happy or angry, she always wore the same serious expression. As soon as she familiarised herself with our physio department, she seemed to enjoy her visits. It made me feel really sad because when Alison wasn't being aggressive, she was a lovely little girl.

The purpose of Alison's physio was to strengthen her legs, so we encouraged her to walk as much as she could. Alison loved individual attention and was happy to stroll around the unit, holding onto my hands as I counted to 10. She would imitate my voice and tell herself how clever she was.

"Is the sun shining, Shell?" she asked, having been used to daily reports on the weather. If it was a sunny day, Alison would then say, "Do you think you could take me for a walk in the sunshine?"

How could anybody resist such a request?

Alison wore green pumps and a coat that we had to squeeze her into because it was so small. Many a time her hand flew out to scratch me or pull my hair. I kept hold of her hands whenever I lifted her up, always talking to distract her, but I never told her off like everybody else did. I'd slowly release her hands and if she suddenly remembered and tried to lash out, I would take hold of her hands and continue talking, ignoring what she was trying to do. This certainly didn't stop her, but her attacks on me were less frequent.

Because Alison was so vicious with the other children, whenever she was left on the ward she had to sit in a hug square playpen on her own. I suppose unless Alison had a one to one relationship with a nurse, it was inevitable, but I felt desperately sad for her when I went to collect her. Sometimes she would be sitting in the corner of the playpen with her legs crossed, head drooping onto her chest like a discarded puppet.

"Hello Alison." I would whisper as I sneaked up on her.

"Hello Shell." she would answer, and immediately follow with a barrage of questions as I lifted her out of the playpen. I felt that it was only to be expected that she would attack people, given the long stretches of time she spent in her playpen with no physical contact.

Everybody Pulling Together

The sad thing was the longer Alison stayed in hospital, the more difficult her problems would become until they were so serious she might not be accepted anywhere. Despite the obvious affection the nurses had for her, Alison needed a lot more scope to develop, although her age was against any great change.

It was about this time I started to enquire about Alison's history. She was born in 1968 and needed an immediate operation to remove a lump in her neck, a cystic encephalocele. A Spitz Holter valve was inserted to assist drainage of the cerebral fluid. Alison went to live at home soon after the operation, where she stayed until she was eighteen months of age. Alison was then admitted to a residential nursery. By the time Alison was almost two years old, she had outgrown the nursery and another home had to be found. She was then admitted to a children's home 60 miles away. The home, for severely physically and mentally handicapped children, had 150 beds, mostly cot cases. Alison stayed there for two years and at the age of four was moved to a local authority home for mentally handicapped children in her own area. The home was mostly for short stay children and the staff had great difficulty preventing Alison from attacking other children. Four years later, when they could no longer cope with her vicious behaviour, she was admitted to the hospital where I met her.

News came that the smaller hospital school was closing down and the children would be transferred to the large hospital half a mile away. It was suggested the children would benefit from better educational facilities. I had serious reservations about Alison being admitted and felt that going to a larger ward would take her to the point of no return.

I had a word with Alison's teacher and told her of the new Barnardo's home that was shortly to open, feeling that Alison would benefit from being in a smaller unit. Her social worker met my proposal with enthusiasm and promised to bring the matter up at Alison's case conference with Dr. Arya, the hospital psychiatrist. I couldn't help noticing—and not for the first time—how the older professionals were open to ideas.

By the time the case conference came around my job had finished.

Dr. Arya gave me his permission to take Alison home for weekends and school holidays, recommending I continue with this support when she was admitted to the unit at Barnardos. Alison's area social worker agreed as did the hospital social worker. Matron was absent and the ward sister said that of course it would have to be cleared with matron—until Dr. Arya reminded her that it was he who ran the hospital and not matron.

Alison's area social worker was about to retire and brought along the man who was to replace her. I knew the fostering officer in Liverpool because I recently fostered a disabled boy at weekends to give his mum a break. I rang the fostering officer and told him the news and he was keen to get the ball rolling. Two days later, I received a copy of the letter my fostering officer sent to Alison's social services department agreeing to supervise Alison's stay with me.

Easy Peazy Lemon Squeazy—Not!

I telephoned Matron a week after the conference to see if I could bring Alison home for the day. Unfortunately, she was not very pleased. In fact, she hit the roof.

"Who do you think you are?" she asked me angrily. "Just walking in here and taking a child to a strange place—removing her from people who care about her, and expecting her to adjust."

"But Alison knows me." I told her. "I've had Alison almost every day for the last few months."

"Who gave you permission to do this?" she asked.

"Dr. Arya said I could at Alison's case conference."

"What were you doing at the case conference?"

"I was invited." I told her warily.

"If you want to take her out, I want two days notice in writing (as if I could ever forget!) and I'll see Dr. Arya about this!"

I hung up the phone. When she said jump, I had to jump. Within an hour I had written the letter and posted it.

Two days later I received the following reply.

'Dear Miss Shearon,

Thank you for your letter received this morning requesting permission to take Alison Jones out for the *day on Friday.*

I am writing to inform you that Alison is to be transferred to Dr. Barnardo's tomorrow, Wednesday, and I would advise that you give her a settling in period before you approach the Superintendant with a view to taking her out.

I should also like you to approach Alison's Grandmother who loves her very much and takes her out.

I am glad my assessment of Alison proved to be correct.'

I folded the smug letter back into the envelope.

So poor Alison was to be moved that day! Just like that. There would be no introductory periods? I felt so sad. Everything she had been familiar with was now gone (Again).

I thought it was supposed to be about Alison, but Matron had made it all about herself and I got the feeling she didn't care where Alison went just so long as she didn't come to me.

15

Her Life in His Hands

Following Matron's words of wisdom, I did as I was advised and kept my distance. After two weeks, I rang the Superintendant at the unit and was told that Alison had not settled as well as expected.

"Can I visit her?" I asked, but the Superintendant told me she would like Alison to have more time to settle in. I disagreed, but kept my thoughts to myself. Had I been in her position, I'd have asked all of the ward staff to visit, knowing how much Alison must have missed their voices and smells and everything she'd been familiar with. Then came the thunderbolt. The Superintendant told me Mr. Davison, Alison's new social worker, had left instructions with the staff that nobody from Alison's past was to take her out for at least six months. The reason for this unreasonable stipulation was to allow Alison to settle into her new home. Today, as then, it beggars belief.

At the end of the third week, with a little gentle persuasion, I was allowed to visit Alison. The staff member, who opened the front door to me, looked so miserable. I was baffled at how someone working in a brand new facility, with only a small group of children, can look so gloomy. I'd have been in seventh heaven.

"Who gave you permission to visit?"

"It was arranged yesterday." I told her. "They must have forgotten to tell you." She didn't seem convinced, but finally stood aside to let me in. I followed her through the hall and into a small lounge. I smiled sadly when I saw Alison. She was sitting on a chair in the corner with her head drooped onto her chest.

"Hello, Alison!" I said softly. I lifted her up and then sat down with her on my lap.

"Hello." She quietly replied. There was no barrage of questions or requests to go walking in the sunshine—just a 'hello'. I wrapped my arms around her cold, goose-bumped limbs. I tried to ignore her chilly-looking cotton dress, which was open to the waist with nothing underneath it. Alison still had her little green pumps on with one of the ribbons missing, and a pair of ankle socks. It was the first week in November.

The home had only been open for three weeks and the children were trying to cope with their new move in different ways. I recognised two little boys from the large hospital, one of whom was throwing Fisher Price toys aimlessly. The other, was almost bouncing off the walls with pent-up energy, having been used to the open space of the hospital ward.

I stood up and gently lowered Alison until her feet rested on the carpet. Clutching my hands tightly, she began to take small steps around the room. Two housemothers and a psychologist were sitting in the corner with a young girl who had Down syndrome. They were obviously enchanted with her and as I glanced over at them one of the housemothers looked at Alison in surprise.

"I didn't know she could walk." She said nudging the person next to her.

"Oh, she's quite a busy little bee." I told them. "She enjoys being on her feet and usually counts to 10 as she walks, don't you, Alison?" There was no reply. Alison remained silent and kept her head down.

"Hasn't she got any decent clothes?" I asked, hoping my directness wouldn't offend them. One of the staff shook her head. "We've been trying to get money out of the Social Services and they won't budge. She's hardly got anything!"

I glanced down at Alison as we stood hand in hand, hoping she wouldn't get too withdrawn as she tried to cope with her new environment. Strange as it may seem, I was worried because Alison had stopped scratching and pulling hair. My intuition told me this 'problem' had stopped too soon to be for the right reasons and, daft as it may seem, I think it would have helped her if she'd brought her playpen with her and been weaned out of it, so to speak.

My attempt to strike up any conversation with the housemothers had failed. I was hoping they would bombard me with questions about Alison, but nobody seemed interested.

I bit my lip as I left the home, trying to hide my disappointment. It had been so different to what I had expected – and so had Alison.

The next time I visited with a friend, the children had just returned from a walk, and poor Alison was still dressed for a summer's day as she sat huddled in the chair with her legs crossed. The two young boys from the big hospital were a bundle of fun, but I watched with growing concern at the way the toys flew across the room. Alison was a sitting target. She was blind, for God's sake; she wouldn't even see them coming. I must have met a different shift on this day because the housemothers were more pleasant and chatty when they came in and out of the room to take the children to the toilet. Poor Alison seemed just as quiet as before, if not quieter.

"She's perished, Mish," my friend said gently squeezing her hand. "And find out what size shoes she is and we'll go and buy her some. She can't walk about like this." He whispered.

Looking back now, I suppose we could have left the money for the staff to buy her shoes but I was afraid the problem would then be that nobody was going to the shops.

We guessed Alison's shoe size (because she wasn't allowed out) and bought her a little pair of blue shoes. I told the man in the shoes shop that the child was ill in bed and he cleverly suggested that if the shoes did not fit then I could draw Alison's feet on a piece of cardboard. This tip came in very useful because the shoes *were* too small.

My friend, Paul, handed another pair of shoes into the home one evening on his way to visit me. The housemothers at the home couldn't try the shoes on Alison because it was half-six and Alison was in bed. Paul asked the staff to ring and let us know if the shoes fitted, but nobody bothered. In fact, nobody phoned for the next two weeks. Still concerned about the child's apathy, I rang her social worker. I explained as best as I could about how withdrawn I thought Alison was and that she needed more individual attention. He flatly refused my request to bring Alison home for one afternoon a week, insisting that Alison needed six months to settle down. With great difficulty, I managed not to argue with him. I wanted to leave the door open, and I had the feeling if I said any more he'd have slammed it in my face.

I decided to stop visiting Alison until her six months were up. Resentment was creeping in from the care staff: I wasn't a relative, nor was I calling in an official capacity—I was just a bloody nuisance. I was also frightened of preventing the staff from getting to know Alison and resenting her instead.

I wondered whether Alison's social worker saw all his clients twice a year, and planned their lives six months in advance. Maybe that was the only way he could keep his "cases" in order.

I used to ask myself time and again, why does it have to be this way?

Skin and Bone

When Alison' six months were over, I rang Barnardos and was told that she had been very ill and was in the paediatric hospital.

"What happened to her?" I asked.

"She just stopped eating and drinking and lost so much weight she became very dehydrated."

I thanked her quietly and hung up the phone.

My enquiries at the children's hospital didn't get very far. The nurse told me Alison had been discharged from there too and had been (dumped) sent to the big hospital for the mentally handicapped.

"What was wrong with her?" I asked anxiously.

"I'm afraid I'm not allowed to say." She said to my annoyance. "That's confidential information."

By the time I found out which ward Alison was on at the big hospital, I was shaking. I asked the nurse how Alison was.

"She's still very ill," she answered and waited for me to speak.

"Would it be ok if I visited her tomorrow?"

"Well," she said despondently, "if you knew her before, be prepared for a shock."

What a strange thing to say. I thought as I hung up the phone.

When I went to the hospital the following afternoon, no amount of preparation would have lessened the shock. I walked into the day room, smiling when I saw some familiar faces of children I used to take for physio, but after scouring the faces I couldn't see Alison.

The nurse I spoke with in the office came into the ward.

"Where's Alison?" I enquired, trying to make myself heard above the background noise of the children.

"There she is." The nurse replied pointing to the side of me. I looked down and gasped in horror at the scrap of skin and bone that was lying on the bean chair. She looked like someone from the Third World. I had seen her already and not recognised her.

"What's happened to her?" I asked the nurse as I stooped down to lift her out of the bean chair. I was choked. She'd lost so much weight and could no longer sit up on her own, let alone walk. The nurse shrugged her shoulders.

"I told you to be prepared for a shock, didn't I?" She said gently. "As far as any of us know, Alison became dehydrated after refusing drinks for about four weeks."

I cannot describe how I felt. I knew they were personal feelings I had to deal with myself, but I will never forget the sorrow that clouded over me as I held Alison in my arms. This was her third home since she left the hospital the previous year, going from one stranger to the next.

She was just another lonely child in care.

My heart ached for her. Why on earth was she in such a noisy and impersonal environment when she was still obviously very ill—so ill, in fact, that she was only being fed on watered down orange juice?

I took her into the dormitory where I put her on her bed. She was freezing; her legs were bare and I stifled a sob when I thought about the empty bedroom at home.

Alison's hair had been cut very short and I suspected her head had been operated on. I knew sometimes a Spitz-Holter valve can become blocked or misplaced, but careful observation by the staff should detect this straight away. For example, if a child became lethargic or their eyes suddenly became glazed, then they would need to be admitted to a hospital immediately in case the valve needed to be corrected. Alison looked like she'd had a stroke and even though all the signs indicated a blocked valve, I put it out of my mind never imagining a blocked valve could have gone undetected by the staff in the unit.

A nursing assistant came into the dormitory and walked over to where I sat at the side of Alison's bed. She reached to the shelf above Alison's head and took down a jug of orange juice, then took a teaspoon out of her pocket.

"Open wide!" she said cheerfully. I watched full of anguish as the cold orange juice ran down the side of Alison's mouth onto the back of her neck; the nursing assistant hadn't even bothered to sit her up.

I left the hospital in tears. So that was the extent of Alison's 'care'— cold watered-down orange juice. It was deplorable.

To me, Alison had died. I knew she would never again pull my hair as I told her how pretty she was and that no more sounds would ever pass her lips. The only comfort I could find was that God had taken her spirit and left her breathing body behind as an example to us all to treat children in care with a little more tenderness and understanding.

I was shaking the next morning when I rang the hospital social worker. She didn't know what had happened and said she would not like to commit herself, adding that one didn't know what had gone on in the child's mind.

16

Treading Very Carefully

I wanted to ring Mr. Davison but kept putting it off because I did not trust myself to speak to him. When I eventually rang, I almost regretted it as I listened to his cool voice on the other end of the line.

"Oh yes, she's been ill, hasn't she?"

"Have you seen Alison?" I asked him.

"Well," he said casually, "I haven't had the chance yet, what with one thing and another." I bit my lip to stop myself vomiting abuse down the phone.

"But Alison was in the hospital for sick children for two months." I said incredulously. "Are you telling me you didn't visit her once?" He started to sound a bit irritated with me.

"Like I said," he replied, "what with one thing and another." I changed my attitude realising it would serve no purpose to antagonise him. I told him I understood how busy he must be.

I was revolted at my lack of sincerity and was becoming a master at keeping my cool. Mr. Davison refused my request to look after Alison at home, telling me Alison was in the best possible place, receiving expert care.

"But don't you think Alison has the right to live in an ordinary home like any other child?" I asked him but I knew I was wasting my time; we were on different wavelengths.

That afternoon I stopped at the jewellers on my way to the hospital to buy Alison a Saint Christopher medal. She looked so lonely the previous day when I left her lying on her bed in the middle of an empty dormitory. This time when I left her, I tied the St Christopher medal and chain around the bar at the head of her bed, and somehow she didn't seem so alone.

I strolled towards the hospital lodge and looked across to the out-patients clinic. I could see Dr. Arya through the window. When I arrived home, I rang him. Dr. Arya had been very fair with me in the past, and I trusted his judgement. He listened to my concerns and invited me to his clinic the following afternoon. When I met Dr. Arya, he explained that Alison's future was to be decided at a case conference in a week's time and suggested I attend it.

In the meantime, I continued to visit Alison and found it an enormous strain to be pleasant when I could not really accept what had happened. My discreet enquiries about events which had led up to Alison's physical deterioration came up against a barrier of silent officials who convinced most people that Alison had a condition whereby she became dehydrated very quickly. The staff's acceptance of this situation left me wondering at my own sanity. I wanted to bring to light the mistakes that had been made. How can lessons be learned, if mistakes are hushed up to protect the staff. Was nobody answerable for Alison's precious life?

Most of the ward staff were cordial but unfortunately there is always one bad egg and it's that bad egg that tends to give everybody else a bad name. This particular woman was not a trained nurse, but was still occasionally left in charge of the ward. One day when I went onto the ward, she was sitting in front of the TV knitting, as the children crawled around her feet. That mightn't have been too bad except that she had a cigarette hanging out of her mouth. When she was in charge her attitude tended to rub off on the other ward staff. She treated me with casual disregard. I'm sure she thought if she ignored me for long enough I would go away. Not a hope! I never criticised her, and nor did we communicate very much. Sometimes our eyes would meet, and they said it all; after all, the eyes are the windows of the soul.

A Power Struggle

The day of the conference, my stomach was in knots as I sat watching the various people arriving: the two housemothers from Barnardos, the hospital social worker, the physiotherapist and several other 'professional' people. When Mr. Davison, Alison's Social Worker arrived he went into Sister's office with Dr. Arya, where I could see them through the glass.

I was edgy as I stood looking out of the window. I could see a nurse in the distance pushing a child in a large buggy; as they go nearer I could see the child was Alison. *Is there no end to Alison's suffering?* I screamed inside. I watched her being wheeled through the snow. Alison had on a little pair of ankle socks, a sleeveless cotton dress, with a poncho on top. I wondered whether the nurse would dress her own children like that; if she had they'd have been taken off her and put into care.

Alison was perished when I sat her on my knee. She immediately closed her icy hand around my finger. Mr. Davison didn't come into the conference. I could see him arguing with Dr. Arya in the office. Within minutes he walked out, shouting at Dr. Arya and slamming the door behind him. He went out of the building and I never saw him again. The social worker, who should have been at the heart of Alison's case conference, helping to plan Alison's future, and improve the quality of her pitiful life, had just abandoned her.

When the meeting began, Barnardo's staff said they were prepared to keep Alison's bed for the next six months. One of the hospital staff addressed them: "Just for my own information, before Alison was admitted to the children's hospital, did it occur to any of you to measure the child's head?" Barnardo's staff shook their heads. It then occurred to me why Alison's illness had been treated as 'confidential'—as someone later confirmed; Alison had suffered a valve closure. She had been so dehydrated by the time she left Barnardo's her weight was a mere 1 stone 8 pounds.

Unfortunately, when Dr. Arya put forward my request to look after Alison at home some of the ward staff took it as a personal criticism. (And some of them were probably right!) I was not very popular with the physiotherapist, who'd been my boss at one time. Our differences hadn't been that serious—I simply objected to her request to have a child admitted to the hospital for physiotherapy, when during the child's stay they would hardly receive any treatment.

The physiotherapist was an exhibitionist and these requests, which usually took place in conferences at the out-patients clinic, were purely an attempt to assert herself amongst her colleagues and, unfairly, misled the parents. Being the parent of a disabled child myself, I probably objected more than most. It was the physiotherapist who spoke out when Dr. Arya mentioned my proposal.

"Actually," she said smugly, "It's a pity the person who cares about Alison the most isn't here to represent her." The knitting nurse that wheeled Alison to the case conference in the snow, sat beside the physiotherapist, nodding her head in agreement.

It was a few seconds before I realised they were talking about an elderly nursing assistant who used to look after Alison on the ward in her old hospital. I knew her and she had actually given me her blessings with the child, telling me she was not in a position to look after her.

"I don't mind taking a back seat if someone else wants to offer Alison a home." I told them. And I really didn't. For someone, anyone, to take Alison home would seriously have warmed my heart.

People started coughing and shuffling about. They had embarrassed everybody with their pettiness. Dr. Arya was obviously irritated with them both and said that I was the person representing Alison.

The meeting moved on with everybody putting their various proposals forward. I listened expressionless as the physiotherapist recommended Alison remain in the hospital for at least six months because she needed intensive physiotherapy.

I knew then that I had no chance; not a hope in hell.

Dr. Arya announced Alison was to remain in the hospital for another six months because she was too ill to be discharged. I was given permission to visit whenever I wanted.

It was with a lump in my throat that I quietly accepted his decision.

It was a safe decision; six months' intensive physiotherapy? What about six months' intensive love and care? Did they not realize that was also the food we needed for life? I could have brought Alison to the hospital every day for treatment or, God forbid, and not wishing to undermine the brilliant physiotherapist, but maybe, just maybe, I could have done the exercises with Alison at home each day.

Everybody wanted a little piece of Alison. I could have, would have shared her with them, but they did not want to share her with me. They did not like me. They were all part of a pecking order and knew their place; I wasn't. I was a free spirit. I could almost hear them asking, "Just who does she think she is?"

I don't think Alison's social worker left Dr. Arya with any choice. Mr. Davison had turned his back and walked away. Two fingers to us all, including Alison.

When the conference came to an end, I shuddered when I saw the knitting nurse wheeling Alison's buggy in to push her back to the ward. I stood up, the child still clinging to me, warm and snug in my arms, cheek resting on my shoulder.

"Would you like a lift?" I asked her, trying to make an effort. "It'll save you having to walk through the snow." She willingly accepted.

The Definition of Care

A week after the conference, I arranged to visit the ward. I arrived mid-morning to find Alison lying on a bean chair in the middle of a noisy day room. She looked so vulnerable as she laid there, her big blue eyes unable to see the chaos around her. Two children lay sprawled on the floor with their heads resting on the bean chair beside Alison's blonde curls. My stomach turned when I lifted her up and saw teeth marks across her fingers. Needless to say the knitting nurse was in charge. When she came into the ward I asked her if she'd seen the marks on Alison's hands. She strolled over to where I sat with Alison and looked at her hand.

"Oh," she said casually, "One of the children must have bitten her. I'll have to keep an eye on her in the future."

It seemed strange being on the other side of the fence. I wondered how many attempts to move children out of hospital failed because of short sighted, cold-hearted, arrogant people, like Mr. Davison.

I was aware that this experience had clouded the nurse's attitudes to the benefits of life in the community as opposed to hospital care. Some were smug: others had been so alarmed at Alison's physical deterioration that they were convinced it was through lack of nursing care. Who could blame them?

Two months later a representative from Barnardo's assessed Alison and decided she was too severely disabled to return to them. They had to let her bed go. She was on the scrap heap now. Still—she had been everywhere else; it was the only place left.

I continued to visit. When Marie was with me, she walked around like she owned the place. She'd lose herself in the dormitory and put her monkey to bed.

Each day Alison was getting a little stronger. I was thrilled when I went onto the ward and she was propped up in her feeding chair, wearing the little blue shoes we'd bought her.

"Oh, she looks nice today!" I told the nurse.

"They brought her things yesterday." She told me with a look of disgust. "They didn't even ask to see her."

"You mean the staff from Barnardo's?" I asked.

She nodded. "They just dumped her things in the office and left."

"But their job is done now." I told her. "Alison is your department and besides," I added, "maybe they didn't feel welcome." The nurse stopped and looked at me.

"We didn't say they couldn't see her!" she told me defensively.

"Maybe not," I said, "but did you say they could?"

"No." She said quietly.

"Well then," I told her, "you probably just misunderstood each other."

M arie was 14 and the hospital was my backbone. The short-term care for Marie was the only means of support I had. Any plans to fill the gap in community care would take a long time before they catered for the Maries and Alisons of this world. They were way down the priority list. I didn't believe using the hospital for Marie did her any harm, at least not on a short-term basis. Besides, I would always be looking over Marie's shoulder wherever she went, not that she needed me now. Her wilfulness and lack of tolerance in situations she did not like meant she would always be last in the queue and first on the bus. She was one of the lucky ones. I wouldn't want it any other way.

My involvement with Alison had left me shell-shocked. I was now a woman on a mission, determined to try and make a difference.

Later that year, Alison was moved to a ward for delicate children. She lived there for four and a half years. Then, in the late 80s a scheme to foster some of the hospital children into families at weekends was initiated. Alison was finally given a taste of what most children take for granted. She died 6 months later. She was 16.

Part Two

17

On a Mission

I got married as soon as we moved to Lincolnshire. My husband Paul and I bought a cosy two bed-roomed terraced house in a row of about twelve. Although we wanted a large house to take in more children, property prices were way out of our range. A few months later the house next door went up for sale. Brilliant! We wheeled and dealed with the owner, and talked him into giving us a private mortgage. The house had been modernised and all we had to do was knock an opening through the dividing wall. Two months later, we had the keys.

Ulterior Motives

We had already introduced ourselves to the Social Worker at the local disability hospital. She had visited our home several times and responded to our plans with enthusiasm. I also wrote to the local Fostering Officer enquiring about fostering disabled children. Unfortunately, the social workers were suspicious because we specified what type of children we wanted. When I said the child didn't have to walk, or feed him/herself, or be toilet trained, I was met with raised eyebrows. One particular social worker said that sometimes children are easier to look after when they don't walk because you don't have to be running all over the place after them.

"I hadn't really thought of it like that." I told her.

"I suppose if they don't walk you'll get the mobility allowance too?"

"I don't think foster parents are entitled to mobility allowance," I said as calmly as I could.

If I asked ask for children who live in a hospital, there are going to be those that don't walk, don't feed themselves, and are incontinent, but if they have to overcome those problems before they can leave hospital, then they'll be there forever. There are people who'll take the bright kids. What about the others?

When I rang the Fostering Officer at the local social services, the woman informed me that she had never received my letter. She came to meet me, filled in some forms and sent off for my notes and references.

That evening, when Marie arrived home from school, I took her to meet Paul from work. On the way home, we called into the pet shop to buy a goldfish. I tried to arouse Marie's interest, but she wasn't impressed and tried to put her foot through the glass. She wanted to leave. I was used to this kind of behaviour and just kept her far enough from the glass to avoid her outstretched leg. We were looking at the lizards in the tank. I turned around to check on Marie and saw a man bending down quite near to her, looking in the aquarium. As I stood near him, and before I could stop her, Marie put her hand up the back of his T-shirt to tickle him and the poor man got such a fright he nearly went through the glass. We laughed all the way home as she skipped in between us.

Two Into One

I was jumping up and down like a big kid when the first brick fell out of the dividing wall and we could actually see into next door. Slowly, brick by brick, the dividing wall crumbled to the floor, and Paul refused to stop until it was finished and our two houses became one. I did my little bit—moved some rubble out of his way and supplied the tea and sandwiches. We spent the following day clearing up the mess but it was worth it, I thought, as I spat out the dust from my mouth. I was glad Marie had gone for a week's respite and wouldn't be affected by the muck and dust.

Next, the electricians came and rewired the two properties as one. At the same time the upstairs wall was being knocked out to make an opening into next door. It was great; our house was suddenly twice the size and we had two stairways. When I think of the wasted journeys I had, traipsing up and down the stairs with cups of tea for the workmen, only to discover when I reached the top that they'd gone down the other side. We laughed about it and thought of all the fun Marie would have as she went on her little walks about the house.

That evening, we put the finishing touches to the playroom. We laid the carpet and brought in Marie's light blue piano that we'd bought her the previous year for her birthday. The piano brought Marie hours of pleasure as she sat banging the keys. By the time the room finished, it was past midnight.

Emotionally Disturbed

One thing about Marie was that we could never take her for granted, though after living with her for so long I could usually tell at a glance what kind of mood she was in. Either way, she kept us on our toes. Marie and I could be sitting in a café enjoying lunch and if someone came in with a noisy child she would put her spoon down and refuse to eat. Whenever she did this we left her, accepting that if anything upset her, she couldn't eat. To have forced her would have made her angry, and she probably would have slung her plate across the table. I just talked to her now and again to distract her attention from the noise. If, for example, I whispered, "Isn't that little girl naughty, Marie?" she would laugh quite loudly with tears in her eyes. As long as she laughed, she was releasing some of her tension. To avoid this kind of situation would have been impossible—it was part of everyday living. I was happy that Marie was at least able to sit through the meal even if she didn't eat it.

Even when Marie was in a dozy mood, her little idiosyncrasies kept us on our toes. She was enchanted by the strangest things. Often I found myself checking on her as I followed her eyes, and more often than not she would be fixating her attention on an object—the top of a sauce bottle or a man's buttonhole in his jacket. Marie delighted at the things most of us would ignore. Past experiences told me to distract her because it isn't always obvious to other people that she has a learning disability. Some people became offended and thought Marie was being rude staring at them. I learnt my lesson some years ago when I was travelling on a London underground with her and I heard someone say, "I'll fucking punch her in a minute." I quickly glanced up from the book I was reading to see where the threat was coming from. There was a group of girls looking our way and I was shocked to see they were talking about Marie. Marie had been sitting staring at them, and one of the girls was getting quite angry with her. I quietly told Marie to stop staring, closed my book, took her hand and stood up to go. Fortunately the next stop was ours anyway!

"She's as lively as a cricket today," Sister said when we went to collect Marie from her week's respite at the hospital. "She hasn't stopped singing since we brought her own clothes out of the wardrobe and she realised she was going home." Marie latched onto our hands overcome by a mixture of emotions, not knowing whether to laugh or cry. She kept requesting to go on the bus. In fact we owned an old mini bus.

"Has she been all right?" I asked Sister.

"Most of the time she's been fine," she replied. She was getting Marie's medication out of the cabinet. "She gets a bit noisy at times with her screeching," she said, returning the cabinet keys to her pocket. "But then, that's Marie isn't it?" she grinned.

"You don't think she's emotionally disturbed then?" I joked.

She raised her eyebrows and shook her head. "Well," she pondered, "that depends on your perception of her!"

On Marie's last visit to the hospital, we had been unable to collect her and had arranged for her to travel with the hospital transport. When she was due home, Sister had telephoned me.

"I'm sorry, Mrs. Daly," she said, "but while I was having my lunch the ambulance arrived to collect Marie and they refused to take her because she was screeching. They said she was too emotionally disturbed.

Even though Marie was not particularly distressed, the ambulance driver's response didn't surprise me. I knew the drama Marie was capable of creating. I also knew it was purely for effect and she had no deep rooted emotional hang ups. One of the reasons I liked using the hospital was because the staff knew and accepted her. I had every confidence in them. And, until an alternative was found, it was all I had.

Paul, Marie and I stopped at a café on the way home.

"She's got lots of bruises this time, hasn't she?" Paul remarked. I watched him cutting up Marie's sausages.

"I know," I replied, looking at Marie's elbows across the table. "I wish she would look down when she walked." When we had collected Marie one of the nurses told us she was tripping over the patients' feet all the time; her poor arms and legs were black and blue.

18

In It For The Money

The next time the Fostering Officer came to see me I think I overpowered her with my enthusiasm. I showed her around our house which was now twice the size and explained what we had to offer. Unfortunately, she had other things on her mind. She asked me if I would consider taking a three year-old boy. The child was living in a foster home, and, because of his difficult behaviour, was classed as unfosterable. I gulped. The little boy's name was Richard; he was in need of a long term foster home. I said it was not really what I wanted to do but I'd give it some thought. I was thrown into confusion after the fostering officer left. They made him out to be a little monster but weren't most three year-olds little monsters?

I hoped they used our home as a last resort. I couldn't see how an unmanageable little boy would benefit from living in a house with severely disabled children, who would most likely present challenging behaviour. It would be different if he was our own child, but this little boy was already disadvantaged by being removed from his natural parents.

Over the next few weeks, we had many different social workers calling to our home. My husband and I must have seemed a strange pair—very naïve indeed; two people with their heads in the clouds who wanted to change the world. A few of the social workers were mildly interested; the others were baffled. "Why mentally handicapped children?" most of them asked. "Don't you think all children in care are handicapped?"

The Fostering Officer from the local Social Services called to see us. She had received my references and said she wondered if I was too qualified to foster (whatever that was supposed to mean!).

The Social Services held many meetings to decide how best they could use us. We were not invited to these meetings and were given bits of tittle-tattle from the various officials who visited our home. Then Yvonne, the hospital Social Worker, came to see us. She had been making enquiries about having a little boy who lived at the hospital placed with us. She called straight from a meeting with the local social workers who told her that when Richard, their three year-old, was placed with us, we could not have any more foster children for at least three to six months. They also told Yvonne to back off, that she was on their territory, that we were their foster parents, not hers. I found their attitude very disappointing and hoped things would improve. Some hope!

Our little 'unfosterable' foster child was a great success. I was told there would be no parental contact, and yet his mother came to see him quite often. The two of us devised a plan and she spent every other afternoon combining her efforts with mine in trying to 'tame' him. After eleven weeks, Richard waved us goodbye as he walked up the road holding his mum and dad's hand; he was going home for good. He was the one and only child the local Social Services ever placed with us.

I have always been a great fan of the Beatles. Like many people around the world, I was devastated when I heard John Lennon had been shot dead. It was also the day my pregnancy was confirmed. We were naturally thrilled with the news, but I remember the day being tinged with sadness for the loss of such a charismatic and humane person.

Being pregnant made me more determined than ever to continue our struggle to foster. The baby, to me, was a gift from God; it was also a test of our convictions. I was unshakable, and memories of Alison were always in the forefront of my mind.

Marie's Transition

When Marie was almost 16 and due to leave school, I was looking at what was available for her in the form of day care. The Social Services are responsible for providing day facilities in the community for people with a learning disability when they leave school and are no longer the responsibility of the Education Department. This facility is in the form of an adult day centre. Because more learning disabled people are living in the community, the Social Services were slowly recognizing the need for special units for people like Marie, with severe challenging behaviour, requiring maximum attention. Their response to this need (in our area) was what they called an ISU (Intensive Support Unit) which had recently been built onto the Day Centre.

When I discussed Marie's future with her teacher, the teacher told me she didn't think Marie would like the ISU, and would be better occupied watching people in the main workshop where there was more activity. I felt that going into the Unit could have been to Marie's advantage, depending on the skill and understanding of the staff. I knew from experience that if she is in a situation that she disliked, she quickly reverted to her old habits. I thought the workshop would be too noisy for her and she would probably spend most of her day screeching.

The ISU stood apart from the main workshop. When I visited the unit there was a group of people watching TV. One of the instructors came over and introduced himself before explaining how the unit was run. It was built to accommodate ten people and had four vacancies, which meant lots of attention for those already there. I was shown various programmes on the wall which represented the days' activities. TV programmes were watched throughout the day—some lasting only five minutes, but everyone had to sit and watch them. *Why?* I thought they would have problems with Marie over this; she had never responded to the TV. I hoped a lot of what they did was optional because when people leave school, even if they do have a learning disability, they have the same rights as everyone else and should be allowed a certain amount of freedom in how they choose to occupy themselves.

The instructor then told me the names of the people in the unit and whose parents were overprotective. As I stood there listening to him discuss the students and their parents I couldn't help feeling disappointed. He could well have been talking about me in my absence and I didn't like it one little bit. I was unimpressed and decided to look for an alternative, not realising at the time there wasn't one

Since Richard had gone home, nobody from our local Social Services approached us. I had made it clear to them when Richard first arrived that we would only accept children with a learning disability in the future. And they just didn't have any. So where were they?

19

Patrick

In the middle of August, when our baby was two weeks overdue, the doctors decided to induce me. I eventually had a little boy delivered by Caesarean Section. I couldn't believe he was ours when I looked at him through sleepy eyes, stroking his little mop of silky black hair. He'd been worth all those hours of agonising labour—until, after he refused to be dragged out by forceps, the doctors decided to delve in and get him. We called him Patrick!

I went home when Patrick was twelve days old. In no time at all, we had become accustomed to our tiny addition and life went on as usual. Marie was in seventh heaven. She would sit on the chair for hours at the side of the baby's pram, holding his bottle when his feed was due and tutting in disgust when I changed his nappy. She tapped his back very gently while I held him, trying to bring up his wind. When all his little needs were seen to, she would sit looking miserable as she once again guarded his pram waiting for the next burst of activity.

From the start I had to tell her not to touch Patrick's pram; she had no sense of danger and could quite easily hurt him. She understood this rule which was why I never panicked when I left her in the room alone with him for a minute, because she usually did as I asked her.

I could not go out of the room and leave Patrick sitting on his bean chair or in his baby bouncer, because in the bean chair Marie could quite easily sit on him without realising. She had almost done it to Sam, my sister Liz's little boy, and we had just caught her in time. If I left Patrick in his bouncing chair, it was likely that Marie would trip over him because she didn't look where she was walking. So although she would do as I asked her, I couldn't leave her to use her initiative because she didn't have any. She was never allowed to put the monkey in Patrick's pram when it was empty because I knew she would probably do the same thing when he was in it.

We spent the last of the summer taking Patrick for walks in the pram; Marie always pushed him while I hung onto the side—(like the Nanny!). People said the strangest things. I had been warned over and over to expect Marie to be jealous, but knowing Marie the way I did I knew she would be so involved in helping me with his little needs that the advantages of Patrick far outweighed any disadvantages. People also said the oddest things to us when they met us in the street. For example; "Is the baby all right?" and when I answered "Yes," they would say something like; "I bet you were relieved, weren't you?" It took me quite a long time to realize they were actually asking me if my baby was handicapped like my daughter. Another question was, "What are you going to do with her now? Are you still going to keep her?" Marie would look at people, sometimes smiling as she held onto Patrick's pram. I was glad that she was unable to understand because cruel words could never hurt her.

My friend's little boy started coming to us before and after school to fit in with his mother's working hours. By this time, I was looking for someone to help me at home. Our young paper girl was ideal, especially when I saw her trailing up the street each evening with groups of children following her. I made her an offer she couldn't refuse, so she gave up her job and came in to help before and after school hours.

Patrick had many names—Marie called him 'Padwick', little John called him 'Battery'—and things worked out surprisingly well in our lively (sometimes chaotic) home. When their dad arrived home in the evening, I didn't get a look in as he took over with the kids; we both loved having them around.

Sunday People Revisits

That weekend we were in the *Sunday Press*. My now friend, author and journalist, James Copeland had come down to do a catch-up article about the tiny new addition to our family and also wrote about the empty beds we had waiting to be filled with foster children. Unfortunately, the issue which sparked off the story was not mentioned ('The Silent Minority' TV documentary by Nigel Evans). However, the article stimulated various reactions and two days later the Fostering Officer called to see us from the head office at Lincoln. He apologized for the way we had been treated and said that the Lincoln office were going to take us under their wing, and we would bypass the local Social Services.

Having worked with his wife in a village for special needs children while having two youngsters of their own, he understood our enthusiasm, assuring us that we'd have his backing with whatever we wanted to do. This was very good news which also gave Yvonne, the hospital Social Worker, the green light to get involved in our scheme.

She rang one day informing us that her colleague at the hospital was looking for a long term foster home for a thirteen year old girl.

"Do you think this is the third time lucky?" I joked.

"Let's hope so," she replied.

20

Judy

Judy had a mental age of about 2½ and had lived in a hospital since she was five. Previous to that, she had lived at home. After years of living in the hospital, Judy needed a more homely environment. After an introductory weekend, she was admitted to a Home for mentally handicapped children. She was 11½.

Most of the children had been at the Home for a long time and were familiar with the social standards expected by the staff. Instead of these children being moved on to foster homes to make room for the Judy's of this world, they tended to be permanent residents.

Unfortunately, because of Judy's behaviour problems and (I think) her difficulty in adapting to such a different environment after such a short introductory period, the staff at the Home decided after a six month trial that they could not cope with her, and she went back to live in the hospital.

When Judy came to visit us, she was accompanied by one of the nurses that was doing a case study on her, and her Social Worker. She didn't walk through the door when she entered the room – she came in like a gust of wind, dragging Chris, her Social Worker with her. She stood in the middle of the floor with her long wavy ginger hair falling in ringlets down her back, a fringe almost covering her eyes. Her nose was running and she'd rubbed it all over her face which didn't exactly make a pleasant sight but she looked a bundle of fun as she stood there laughing at us with one finger stuck in her mouth as if she was about to make a decision.

"Well," Judy's Social Worker said as he headed for the front door, "I'll collect her in an hour."

"Coward," I teased as I watched Judy clear the top of the piano with a sweep of her arm.

In a way it was a relief having her nurse around to see how he dealt with her but, unfortunately, when Judy (who was very excited and showing off) tipped the record player over and started ripping the pictures off the wall, he didn't seem to notice; he was rolling a cigarette.

"Does she understand what you tell her?" I asked him. I was watching her throwing the lid of the record player up at the wall so it bounced back down again. Her eyes were full of mischief. She looked at each of our faces to see what effect she had on us.

"Well," he said, licking the cigarette paper and sealing it, "sometimes." I laughed thinking what a great help *he* was.

Marie thought everything Judy did was hilarious and her loud approval only seemed to encourage Judy to be all the more silly.

"Would you like the records on, Judy?" she was asked her. She immediately responded with a smile.

"She doesn't speak at all," the nurse said as if he suddenly remembered the purpose of his visit.

"She gets by all the same though, doesn't she?" I said. The hour flew, and by the time Chris returned, Judy had us all running around in circles. She did the daftest things just to make sure she had our undivided attention.

It was a cold January morning when I collected Judy from her ward a few weeks later. She strutted on ahead of me to the mini bus, insisting on carrying her own overnight case. Christmas had come and gone and little David, my friend's son, had now left us to take up his long awaited place at residential school.

Judy was much calmer and sat quietly during the trip home. She understood that we understood that she knew better than she let on.

"Why don't you show Judy your toys, Marie?" I suggested when we arrived home. I was on my way into the kitchen to switch on the oven. They both followed me and stood in the doorway. Marie seized her opportunity.

"Doose," she ordered as I took Patrick's bottle from the fridge and dipped it into hot water.

"Would you like some juice too?" I asked Judy as she stood holding Marie's hand. She smiled in response and followed me with her eyes to see what I was doing. Her face was full of expression – because of her lack of speech, she was used to using it to communicate with people.

We had three cots—one in Patrick's bedroom and one in each of the downstairs rooms. This meant we could have Patrick around for most of the time. After the girls had a drink, I could hear Patrick cooing to them as they stood beside his cot. When his bottle was ready I lifted him out and prepared to feed him. Judy looked at me questioningly, but Marie walked to the chair in the sitting room where she prepared herself to watch her little brother being fed. When Judy entered the room with me, Marie beckoned to her; "Shub ober," as she made room for Judy on the same chair. Marie loved to share and was very good natured; she was never jealous and loved the stimulation sharing brought her.

When Patrick was fed and I was putting out lunch, Marie took her apron off the door, and gave it to me to tie on her. I rooted out one for Judy and she was soon sitting cheerfully at Marie's side wearing one of my spotted overalls.

The meal passed with surprising calm. Only once, when I asked Judy to wipe her mouth, did she try to test us. She threw back her head to laugh at us, letting the food pour out of either side of her mouth. We ignored her after that; she was obviously doing it for effect.

During the afternoon, she sat with Marie at the table doing jigsaws. I was amazed at her capabilities. She studied the picture intensely before tackling the pieces.

"Again," Marie requested each time she completed a puzzle and Judy happily obliged, smiling at her new friend who sat holding a monkey.

The rest of the evening we spent pottering about the house. The two girls complemented each other; Judy enjoyed the novelty of having all the toys around her, being able to play with whatever she wanted whenever she wanted. Marie enjoyed sitting and watching, stretching her neck occasionally when Judy blocked her view.

Judy only had one habit that we objected to: her constant hair chewing. When I asked her to take the hair out of her mouth, she became quite agitated and blew raspberries at me. Later on, when they were in their nightclothes watching TV, we sat Judy on a chair and brushed her hair down her back, making it less available for her mouth.

After Judy spent three successful weekends with us she came for half term. She really was no trouble. She seemed to appreciate everything we did for her. Her favourite pastime since she'd first arrived was dressing and undressing an old doll she'd found in the toy box. She did this for hours and never seemed to tire of it so I sorted out some baby clothes and put them in a carrier bag for her which she kept at the side of her chair. But if any of us went near, she stopped what she was doing and held her doll tightly so we couldn't take it from her. She eventually realised it was her doll and, unlike on the ward, she didn't have to share it with lots of other children. On the day Judy was to return to the hospital, Chris, her Social Worker, called and seeing she was so happy, arranged for her to stay with us. We laughed at the surprised look on Judy's face when she stood up to leave with him before realising she didn't have to go. Her face was a picture as she stood there wringing her hands with pleasure.

"Are you going to say goodbye to Chris?" I asked her. Infected by our laughter she strutted across the floor and pushed poor Chris over the step as she tried to close the door on him. It was all taken in good fun. Chris walked down the path pretending to be disgusted as he straightened his leather jacket.

When Chris left, I watched Judy curiously as she approached the cupboard in the playroom and lifted out some magazines. Standing there holding Patrick, I was intrigued. From the bottom of the pile she brought out a carrier bag; in it was her old doll that she had was hiding until her next visit...

We were now into February 1982.

House of Fun

Weekend trips home to Liverpool in our old mini bus were quite a regular event. Bottles, nappies, steriliser, wheelchair, toys and children would all be waiting eagerly to be loaded into the bus. My family were scattered throughout Liverpool and Cheshire. Waiting patiently for us to arrive, they never knew how many children I was going to turn up with. They were well used to me and made us all most welcome. Flying visits were all we could manage but they were worth the effort. Returning home on Sundays, we were a little tired but refreshed.

Judy was settling very well—so well, in fact, that she was starting to put us to the test. She hated the sound of a firm voice and would flare up at the least sign of any disapproval of her behaviour, using her screeching as a weapon against us. Her biggest difficulty seemed to be having to cope with our slower pace after being used to the hospital's inevitable routine which was so rigid, especially at meal times. She could be sitting quite happily eating her lunch, but if she caught sight of her pudding she would shovel the rest of the food into her mouth. Any requests we made to slow down brought screeches of resentment which were so loud that I had to move her from the table. Then we felt guilty in case Judy saw it as another rejection. However, our clever little Judy didn't mind one bit; in fact, the arrangement suited her fine. Peeping through the door after a particularly noisy commotion, I saw her sitting watching the TV. She'd turned it on and left the sound off! I smiled at her shrewdness and laughed at her spirit.

Marie took it all with a pinch of salt but only because we made light of it and kept distracting her. Having Judy around made me realise how difficult it must have sometimes been for Marie at school. Over the years I had learnt she could cope with noise, but only with the help of someone steering her through it. I have learnt a lot through Marie; the most rewarding thing she has taught me is how to accept and respect people's individuality. We were very careful with Judy and only disapprove of her behaviour when it was intolerable. Our expectation of fostering was not to have a group of perfect children. On the contrary, we welcomed the difficult to place children and hoped with all our hearts that we could provide what they needed, which was basically a warm and loving home. Too often I have seen children admitted to homes and hospitals where the staff have let their enthusiasm run away with them by putting the new children on 'programmes' before they have allowed themselves time to build a relationship with the child. This is simply because of their ideas of how the child should be, and often the poor child ends up with more problems than he or she had in the first place.

However, I had to try to encourage Judy to stay at the table until we had all finished the meal. She would push her chair back to leave the table before she'd finished chewing the last mouthful. She objected quite strongly to our request for her to wait and would put her hands under the table, trying to turn it over but we usually continued eating with our elbows firmly holding it down, trying to ignore her. After a while I realised once again how difficult it must have been for her and thought perhaps we were expecting a bit too much of her having to sit there with nothing to do. In the end, I gave her a picture book to look through. Sitting across the table from her I was very moved when she smiled her appreciation over the top of the book.

Judy swallowed her drink in one go. Her eyes would look over the top of her cup as if she was rushing to finish the drink before I stopped her. She would then end up with a red face as she coughed and spluttered. However, Marie was not allowed to behave like that so it wasn't really fair to let Judy. In the end, I gave her a cup quarter-full. She still rushed her drink, but didn't have the same dramatic effect. Each time she finished, I gave her another little drink. She was so pleased thinking she was having a treat. After a few weeks I started filling her cup up again and she forgot all about the race.

Marie followed Judy everywhere, frightened of missing anything. She loved watching her play with the toys, sometimes handing Judy something to wind up.

"Come on, lazybones," I'd tell her jokingly, "do it yourself." But Marie got more pleasure from watching. Most of the things Judy was able to do, Marie found difficult; she'd never been able to fit two pieces of a jigsaw together, so Judy was very stimulating company.

When Patrick went to bed at night, we'd tidy all the toys away. Judy was a great help; she was so thorough that ages after Marie and I had gone into the kitchen to make the cocoa, she was still picking bits off the carpet. She was so helpful that once she got the dish cloth and started washing the wooden panels in the sitting room. Unfortunately, the cloth was full of spilt milk and I looked on in horror as the walls turned white, knowing I'd have to wait until she'd gone to bed before I set to cleaning it.

One evening I was developing some photographs in the kitchen. The kitchen was almost in darkness except for the low darkroom light in the corner. Marie and Judy stood in the doorway.

"What's the matter, Judy?" I asked when it became obvious she was trying to tell me something. She about-turned and went into the sitting room. I thought she'd gone to watch the TV until I heard the drawers in my desk opening and closing—then giggles—then she came and stood in the doorway and handed me a candle!

Marie's Visit to the Adult Day Centre

Patrick was five months old and Judy was living with us permanently, when I took Marie to meet the Manager at the local ADC (Adult Day Centre). I knew from looking around the ISU (Intensive Support Unit) that the emphasis was on group activity, and because of Marie's wilfulness and lack of concentration, I thought it would be too long a day for her to have to conform to this idea.

When I met the Manager there was definitely a chill in the room. She said how difficult I'd made things for her staff by keeping Marie at home and asked if we were able to do anything at all with her. *Now there was a million dollar question.* I didn't appreciate being talked down to but I had learned not to react. I had requested a part time place for Marie on the application form, but the Manager didn't bring it up for discussion, and made arrangements for Marie to go full time. Who was I to have any say in the matter?

Having always been an early riser, busy mornings were no problem. With Patrick dressed and fed, and the two girls ready to go we usually had an hour or so to bomb the playroom.

Judy was the first to depart in her taxi. Beautifully dressed in the clothes, her parents bought, hair no longer falling over her face but held back with a brown velvet band, bag over her shoulder. I had very tentatively introduced a diary between school and home to avoid the many misunderstandings created by verbal messages through third parties. It worked very well. In fact, Judy's teacher took a great interest in her and often popped in after school for a chat.

After Judy left in the mornings, I would put on Marie's coat and she would stand by the window waiting for the bus to reverse down the street to take her to the centre.

"Not 'ere yet!" she'd keep repeating impatiently. And then I would hear, "Oh, Mam!" and then an even louder, "bu-dy-ell!" I knew the bus had arrived.

Marie seemed happy enough. She arrived home in the evenings, kissing the walls and doors and chatting to herself. I had always used a diary for Marie too, but the ADC staff met my proposal to continue with this arrangement with raised eyebrows, and then reluctantly agreed. In the diary I was informed when Marie needed 20p for an ice cream, but not when she was coming home from the Unit two hours early—when she needed more elastics for her hair, but not when she was throwing her food at them. I was given no information at all and consulted about nothing. I was later to learn that I had the reputation of an upstart. Not sending Marie straight to the Day Centre when she left school had confirmed their beliefs. Just who did I think I was?

"Aren't You Bothered About Bringing The Baby Up With THEM?"

Eight weeks after Judy was placed with our family, Linda joined us. Linda was 12, and came to us from a children's home. Her short black hair was a mass of knots at the back where she rocked herself to sleep at night. When she spoke, there was hardly any eye contact and she looked down at the floor for most of the time. I used to tease her, saying, "Let's see your lovely face," and she would giggle shyly when she raised her head to meet my eyes. However, this lack of eye contact in no way impeded her speech and Linda never stopped talking. She was also very motherly and wanted to do everything for the girls. I explained to Linda how Judy preferred to do some activities on her own. For example, Judy objected to Linda's kind attempts to help her with her jigsaw. And Linda had to accept that, although the girls were not as skilled, they were just as capable of asserting themselves and refused to accept her well meaning bossiness. Then there was Marie whose friendly and affectionate nature appeals to most people; Linda was no exception. She looked on helplessly when Marie struggled to undress herself, but I had to be firm on this because Marie, being the way she was, would quite happily let anybody do anything for her. Too often I had seen Marie put in other children's care at school, with alarming results as they walked her into doors and dragged her over steps. Once, at an Open Day, I watched helplessly while a child dragged her over a stack of wheelchairs, and the teacher wasn't even looking Marie's way as she stood up crying and was walked back to class on the hand of the brighter child.

"Aren't you bothered about bringing the baby up with them?" people would ask, but the girls treated Patrick like a prince and from the start I had very firmly forbidden them to touch him unless I was in the room. They accepted this, so if he dropped his dummy, Judy or Linda would come running out to let me know. He had them all running around in circles. They dashed about the room trying to pick up all his baby toys and put them in his cot before he slung them all out again and they all laughed helplessly.

They each had their little jobs to do. As soon as I went to change Patrick's nappy, Judy jumped up and got me his changing mat from behind his chair. Even if she was in the other room and she heard me talking to him, she'd appear in the doorway to check if I needed it. Marie would hold his bottle for me, but it was Linda whom I had to watch because she was always trying to pinch Patrick's clothes for her doll which was why she always insisted on folding them.

"Oh look at this, Michelle," she would say, holding one of his garments in the air. "Isn't it lovely?" Then she would say, "I think it's too small for Patrick though, don't you?"

"Hey, never mind," I would answer playfully, "just lay off and put them in the cot."

"Oh okay, darlin," she would answer loudly as she laughed at her own cheek.

The three girls got on extremely well; perhaps because they were all so different they complemented each other.

Not long after Linda came to us, we bought her a budgie for her birthday. She was ecstatic about it and called it 'Lion'. The day it arrived we placed it on top of the piano in its cage. Then I set to trying to arouse Marie's interest.

"Come and see the bird," I said, almost dragging her across the playroom floor. She stood there very unimpressed before returning to sit with Judy and singing; "Hatty-bird-day-to-you."

Judy was different again! She was intrigued with it and wouldn't leave it alone, standing at its cage for hours and jumping if the bird so much as flapped its wings. When the bird was sitting on the far side of its cage, Judy would wet her fingers and stick them through the bars, making the bird food stick to them as she tasted it. One day, I heard a sudden scream and went to investigate. I nearly collapsed with laughter when I saw Judy running around the room with the bird perched on her head. She'd let it out of its cage. I think Judy learnt a lesson and was careful not to get too close after that incident.

There was no getting away from it though, the girls were a bundle of fun.

Prejudice

One day, not long after Linda had arrived, her Social Worker, who was recently promoted to Fostering Officer at Lincoln, rang me. She'd been to a meeting at Head Office with the fostering panel, and, amongst them were two social workers from the local Office. One of the social workers placed Richard with us, and the other dealt with families of learning disabled children in the area. Imagine my surprise to be told both these social workers had expressed their concern to the Divisional Director that we were allowed to foster two mentally handicapped children. They wanted to know who would take the rap if anything went wrong. The Divisional Director had apparently reminded the two social workers that we were coping with a child one of their Homes had given up on. They had then both expressed their concern about the effects living with disabled children might have on Patrick. I was aghast and thought they should concern themselves with more important things—and leave our son's welfare to us. It was only months later that I realised I should have taken them more seriously. I underestimated the lengths to which they would go to prove a point.

22

Parents with Ideas are Upstarts

In my attempt to show the Day Centre staff I was not an upstart, I was turning a blind eye to things I should have pointed out. However, when Marie arrived home with her bra around her neck, I decided to ring the Instructor. I didn't know how this happened, but felt the Instructor should be made aware the incident because Marie was so vulnerable, and unable to protect herself in any way from being exploited.

"Do you think she's improved at all?" the Instructor asked me. I am wary of staff, who after only a short time, feel they need to get results to show their own effectiveness. Marie was just 17, and I didn't kid myself about her potential. Her development over the years had been very slow. Before I could speak, the Instructor went on to tell me that last time Marie went swimming, she had an epileptic fit.

"But she went swimming two weeks ago," I told her, thinking we must have our wires crossed.

"Yes, that's right," she answered.

I was flabbergasted. "Why wasn't I told?" I asked her. "Why are you only telling me now?"

"I forgot to send the diary home with her on the Friday," she told me casually. "And when I returned after the weekend, the urgency seemed to have gone out of it."

I mentioned about Marie's clothing being loosened. The Instructor said she didn't know how this could have happened, but would look out for it in the future.

Had Marie had fits every week, I could have accepted the oversight but as far as we knew this was her first one she had at the Unit. It wasn't enough to supervise Marie; I expected the staff to have a bit of feeling too. I decided it would be a good idea to have a chat with the Instructor. I sent a note in the following day suggesting this. It was Open Day when I met up with her.

"By the way," she said to me, "The swimming will be on Tuesday now instead of Friday." I gulped. I didn't want Marie to go swimming any more, but somehow I didn't think the Instructor would understand.

She didn't. I told her I was concerned after what happened the last time she took Marie swimming. It is the only time Marie fits and these fits are usually brought on by a rapid drop in her body temperature. *She should have told me.*

"But I apologised for that," she said angrily, "and what happens if she has a fit doing something else? Are you going to stop her from doing that too?" I tried to reason with her, asking her to see it from our point of view.

"She'll have to go swimming," she said. "All of the group go."

"That doesn't matter," I told her. "She can have a day at home on the swimming day." She raised her eyebrows and pursed her lips before speaking.

"You just remember this," she almost snarled at me, "I didn't have to tell you at all." *How many times has that been said to me over the years?* And with that bit of frightening information, the Voice of Reason left me standing in the middle of the floor and walked away.

"Round them up," she shouted to her assistant. I looked on in amazement as the people in the Unit stood up to go over to the big hall.

The following day I wrote to the Instructor, telling her that if she did not feel answerable with regard to Marie's welfare, then I was not happy about her taking Marie on holiday. I asked her to return Marie's holiday bag.

The bag came home with Marie on the bus the following evening with a letter from the Manager asking me to keep Marie at home the following week because although the ADC was still open, the Unit would be closed.

Teamwork

The secret of our success was teamwork. Though we made every effort to give all of the children their fair share of attention, we never forgot that unlike Marie and Patrick, who were in our sole care, Judy and Linda were in the care of the local authority with their two Social Workers, Carol and Chris, acting as their guardians. They were required by law to visit the two girls at least every six weeks. Their visits, in fact, were far more frequent, and because they were so helpful and supportive, we looked forward to either of them popping in whenever they were passing.

We still came under fire, especially from Social Workers at the local office, not only because we fostered two mentally handicapped children but also because we were given special allowances to cover the cost of their needs. I didn't pay too much attention to what people said, but being accused of looking after handicapped people for money touched a raw nerve. I mentioned it to Carol when she called one day.

"Take no notice of them," she said in disgust. "You've only got to look around your house to see where the money goes."

At the beginning of the school holidays, we employed Rachel, a young graduate, to stay with us until September, when she was going on to teach. By this time, I was two months pregnant. We were very happy with the news because we'd wanted the children close together. Rachel's presence in our family made an enormous difference to me. I had never allowed any of our helpers to look after Patrick and did everything for him myself, so that in years to come I would not have to wonder if he'd had enough of my attention.

23

Showing Me Who is the Boss

Unfortunately, my relationship with Marie's Unit staff was still very strained. In an effort to improve the situation, I had telephoned the Manager to arrange a meeting. She had sent me a letter telling me she was going on holiday and would contact me with an appointment when she returned, but she never did. Marie still only attended the ADC four days a week, staying at home on the swimming day. This arrangement had worked out very nicely because it allowed Marie to have a day on her own with Patrick and me, though I have to admit, by this time Marie had become so used to having Judy and Linda around that she missed them if they were gone for more than a few hours.

I should have known it was all too good to last.

Carol, Linda's Social Worker, who had by this time been promoted to Fostering Officer at the Lincoln office, telephoned me one afternoon requesting to call and see Paul and me together that evening. She sounded a little subdued, but I didn't pay too much attention; it was half term and I was busy with the children.

Carol and I had a very good relationship, and not only were we alike; we also shared the same birthday (the same as Hitler's!) However, nothing could have prepared me for the bombshell she brought with her that evening.

The manager from the Centre had contacted the local Social Services with many concerns about Marie—screeching and pulling hair—bruising on her body—weight loss and aggression. The staff felt this behaviour was a result of Marie's unhappiness at home. The District Officer at the local Social Services had refused to let any of his Social Workers deal with the problem and had referred it to the Director at Lincoln because he felt that Marie's problems were due to our fostering two other mentally handicapped children. (Would they ever let it go?)

I thought that after having Marie for all these years and dealing with professionals, that I was open minded and nothing would shock me. I was wrong. Carol went on to tell us that the Centre staff had been making notes of bruising on Marie's body for the last three months and the staff in the Unit felt she was seriously emotionally disturbed. They had even reported me for not allowing Marie to go swimming.

Before she left, Carol added insult to injury when she told us of the events which led up to this. The Director at Lincoln had asked Carol to look into the matter. She had then reluctantly visited the Centre and spoken with the Manager. Finally deciding the problem wasn't hers, she told the Manager to handle it herself in the proper way (i.e. by sending for me to discuss it with her). Carol explained to the Manager that she and another Social Worker visited our home regularly and were quite happy with the general well-being of our family. However, the Manager did not contact me and with the matter unresolved, the local District Officer sent in another complaint to Lincoln. This time Carol (not the Manager) was ordered to look into it.

We felt so humiliated, especially when we learnt of all the people who had known before we did. Nobody had given us a friendly warning. Even Carol, though perhaps meaning well, had made a special twenty mile trip from her office to discuss us with the Manager, almost driving past our home which is only five minutes' drive from the Centre.

The most annoying thing was that they were describing the Marie we all knew. Had they been less arrogant and given themselves time to get to know her, they'd have seen this for themselves. The lack of skill and understanding by the Unit staff seemed to defeat its purpose. The hardest thing to accept was the noted bruising on Marie's body. Carol was unable to enlighten us on this, saying she would have to ring them and find out what they meant.

"Even if the allegations are untrue," Carol said, "I want you both to think very seriously about this because we have to think of our reputation in the type of foster parents that we select." I didn't know whether to laugh or cry – or just to thank her for the vote of confidence.

Before Carol left, she said she'd give us a couple of days and then she'd be back for some answers.

Was it any wonder the hospitals were full if people have to put up with that kind of attitude?

That weekend, Paul and I were as miserable as sin. Early on Saturday morning, we all went to the park but sat like two strangers on a bench, deep in thought as the children played around us.

I was frightened when I realised the powers Social Workers had. Watching Patrick running across the grass, I wondered what steps they were allowed to take if ever they thought the girls were affecting him. I thought I could put up with a lot; I could not put up with this. If being a foster parent left one open to all kinds of accusations and spite, then we were obviously were not suitable candidates. Every time I looked at Marie, a lump rose in my throat. I had to bully myself to try and accept that they were only doing their jobs, but it was difficult. Carol had phoned me the day before to ask our permission to visit us with a senior Social Worker. I was looking forward to straightening things out and clearing our names.

The dreaded Monday arrived and Paul took yet another afternoon off work so we could be seen together. Deep down, I found it rather degrading having to explain about Marie's mental and physical condition and the behaviour problems which can arise from time to time. The senior Social Worker was angry that the Day Centre Manager had passed the buck onto the Fostering Department at Lincoln instead of dealing directly with me. Carol then told us that Marie's bruising had been on her hands and lower arms. I was stunned.

"But she's always got bruises there from when she pinches herself if she's cross; they know that," I said incredulously. "So why did they suddenly start writing it down three months ago?" It slowly dawned on me that three months ago had been our disastrous Open Day when we had stopped Marie from going swimming.

Marie did not return to the Centre. What was the point? They couldn't cope with her, nor could they accept that to all intents and purposes that I was Marie's mother. It just didn't sit right with them. Carol said the Centre staff were prepared to sit around the table and talk with us, but to me, the damage was done; the situation had gone way past that stage. They could all go to hell.

"But they don't want you to remove her," Carol said. "She's so happy there and has improved so much." I think that must have been the understatement of the year!

"She's Eccentric"

When you think you're as normal as the next person and then someone comes along and gives you a character assassination, it's devastating. I know it shouldn't be, but I found it so. The Manager had said I was difficult, unapproachable—but what threw me was being described as eccentric. I thought only elderly people acquired such descriptions. How could I, at the age of twenty-nine, be so?

Given that period of my life again, I would sit and laugh at them all. It would no longer matter what they thought of me, and as far as Marie went I knew they would stoop to any level to prove they are the experts and are always right. It has been my experience that if you have a child with learning difficulties, the Social Services don't like it if you don't put yourself in their hands. Even though I'd looked after Marie for ten years and had managed without their 'support,' they could not accept our situation. Their concern was that even though we had Social Workers looking after the foster children's interests, there was no Social Worker looking after Marie's.

Many letters were exchanged.

Despite my depression, I still had enough fight in me to go and see my solicitor. He wrote to the Director at Lincoln asking for some justification for the accusations against us. A few days later we received the following reply;

> 'Thank you for your letter informing us of your instructions from Mrs. Daly. The circumstances are that Mrs. Hardy, as the Manager of the ADC, where Marie was attending, reported to the fieldworker that bruising had been noted on Marie over a period of days. Mrs. Wilson, Fostering Officer who supervises two children in Mrs. Daly's home was asked to discuss the matter with Mrs. Daly from the point of view that Marie was falling about more often. It was intended to discuss possible reasons for this and other matters noted

in Marie's physical condition and attitude. However, Mrs. Daly saw this discussion as implied criticism of her handling of Marie and regrettably in my view, has chosen to withdraw Marie from the centre.

Mrs. Wilson, with the senior Social Worker, Mrs. White, will be visiting Mrs. Daly again and I hope it will be possible for Marie to be allowed to attend the centre again.'

I felt like banging my head against a wall. The reply was from the Director of Social Services. He eventually came to see us and apologised for what had happened. He agreed that we should have been contacted initially by the ADC staff and he would inform them of this. He also said that a lot of water had gone under the bridge since he had written to us, adding that he would not expect Marie to return to the Centre as we probably had no confidence in the staff. How right he was…

I looked after all the children up until three days before my second baby was due. Ideally I should have been able to go into hospital without anybody needing short-term care. It was their home too, and having a baby was such a natural event for them to experience. Instead, my wonderful Irish midwife arranged for me to go into hospital a week earlier than the obstetrician had planned in order for me to organise everybody's short-term care. Even though the Social Workers had said I over-reacted, I was very nervous about leaving the children at home while I was away. I had visions of returning home to find everybody had been taken into care, including Marie and Patrick. I was having another Caesarean section and expected to be in for at least two weeks. I was taking no chances.

Judy went into a children's home, Linda went to stay with her grandparents and Marie went onto her usual ward at the local hospital for mentally handicapped children. I felt such a failure.

Anna

Anna was born on 3rd February 1983. She was a bonny little thing and, like Patrick, had a mop of black hair. Then came all the cards, flowers and telegrams and what should have been a wonderful occasion was tinged with sadness when I thought of my little boy at home and the three girls staying in separate places.

"I want to sign myself out," I told the Ward Sister the day after Anna was born. She was very kind and very shocked.

"But you can't go yet," she told me gently, "don't you realise you've had major surgery?"

I nodded. "I have to go," I told her.

"Will you at least stay and see the doctor?" she asked me anxiously.

I agreed because I didn't want anybody to think she'd upset me, and blame her. The doctor arrived and, despite her efforts to make me stay, she knew I was determined to go and that I'd only waited to see her out of courtesy.

"You seem sensible enough," she finally said, "but please take it easy when you get home". They must have thought I was crazy!

Broken Spirit

It was so difficult trying to pretend everything was normal when our spirits had been crushed. We rented a house near our families up north at the beginning of the summer holidays and toyed with making the move permanent. What kind of environment was it to bring children up in when I was frightened to leave them in the house when I wasn't there?

When Judy's parents were told of our plans to move, they decided that they didn't want her to live that far from them. We were very sad about this, but knew that the fourteen months she'd spent with us would have helped her enormously to adjust to a children's home. It was a very sad day for us all when we piled into our blue minibus to take her to the home.

Our new house was a lot smaller than what the children had been used to, and they desperately missed the play space. Despite our great efforts, none of us liked it.

The week before Linda was due to start her new school, we went to have a look around the ADC. We were very impressed. The 'students,' as they called the disabled people, were not looked down on from a great height – they were very much on the same level as the staff and treated with the dignity and respect they were entitled to. Instead of monotonous routines, they had one free day when they did as they pleased. We explained what had happened at Gainsborough

Enterprises and they accepted our decision not to have a Social Worker but to deal directly with them to avoid complications. We looked around their Intensive Support Unit where Marie would most likely be going and breathed a sigh of relief at the brightly coloured toys along the shelves. I knew straight away that she would like it and the staff would accept her for what she was without expecting her to grow up overnight and be the adult her eighteen years told them she should be.

For the first time in months, things seemed to fall into perspective. I had almost been convinced of my worthlessness and that old suspicion that comes now and again had been lurking about—had I really been selfish in bringing Marie out of hospital and had I really done her more harm than good? And slowly, ever so slowly, it dawned on me—we should have stayed where we were and fought for her rights. At the time, we felt too injured ourselves.

When we arrived home, we sat in our little kitchen. For the first time in months, I felt good. I put on the kettle for some coffee.

"Where would you rather live?" I asked Paul as he sat doing the crossword. He put down his pen and grinned at me; "This house is nice," he said. "But it's not really suitable for all of us, is it?"

We hadn't yet sold our house in Lincolnshire and I was convinced we were not meant to leave it. The funny thing was we'd had to build the dividing walls in an attempt to sell them separately, because most potential buyers had thought they were too big.

We returned within a week, seeming like we'd only had a long summer holiday. Four days later, we had the dividing walls knocked out again and the playroom painted. It was as if we'd never been away. Marie was over in the corner kissing her piano; Patrick and Linda were running up one side of the stairs and down the other. My little blue-eyed Anna was cooing excitedly in my arms. Yes, it was chaos; it was good to be back.

I had a really lovely GP I had been registered with for years, and I trusted him completely. I think he also respected and accepted me for who I was. Soon after we returned, I took Marie to see him and I was surprised when he handed me a letter across his desk for me to read. I acknowledged the Social Services letter heading and began to read. It was from a Social Worker at the local office. In her letter she told my doctor how I fostered two mentally handicapped children and of the problems the ADC had been having with Marie, of the bruising that had been noted on her body and of her concern for Marie's welfare. She went on to explain that even though Carol and Chris supervised me with the two foster children in my home, there was nobody to supervise me with Marie. She finished by telling my doctor that if he was ever worried about Marie, he should not hesitate to contact either herself or the District Officer at the local Social Services. I handed the letter back to my doctor. With a look of disgust on his face, he tore it into tiny pieces and dropped them in the paper-bin.

I was devastated.

So many things were going through my mind when I left his surgery that afternoon. Then a kind of relief flooded over me as I realised I had not over-reacted after all. The letter proved what liars they were. I was thankful that we had returned and shuddered as I thought how that letter would have followed me wherever I went and I'd have known nothing about it. We were obviously meant to return and finish what we had started.

Seeing the Light

I'd always wanted to write a book and tell our story but I didn't know how. Now I'd had enough and felt it was time I learnt. It was just after Christmas, which is my favourite time of the year, when everything stops for the holiday and I go into my thinking mode, that the intention planted itself firmly in my head. So I set up my own little corner of the bedroom, bought a wallpaper pasting table, a dictionary, a thesaurus and some foolscap paper so I could make a copy!

Fortunately, I was a hoarder and had kept every piece of correspondence relating to Marie and my struggle with "officials" over the years. Even the envelopes came in handy when enclosed letters were not dated; at least I had the postmark. I went to Boots and bought loads of diaries, then filled in the relevant correspondence from over the years. This gave me a really good head start, enabling me to fill in the gaps and make sense of things.

Every night when the children were in bed I'd be tap-tap-tapping away. It was so therapeutic, that once I started, I couldn't stop. I turned the pages into chapters and spread the chapters across my pasting table, and soon a book began to form.

Today I say I wrote myself out of a nervous breakdown. I had been so beaten down by the system. I thought I was a crap mother and was led to believe all the snide and slanderous remarks made against me by people who should have known better. It was a revelation.

I finished the book almost a year later and decided to find an agent. It was a long drawn out process and when an agent arranged to meet me in London and then cancelled without any explanation, I sent my book directly to publishers. When Virago sent me a rejection letter, they apologised for keeping my manuscript for so long, saying that all of their staff had wanted to read it. They also said their publishing house was too small for my book and it would simply "get lost" with them. Two readers from Souvenir Press had recommended it to be considered at their editorial board, but in the end, after much discussion, their hands had been tied because my story was not the type of book they normally published.

I'd written to Anne Robinson, a fellow Liverpudlian and the then Deputy editor of The Daily Mirror. I was so touched when she replied, saying how much she had enjoyed reading our story and giving me all kinds of helpful tips on how and what to submit to publishers.

I ended up with a handful of rejection letters from people who praised the book, describing it as promising, but also saying that their hands were tied because it didn't fit into their usual catalogue of publications.

In the end, I decided to put the manuscript away in the drawer. There was no rush to have it published. I was just so happy that I'd written it. I was reborn with the weight it had taken off my shoulders. However, it was only years later that I realised that was only the first half of the book!

24

You Made Your Bed...

I had been foolish to think we could carry on where we had left off. Our fresh application for Marie to return to the day centre was rejected—no vacancies. This surprised me. Before we left the area, I was led to believe there was ample space. I was now being told Marie's name would have to go on a waiting list. They couldn't give any indication how long the list was or where Marie was placed on it.

The day centre Manager and her staff had had their knuckles rapped about their unprofessional behaviour towards us and they weren't likely to forget it.

Still, always the dangerous optimist, I imagined it would only be a matter of weeks before they offered Marie a place. Surely the Social Services would make Marie a priority to enable the fostering to run smoothly. They couldn't have cared less. If only I'd known then that it would be six long years before Marie was once again to take her rightful place in the Unit.

The Social Service's one and only concern was for Linda. Under normal circumstances, that's how it should be, but our circumstances were far from normal. Our lives had been turned upside down. With Marie at home all day, plus an eight month-old baby and a two year-old toddler, it was difficult to pick up the pieces and put the past behind us. The ADC staff were not going to let us forget. I had made my bed and now I had to lie in it. It was a matter of rolling up my sleeves and getting on with it. We'd had so many plans for the future, so many dreams...

Linda was like one of our own children, yet her presence in our home was bringing us nothing but misery. We were five minute's walk from the Social Services office. If any of the social workers had time to kill, they killed it in our house. They often called at teatime when I was busy looking after the children and preparing the evening meal. Sometimes when Paul came home from work, the children would be sitting having a meal at the table while a Social Worker sat on the settee sipping his coffee indifferently. Knowing I'd been on my own with the three children all day, and the social worker bringing no news of any kind of day care for Marie, I knew it took Paul all his efforts not to throw the social worker out.

After the social worker left the rows would start. Finally, after many sleepless nights and much soul searching we asked the Social Services to find Linda another home. Linda had lived with us for two years; we had to live with that decision forever. Though the decision had been a very hard one, by closing the door on the Social Services we not only gained our privacy but also our self-respect.

The children, unaware of any difficulties we had with officials, thought Linda was returning home to her family. They missed her terribly and constantly asked me when she was returning. Many times I wanted to ring the Social Services to tell them that I was sorry, that I would put up with anything if we could just have Linda back. I was being foolish. We'd made the decision and we had to live with it.

A year passed and I employed a young girl to come in and help. With only twenty months between Anna and Patrick, it was like having twins. Far from being the baby, as soon as Anna was toddling about, she was kicking her nappy off and insisting on using the toilet like Patrick and Marie. Bath time was great fun. With Marie's generous dose of bubble bath, Patrick and Anna were submerged almost to their mouths in suds. Marie knelt at the side of the bath— she loved to help. She would get a good lather on the flannel and wash the children's back and legs most thoroughly.

The children were my life. Nothing else mattered to me as long as they were happy. Years of looking after Marie had put an end to any social life we might have had. I was not too bothered; I had learned to create my own interests at home. I loved to read, especially biographies. I was always looking for an opportunity to sneak off to a quiet part of the house and stick my head in a book. Music was another form of escape. I was an avid record collector. From the moment I got up in the mornings, the records were played for most of the day. It didn't matter how low I was feeling; music always lifted me out of my doom and gloom. Just to remind myself there was a world outside of the house, occasionally, when I went out alone I'd have a look around the shops. Instead of testing the new perfumes on the cosmetic counter or browsing in the lingerie store, more often than not I'd find myself standing in the middle of the toy shop winding up all the Fisher Price toys!

My helper, who in the beginning had been very nice, turned out to be very unreliable. Sometimes she'd go home for lunch and wouldn't return in the afternoon. It seemed less trouble to get on with things myself than to wait around for someone who constantly let me down. Apart from the refreshing change for the children, I was quite happy on my own.

I Felt So Guilty

Despite my outward cheerfulness, I was full of inner turmoil. It was Anna's second Christmas and still there was no day care for Marie. I felt so guilty. Without a doubt, Patrick and Anna loved Marie, her gentle disposition and endless patience made them very loving and protective towards her. I know one of the dreaded fears of having a disabled child is their siblings feeling responsible for their care. But there is a great difference in enjoying a child and being burdened with her. Marie was a bind, there was no doubt about that—there were places we couldn't go and people we couldn't see, but I never told the children that. I always used the bad weather or some other excuse rather than Marie's disability, thus avoiding her being resented. Nevertheless, spending day in and out with Marie in their formative years was not part of the plan for Patrick and Anna.

Every few months, I wrote to the Social Services to remind them that Marie was still sitting at home all day but they couldn't give a damn. It seemed ironic that they were hurting the very person they had set out to protect. They had a duty to provide day care, but it seemed they were a law unto themselves. I just prayed the day would never come when I would have to put Marie in the hospital because I couldn't cope with her at home. I dared not even think about it. It would never come to that—surely it would not.

Week after week, month after month, I would anxiously scan through the post every morning to see if there was a letter offering Marie a place in the Unit, but there never was. I knew when I looked at the children I should have put up more of a fight. Though Marie was happy, she was not getting the exercise and stimulation she needed. However, to have battled with officials for Marie's day care would have used up the emotions and energy I badly needed to play the 'happy' mother.

I could also have gone to the Press. That was something else I was unable to deal with for various reasons. Not only did I hate the focus of attention and lack of privacy, I did not want the children exposed to the publicity. It was one thing to stand up for what I believed in, but there was no way the children were going to carry my banners for me.

Most days I tried not to think about the injustice of it all. On other days I felt so despondent that guilt would envelop me. If only I hadn't been so mouthy, if only the fostering had worked out and we'd been able to keep the girls, if only I wasn't so direct with people.

Unable to sleep at night, I would sit by the downstairs window and look out at the moon. The hours ticked slowly by. I felt so tired I didn't know how I was going to get through the next day, but my overactive mind would not let me sleep.

Returning to bed in the early hours of the morning, I used to wonder if the Social Workers would ever forgive me for standing up to them and refusing to be bullied. I wondered too if I would ever forgive them for making my children suffer because of their differences with me.

What we really needed was someone to take on Marie's case. I knew my hands were tied and there was nothing I could do. I could fill a phone directory if I were to list the organisations I rung for help and support. A few gave me unwanted advice and completely missed the point. Some said it was time I 'let go'. Decent residential care for learning disabled adults was very hard to come by. Had I been offered decent day care resulting from a residential placement, then I certainly would have considered it for Marie, but I was not. Hanging up the phone, I'd regret having contacted these organisations because they reinforced the low opinion I already had of myself.

Just Keep Trying

One day I rang the regional office of Mencap in Nottingham. I explained the situation as best I could. There was a sigh on the other end of the phone; "Your lot have a right reputation in Lincolnshire, you know?"

I giggled knowingly. "Well…it is partly my fault because I have this knack of upsetting people." I hadn't reached this stage of my life without seeing the error of my ways. I didn't apologise to him for being me, I simply stated a fact.

"That's nonsense! Shouldn't even come into it," he said firmly.

"You should hear the way I speak to them sometimes—but that's life isn't it? They can't exclude someone from the local training centre because her mother doesn't agree with everything they say. And how long did you say your daughter has been waiting for a place?" he asked. I told him it was 1 ½ years. He went on; "I know for a fact that the ADC in your area is one of the few in the country that isn't fully utilised". He promised to write to the Social Services to ask them what they were playing at. I didn't hold my breath. I knew it could take the Social Services three months to reply. They were, after all, a law unto themselves.

Learning Disability Nursing

Although Marie was 19, she couldn't have been with a better age group. The house was like a toy shop and, to compensate for being housebound on some days, the playroom was also full of garden toys dominated by a big red and yellow slide in the middle of the floor. The children's constant chatter as they flitted from one curiosity to another kept Marie occupied for most of the day. Late afternoon, just when my batteries needed recharging, who chugged hoot hooting cheerfully on the TV screen but Thomas the Tank Engine! Snuggling up either side of Marie on the sofa, there wasn't a peep out of any of them while Thomas and his naughty friends kept them entertained.

Every so often, Marie went into the hospital for a week or two. Using the hospital was only a temporary solution to a long-term problem. With emphasis on care in the community, using the hospital to give the rest of the family a break was far from acceptable, but it was all there was—and, by God, we were glad of it!

For Marie, two weeks on the ward was long enough before her behaviour started to deteriorate and the old behaviour problems began to surface. Yet what made the nurses' attitude different from other professional carers was their realistic acceptance of Marie and her capabilities. Her pretty looks and good manners often suggested a higher degree of intelligence than she had. This had been half the problem with ADC staff. They had refused to accept Marie as she was and had their own ideas of how she should be. I had much more confidence in the nurses who were also trained to deal with complex medical issues.

All these years later I am still an advocate of Learning Disability

Nurse's Training. I recently invited Helen Laverty, Health Lecturer from Nottingham University to give her views on what I feel is a diminishing profession, which I have included in the back of this book.

"They're Such Happy Children!"

I have to mention that my other source of support at that time was still my ever faithful aunty Terry. Marie still went to stay with her for occasional weekends and still got spoilt with kindness and adoration. Most of the children who'd looked after her protectively all those years ago when Marie had first gone to Terry's had now grown up and had children of their own. Marie was always known as 'the little girl from the newspapers', stirring up fond memories and great warmth and affection from the local people. They all loved to see her.

My biggest regret was not being able to drive. I had always wanted to, yet had this terrible underlying fear of being involved in an accident and being unable to look after Marie. When the children came along I knew I should have made more of an effort, but I was just too nervous and felt I was relied on more than ever.

Trips to town at first had been a nightmare. With two toddlers and a disabled young woman, just preparing to go was a ritual. When they eventually had their boots, hats, gloves and snowsuits on and their zips, laces, ribbons and buttons were fastened, we were ready to go.

Marie went in her wheelchair, Patrick held onto one side and Anna (supported by her reins that I held) held onto the other side as we slowly made our way to the shops.

We went at a snail's pace, stopping to inspect every little distraction along the way. Cats were the most fascinating as they ran in between the cars and hid behind the wheels. The children thought they were playing hide and seek with them and waved sadly when we had to move on.

When Anna showed signs of becoming tired, I would lift her onto Marie's lap to give her little legs a rest. Marie immediately came to life. Sitting back in her chair to make room, arms outstretched as Anna sat on her knee.

"Om on!" she'd say, putting her arms protectively around Anna's waist, "Om on, Narna," she coaxed. Up in the comfort of Marie's arms, unaware that I was still holding the reins so Anna wouldn't fall off Marie's knee, the repertoire of nursery rhymes would start as we continued our journey to town.

"Aren't they lovely?" people would remark, "They're such happy children." Their kind words touched me with relief. For the first time in my life, I had no friends living near me. Bridget, my long time friend, lived some sixty miles away, so there wasn't really any yardstick by which to measure the children's development. I just plodded on each day and hoped for the best. Maybe if the children had been naughty and unmanageable, the situation would have been easier to accept, but they were always so well behaved.

On the way home, Patrick used to ride on the foot bars at the back of the wheelchair so he wouldn't feel left out. There was some weight between them!

Still No Room for Marie

As time went by, I slept less and less. I had recently received a letter from Mencap which took away what little hope I had. They had been informed by the Social Services that although there were vacancies in the workshop at the ADC, there was no room in the Unit, and because of the maximum attention Marie required, the workshop would not accommodate her.

I was upset when I read the letter. It was okay for me to struggle on at home for the last two years with Marie at home all day and two little children to look after—for the ADC staff who only worked from 9-4 Monday to Friday, she was too much hard work.

I laughed at the hypocrisy of it all—if I hadn't laughed I'd certainly have cried. Switching off from things was becoming a bad habit with me. It was the only way I coped. For as much as I laughed and joked (and did my crying on my own), I knew I was running out of time and I had to face reality. Patrick was ready to go to Nursery. I didn't want to be having to gauge Marie's moods when we were getting ready to go out in the mornings; he had enough to cope with, starting a new nursery. I couldn't believe we had reached this stage and there was still no light at the end of the tunnel.

Finally, in desperation, I went to see Dr. Garry, the hospital psychiatrist. I was clutching at straws again and hoping that if we provided the transport, Marie would be allowed to go on the wards as a day-patient. Even one or two days a week would have relieved some of the pressure. We were prepared to give anything a go if it meant keeping Marie at home.

Although the psychiatrist was sympathetic, he felt the 40 mile daily round-trip would be too much for Marie to cope with and suggested we let her live on the ward from Monday to Friday, and have her home at weekends. We drove home in silence. Choice is a luxury— we didn't have any.

When you love one of your children as much as the other, it's heartbreaking to have to choose between them. That's how I felt, like I'd been put in the position where I had to decide. Perhaps I should have loved Marie less because she hadn't been born to me, but I didn't.

Sadness replaced my animosity towards the Social Workers. How could I feel angry about such a pathetic group of people who would go to such extremes to prove a point?

Standing in front of the mirror wearing her best pink track suit, Marie had no idea I was getting her ready to send her into hospital. Anna sat near us on the stool holding Marie's hairbrush and slides. Patrick kept watch out of the window for the ambulance which came from 8.30 onwards. Putting his hand conspiratorially to the side of his mouth as he watched Marie, he kept whispering to me that it hadn't arrived yet. He was so funny and so sensible for a little boy. We had the records on as usual and I must have appeared a bit chattier than normal but it took all my efforts to hold myself together. I sighed dramatically as I faced Marie in the mirror.

"Oh, Marie, you look so beautiful," I told her as I released the curling tongs and her mousy hair fell in springy ringlets. She *was* beautiful too; everybody said so. Anna passed me the slide as her eyes rested adoringly on Marie.

"Will she be home tonight?" She asked. I had been over it with them a hundred times but they were both too young to understand. I explained to her once again as best I could. Eyes growing like saucers she searched her little mind for something to say; "What if she cries for us?" I pretended not to hear and sent her off to get some perfume to spray on Marie.

When the ambulance finally arrived, we put on Marie's coat and took her out to the gate. Laughing and joking and being their usual cheerful selves, the ambulance men let the children have a ride up on the ramp with Marie. Giggling happily when they reached the top, they were lifted down as Marie went and sat in the back. Standing the children on the garden wall so they could see, we waved to Marie through the windows as the vehicle slowly drove up the terrace. Beeping the horn when it reached the top, it turned the corner and she was gone.

25

Never Ignore Your Instincts

Thank goodness our lack of contact with the outside world in no way impaired Patrick's development. Though a little shy at first, when the time came for him to start Nursery, his feet hardly touched the ground when he ran across the playground. He was a very happy child with a great sense of fun. His appearance was almost comical with his big brown eyes and mop of dark curly hair. Sometimes I wondered if God had given me extra happy children to enable them to live with Marie.

Unlike Patrick, who had everybody eating out of his hands, Anna liked to sit back and weigh people up. She was extremely observant for such a young child and seemed to know straight away whether or not people were sincere. Strangely enough, Anna and Marie had the same colouring—lovely blue eyes and light brown hair.

"Can't you tell they're sisters?" I was often asked (much to my delight!) And, of course, as far as the children were aware Marie *was* their big sister.

"Is Marie coming home today, Mummy?" that was the question I was greeted with each morning. Unaware of Marie's plight, the children thought she was having a wonderful time at the hospital but they missed her enormously and looked forward to her return on a Friday evening.

Each morning, after we took Patrick to Nursery, Anna and I went shopping. It was on one of these trips that her foot got trapped under the foot rest on her buggy and the poor little mite broke a bone in her foot and ended up with it in plaster. From then on, Anna had to go out in Marie's wheelchair, and, just like Marie had done for Anna, she shoved over for Patrick, enabling him to have a ride to school each morning.

When Fridays came around, the whole day was taken up waiting for Marie to arrive. The 20 mile journey could take up to two hours as the ambulance drove around the countryside dropping patients off. However, there was always one of us looking out the window; we were all dying to see her. As soon as the ambulance was spotted reversing down the terrace the door was flung open and the children waited on the wall to welcome Marie home. The joy on their faces made me almost eat my lips to avoid crying, especially the day I lifted Anna onto the wall and she had Marie's slippers in her hand.

Marie was so happy to be home but she was pale and tired looking. She ate anything and everything. She was so unsettled on the ward she almost exhausted herself and was usually starving because she'd hardly eaten. The children adored her and did everything possible to make her comfortable. After Patrick had struggled to remove Marie's shoes, Anna put her granny slippers on (usually on the wrong feet). I didn't have the heart to tell her as she puffed and blew struggling to fasten the zips.

With everybody comfortable, they'd sit on the settee either side of Marie and open the box of Maltesers for her. When everyone was munching away, the fun would start.

"Mmm. Mice!" Marie would remark when she offered Anna or Patrick a chocolate. Opening their mouths when it almost reached their lips she would change her mind and put it in her own. Of course they knew what she was up to; she'd done it to them so often, yet they always fell about laughing just as she had when I'd done it to her in the past.

Marie's diary was very helpful and a great source of communication between the hospital and home. Her behaviour varied from day to day depending on how bored she was and what kind of mood she was in. One day's comments went: *'Screamed for approximately half an hour this morning, pulling her own hair to make herself cry—stopped for a while then started again. Ripped her tights and pulled a button off her dress, was changed into trousers after lunch and spent the afternoon playing quite happily'.*

Looking at her sitting with the children one would never have guessed she could be so badly behaved.

"Have you been carrying on for the nurses?" I would ask, pretending to be cross. Glancing over to me with her mouth full, she didn't have a care in the world.

"Tut, tut, tut," she'd say casually before turning to her little brother and sister and offering them another chocolate. "Mmm," was all she said for the next hour, obviously delighted to be home once more.

Constant reinforcement was the reason for Marie's good behaviour at home; too few nurses and too many patients was the reason for Marie's difficult behaviour on the wards. We were swimming against the tide. Quite apart from anything else, I was worried about the infection she was bringing home from the hospital. Dysentery was the biggest nightmare. It was not unusual for one ward or another to be in isolation because of it. If Patrick and Anna were to become ill because of some infection Marie caught, then we would all go under.

On Mondays when Marie returned to the hospital, we toddled off to school and got on with our lives as best as we could. Each weekend, she arrived home in a worse state than the previous week. She was always very pale and tired and her mood swings were becoming more frequent to such an extent that by the time she settled down with us it was time for her to return to the hospital again.

Things finally came to a head when she arrived home one weekend in the most appalling state. She had a very high temperature and a nasty scratch on her nose; accompanying her was a bottle of 5mg Valium tablets.

One side of her face was so chapped because she slept for long periods sitting up in a chair, cheek resting on a shoulder soaked in dribble. She had diarrhea, which showed no sign of clearing up after two days. I was panic-stricken. So scared of any infection spreading, I wouldn't even use the washing machine and put the soiled linen and night clothes in a sealed bag in the bin. Our doctor was also concerned and said if there was no sign of it clearing by the next day we would have to take a swab to the lab.

I knew we'd come to the end of the road. A decision had to be made. We'd reached the stage where Marie either came home for good or she stayed at the hospital permanently. I knew deep down what we had to do. I think any mother would have done the same.

Only that weekend Patrick's term had ended and he collected his school uniform in order to join the Kindergarten class upstairs in the private school after the Easter holidays. It was almost as if God had given me a certain amount of time to get myself organised and was now saying to me, "Enough is enough".

I wrote to the hospital psychiatrist, thanking him for his support and informing him that Marie would not be returning to the hospital.

During the Easter holidays, Anna had her plaster removed, enabling

Marie to go back into the wheelchair and the children to have a ride.

The Answer to All of Our Problems

Pushing the children to school each morning, I passed an interesting looking house for sale right opposite Patrick's school. With Marie now at home, it seemed an ideal place to live. I could leave Marie sitting at the window where I could see her from the street and take the children over the road to school. The price was reasonable, though there was a great deal of work to do on it. It seemed the answer to all of our problems: I kept my fingers crossed.

We were all thrilled at the prospect of moving. The house was the back half of a big old Victorian house. Not much of a garden, but who cared—there was plenty of space indoors—large living room, kitchen and dining room, a cloak room and a small room large enough to make a bedroom for Marie. She had always slept far enough away from the children not to frighten them if ever she woke up screaming from a nightmare or cramp in her legs. Upstairs there were three bedrooms and a large bathroom.

The owner, Mr Cochran, was Irish, and still lived in the front part of the building. The entrance to his section was around the corner in the next street. The house we wanted had previously been let as two flats and was still fully furnished. I expected the items to be removed by the time the sale was completed. There was a few bob to be had for that second-hand furniture.

Most mornings when Marie and I walked the children to school we looked across to 'our new house' with great excitement. I would find any excuse to collect the keys from the estate agents just to have 'another' look around.

Kindergarten

I liked Patrick's school, but there was never any information available for parents—no booklet, no news sheet, nothing. It could have been the reason the fees were so cheap, but I would have preferred to pay extra and be kept informed, instead of getting instructions by word of mouth from other parents. Often it was a nuisance but I turned a blind eye (thinking it was just me!); I shouldn't have.

On swimming day, for example, I arrived at Patrick's school only to be told by a helper in the nursery that the class met at the baths. The parents then stayed at the pool to help dress and undress the children. That was all very well; but for me to have stayed at the pool with Patrick would have been impossible because I had Marie with me in her wheelchair. Luckily, his dad had driven us to school that day and we were able to go to the pool, but ordinarily I just couldn't do it. That's what we paid them for – that extra special attention.

As it turned out, Patrick didn't enjoy the swimming session. It was too noisy and chaotic and besides, his Dad took him and Anna to the pool every Sunday, so that was the end of that.

The lady who ran the school also lived on the premises. With only three classrooms and so few children in the school one would have thought she'd have become familiar with the pupils and their parents, but we hardly ever saw her. There was only herself and another full time teacher in the school. Patrick's teacher worked four mornings a week and often the class doubled up in the afternoons. Children who didn't want to go swimming went straight to school on the swimming day and sat in the nursery classroom downstairs until their own class returned.

Little Boy Lost

For a while, things went smoothly, and then something awful happened. Anna was not very well so we arranged for Patrick to travel to school by taxi and I informed the Headmistress of this. We knew Henry, the taxi driver, very well. Often over the years, he had taken Marie to the hospital and continued to do so even after the following incident occurred; that's how much confidence we had in him.

Each morning when the taxi arrived, Patrick climbed into the car like a young prince, looking very smart in his little cap and blazer, a figure of the 'Incredible Hulk' clutched in his hand.

"Here's my driver, bye, Mum!" he would shout as he marched down the path obviously feeling very important. When Patrick arrived home on that last day I knew instinctively that something was wrong when he went and sat on the floor BEHIND the couch. I don't think I'd ever seen him look miserable. I was mystified. During lunch he picked at his food and just sat there looking very sad for the most of the time.

Most afternoons the four of us usually sat around the big table colouring in and it was difficult to get a word in edgeways as they chatted amongst themselves but Patrick remained very quiet and subdued. I playfully lifted him out of the chair and sat him on my knee.

My family had affectionately nicknamed him Pinocchio; (I've got no strings to tie me down!) and here on my knee, head drooping and little legs dangling he did indeed resemble a puppet—a sad one.

"What's the matter, Patrick?" I asked him gently.

"Nothing," he replied sadly.

"I know!" I said cheerfully, "let's play puppets!" I went to the toy box and brought out Sooty. He was definitely the favourite and had them all in stitches. Marie had Patrick and Anna well trained with her tidiness, so when they saw the puppet they put their tops back on the felt tips and cleared their colouring books away. I returned to the table and was met with two bright faces full of anticipation as they waited for the show to begin. I cleared my throat!

"Hello!" I said in a stupid voice

"Hello, Sooty," they replied.

"Did you have a nice time at school today, Patrick?" Patrick shook his head miserably; "Oh no, Sooty," he replied. "There wasn't anybody there."

"What do you mean? How can there be nobody at your school, Patrick?"

"Because, Sooty," Patrick said earnestly, "when my driver left me in the hall I hung up my cap and blazer and went upstairs and there was nobody there."

Alarm bells started to ring in my head.

"Oh my goodness," Sooty said dramatically. "what did you do then?" Tears started to fill his big brown eyes.

"I ran out of school and across the road to find my way home but a van came along and nearly ran me over. He beeped at me and I was scared." Searching my mind for something to say I lifted him back onto my knee and hugged him tightly.

For Marie to go away, for all we went through—for what? To end up with my little boy wandering around the street crying because the Headmistress had decided to have a swimming gala for the whole school and forgot to tell me the building would be empty. The taxi driver, noticing the school was quiet, had assumed the children were upstairs and left Patrick in the hall. I later found out one of the parents had found Patrick ten minutes' walk from the school, standing on the corner of the main road in the pouring rain, crying. I wasn't upset or angry—I was numb.

I rang the Headmistress, who should have brought the matter to my attention and had obviously hoped I would not find out about it. She was so busy being defensive, telling me Patrick should have brought a letter home to me and she had just found it in his desk—*very convenient!*

No matter how incompetent she was at running her school, at the end of the day it was I who had placed Patrick in such a vulnerable position, not her. It was I who had sent him to Kindergarten to enable Marie to live at home, not her.

I felt like I'd been turned inside out. I was an emotional wreck as the days passed by and I thought of all the villains out there who could have wound down their car windows and offered my little boy a lift.

By the time Monday came around I was fit to be tied when we drove to the school to confront the Headmistress. The woman was on another planet. She hadn't a care in the world, and even asked me how Patrick had got to school. I was absolutely livid with her and left her in no doubt what I thought about her school.

Walking around in the pouring rain had left Patrick with a heavy cold. He spent the next few weeks closely at my side until he began to feel secure again and went off to play with Marie and Anna.

It took me quite a long time to recover from the shock. Then, as the weeks went by, I realised if I kept thinking of all the awful things that could have happened to Patrick, then they might as well have. Nobody had picked Patrick up on the street; he had been found safe and sound.

I was not sure whether to go ahead with buying the house, but after a long talk, Paul and I decided to thank our lucky stars things had turned out the way they had. We would put the past behind us and get on with our lives.

I wrote to the Headmistress, sending her a cheque for Patrick's fees. I also told her that we didn't have any bad feelings towards the school. She replied by saying if we would like to return Patrick to her school the following term she would only charge half a term's tuition.

I couldn't care if she charged me double, so long as she looked after him!

With that hurdle behind us, we put in an offer for the house and hoped for the best.

26

Oops, I Did It Again

Three months later, we collected the keys to our new home. What a difference it was going to make; no more treks to school with the three of them on the wheelchair.

I didn't know what to expect when I put the key in the door. With Marie holding onto one hand and Anna holding the other, we eagerly followed Patrick inside. I was overwhelmed at the sight that met my eyes. Our kind Irish neighbour had left all the furniture for us. We had planned to move in after the builders had put new downstairs floors in. They weren't starting work for five days. My mind was working overtime. With all the furniture still in the house I had only to go home and get the cutlery and bedding (and the record player!) We could have a five-day holiday.

I hardly saw the children that afternoon. Running away from Marie, they hid behind the doors. Sometimes it took her ages to find them as she plodded across the floor. Deathly silence was followed by screams of terror when Marie finally discovered where they were.

It must have been the only time in my life I enjoyed cleaning up. With a bucket of hot water and a cloth I set to washing down the doors and ledges. Standing in the middle of the sitting room I looked up to the ceiling as the loud thump, thump, thump reached my ears. I could hear the three of them laughing and knew they were bouncing on the big double bed. I loved to hear them laugh; it was all that kept me sane.

Falling Apart

Paul and I had been aware for some time that our marriage was over. With great difficulty we plodded on, for the sake of the children, until, finally, we decided to separate. Considering the pressures we had been under, it was amazing we had lasted so long. I only wished we could have carried on pretending, for the children's sakes, but that was impossible. Most evenings Paul came to see the children from work and didn't leave until they went to bed.

I was still communicating with the Social Services on Marie's behalf and I was still waiting for day care. Patrick had settled down in his class and Anna had joined the Nursery for two mornings a week. I still had a niggling feeling about the safety aspect of the school. My heart was in my mouth when I saw a playground full of small children from age three upwards, usually unsupervised and with the playground gates wide open, leaving the children to run into the road. Parents moaned and groaned but, of course, nobody spoke up. I was determined to keep quiet. It took me all my time fighting my own battles, never mind anybody else's. I just warned my children not to go near the school gates and to try to remember to put on their coats if it rained. On reflection, I must have been mad. At the time, it was all there was and I was under the misapprehension that children who didn't go to nursery or playschool were deprived. Yes… I must have been mad!

Losing the Plot

One day, during the school holidays, a doctor called from Nottingham to assess Marie for the Attendance Allowance. This examination was carried out every five years in order to establish whether or not Marie still required the same degree of care to qualify for the Allowance. Most of the doctors who conduct these examinations are retired. Some of them are extremely nice – some are just cantankerous.

I had told the children I was expecting a doctor to visit Marie and they were to play quietly while he was here. We brought all their jigsaws downstairs and spent most of the morning piecing them together as they were spread across the kitchen floor.

I was quite nervous because the doctor was coming. I'd also had cramp in my stomach that morning and didn't feel too good.

On his arrival he walked through the kitchen and past the children without even having the manners to greet them. He followed me into the sitting room, where we joined Marie. I think he made the children feel very uneasy, which was why they came to join us.

He got his notes out of his briefcase and the interview began.

"How old are you?" he asked Marie to my astonishment. I went to tell him that Marie did not understand what he was saying when he put up his hand to silence me.

"Do you know your address?" he asked. I felt incredible sadness when I looked over at Marie who was chattering back at the doctor, trying to imitate his conversation. I cleared my throat.

"She really does not understand what you're saying," I told him firmly. Patrick, who was sitting on the little step near the hall door started to giggle quietly at the idiotic way Marie was being spoken to. Anna, who never took her eyes off the doctor, climbed up on the sofa and sat next to Marie. Linking her protectively, she continued to look in the doctor's direction.

He took off his glasses and looked at me as if I was some tireless child.

"My dear," he said pompously. "The first thing I have to establish is that the young woman actually suffers from a mental handicap!"

He asked Marie another question and the children giggled. Then he told me he wanted to interview Marie alone.

I'd had enough. I ordered him out of the house.

"Look," he said gently when we got to the front door. "If you don't go ahead with the interview you're going to lose a lot of money."

"You'll still get paid, won't you?"

"Not if I don't interview you."

"It's not worth what we have to go through to get it!" I told him.

"I'm sorry we got off to a bad start," he said. "Why don't we just try again?" I suddenly felt sorry for him.

"Okay," I said, "But you're not interviewing Marie on her own."

"Alright," he replied. He was a different man. A nicer—better mannered, man. Why couldn't he have been like that in the first place?

The children were flabbergasted after he left. I rang my mother.

"I've just done the most awful thing," I told her. I explained what had happened and how I'd spoken to the doctor.

"You were right to react the way you did and maybe he'll think twice when he goes into the next house," she said, trying to reassure me. When I put down the phone I sat Anna and Patrick on my knee.

"I was really sorry I had to speak to the doctor the way I did," I told them, "But, you see, this is our home and when people visit us they should have some manners. He forgot his and he just needed reminding about them, that was all," I said, wondering who it was I was trying to convince.

Since my marriage broke up, things seemed to get me down more. I still played the happy mother and managed to hide my feelings, but it took more and more effort just to get through the day.

Patrick and Marie were not well and our doctor came to see them. The following day I could feel my neck and throat becoming sore. Taking it as an early warning and knowing that I needed to muster all the energy I could to look after three children, I rang Paul at work and arranged for him to call in on his way home to look after the children so I could go to the doctors. I then rang the doctor and spoke to the receptionist. Our conversation went like this;

"I'd like to make an appointment to see Dr. Bird this evening please."

"I'm afraid the evening appointments are only for people who can't get in during the mornings because they're working. Do you work during the day?" she asked to my amazement. Not knowing how to answer such a ridiculous question I hesitated.

"No," I finally said, "but just because I'm not in full time employment doesn't mean my time isn't as committed as someone who is."

"Huh!" she said, "who do you think you are?"

"I'm a patient who would like an evening appointment to see her doctor."

"I'll tell you what," she said, "why don't you put your duster down and let it gather a little dust and get yourself along here and leave the evening visits for those who really need them?"

I didn't have the energy to argue with her. "Can I have your name please?" I asked.

"No you can't" she said incredulously. The next thing I knew the phone was banged down on the desk and she was telling the other receptionists about my 'cheek'. Standing in the hall with the phone to my ear the tears ran down my face when I heard them all giggling. The phone was picked up again.

"Hello, can I help you?" a different voice asked. Trying to keep my voice steady I asked for the name of the receptionist who had taken my call. She refused to tell me. I wouldn't let it drop and asked her again. Realising I was not going to be fobbed off she said she would put me back on to that receptionist. When she came back on the phone she refused to give me her name. "Look," she said irritably, "do you want an evening appointment or not?"

I was so upset I could hardly speak, "It doesn't matter," I whispered and hung up. I was so fed up; I didn't know how much longer I could go on.

I gave myself a few days to put things into perspective so as not to be too hasty. Then I wrote a letter to my doctor and told him what had happened. I knew that writing that letter could have left a big black mark against my personality on the doctor's file, but it was worth it for all those poor sods that for one reason or another were bullied by receptionists like that and didn't have the nerve or the energy to speak up.

My lovely doctor came to see me the day he received my letter, apologising for the way I was spoken to. He said he asked the receptionists which one of them had taken my call and nobody had owned up. I recognised the receptionist's voice and told him who she was.

Merry Christmas to You Too!

With Christmas almost upon us and the children in school, Marie and I used to go window shopping in town. Catching sight of myself in shop windows I could not believe my size. Still eating when I felt anxious, the pounds were creeping on. I didn't know myself any more. I had disappeared.

The final blow for that year came two days before the end of Patrick's school term. When I took him back to school after lunch one day, I found there was no teacher in his classroom. The children, from age three up, were jumping over desks and throwing things around the room. An eleven year old girl had been left in charge while the Headmistress gave private piano lessons. I'd learned to follow my instincts. Looking around the room, I knew I couldn't leave him.

"I don't really like to leave Patrick without a teacher," I said to the young girl. "I'll take him home because he's got lots of Christmas cards to write and he can bring them in with him in the morning." I was very pleased with such a sensible excuse. I planned to have a word with the Headmistress when the opportunity arose. Patrick spent all afternoon writing out his cards and the next morning when he was ready for school he took them in, with his little present for his teacher.

When lunch time came, Anna and I strolled over to the school for Patrick. We stood in the brightly decorated hall with the other parents collecting Christmas cards with our names on, which were spread across one of the dinner tables. One of the parents handed me mine. I gave it to Anna to open. She smiled from ear to ear as her little fingers pulled out the card. A letter dropped onto the floor so I picked it up curiously. One of the children burst a balloon. I exchanged a few words of sympathy with his mother as the toddler held out the piece of blue rubber for her to make better. Anna gripped my hand very tightly, having been unnerved by the loud bang. I lifted her up and casually opened the letter in my hand.

It read:

Dear Mrs Daly,

Following the incident of today regarding your removal of Patrick because, and I quote, 'No teacher was left in the Kg classroom', I feel it would be in both our interests if you removed Patrick and Anna at the end of this term.

I—who cried in front of nobody—stood in the middle of the school hall with tears rolling down my face. Hoping nobody would notice, I collected Patrick's cap and blazer from the peg. I took them both by the hand and they skipped out of school, unaware that they would not be returning and all because their mother had opened her stupid big mouth, AGAIN.

There was great excitement in the school and Patrick told us how he'd posted his Christmas cards in the big Santa box which was to be opened the following day. I cleared my throat.

"Hey, Patrick," I said as I gently squeezed his hand, "I'm such a silly Mummy. I forgot to tell you that you were leaving today." It was the best I could do. I'd much rather my children thought they had a crazy scatter-brained mother than let them know they lived in such a rotten world.

"What about all of my Christmas cards?" Patrick said as we crossed the road. "I have to go to school tomorrow to collect the cards from all my friends." Every time I went to speak my voice faltered.

"Don't worry," I managed to say cheerfully, "Someone will probably drop them off for you". That seemed to satisfy him for the time being.

Going indoors and being greeted by Marie's smiling face was too much for me. I ran upstairs to the bathroom and locked the door. Sliding down the wall to the floor I drew my knees up to my chin, hugging my legs. I truly thought it was the end for me. I couldn't bear my children being punished again because of differences with me. I felt like a noose around their necks. I hated myself…I wished I was dead.

I don't know how long I stayed on the floor in that little corner with my face turned to the wall; I seemed to have lost all sense of time. Hearing footsteps on the stairs, I knew it would be one of the children coming to find me. Dragging myself up off the floor, I swilled my face at the sink. Someone tapped on the door.

"Mummy, are you in there?" Anna whispered. I pretended to cough and blew my nose before I answered her.

"Oh Anna, I've caught the most awful cold," I lied. "I'll be down in a minute, love".

I looked at the bloated, red-eyed face in the mirror. I was a burnt-out wreck. Sapped of all my energy and hope, I wanted to curl up and die. Three and a half years and still no day care. I wondered what was to become of us all. Tears spilled down my face as the sound of children's laughter reached me from the playground. I just couldn't take any more.

When I awoke the following morning, my eyes were so swollen I could hardly open them. As the morning went on, the street became alive with cars as the parents came to see the school play.

Most of my time was spent distracting the children from the window which overlooked the school. My face was like a pumpkin and I dared not venture out with them for a walk. We spent the morning blowing up balloons and wrapping the last of our presents. Patrick and Anna didn't mind not going to school. Fortunately, because the house was so large and was heated twenty-four hours a day, there was so much for them to do they were never bored.

At lunch time the doorbell rang. With the children on my trail, I went to see who it was. There on the step stood Patrick's teacher. She smiled at me sadly and said hello. Declining my invitation to come in, she gave me a knowing look and said she was just calling on her way home to give Patrick his Christmas cards…I could have kissed her. His face was a picture when he took the little pile from her.

I later learned she'd known nothing about the incident the previous day and when she had found out, she had waited for the Headmistress to go out before she came over to see us. She left the school at the end of that term. When I closed the door that day, she had restored my faith in humanity. Patrick, as proud as punch, was sitting by the Christmas tree with Anna busy opening his cards. I sat on the couch next to Marie and smiled over at them.

"My goodness, you're a lucky boy," I marvelled. "My teachers couldn't wait to see the back of me and yours are knocking on the door to say goodbye!" They both giggled happily. I looked up to heaven and thanked God…

~ 27 ~

Whistling in the Dark

"**L**adies and gentlemen, we will be approaching Dublin shortly. Please ensure your seat belts are fastened and any baggage is tucked safely away."

Travelling on an Aer Lingus flight above the Irish Sea, my brother and I were off to Ireland for a few days' holiday. With the excitement of a child, I clasped my hands together and stretched my neck across my brother's handsome face. I wanted to get a birds-eye view of this great city. His eyes danced. He sat back dramatically, allowing me a better view through a tiny window.

It was my second visit to Ireland that year. A few months before, driven by a longing to discover more of my grandmother's past, I had spent two weeks in Co. Mayo, on the west coast of Ireland.

I smiled at my brother as the plane started to descend. Despite being ten years older than him, we were very close. At the age of twenty-six, he was the last of the brood at home. The rest of us had flown the nest and travelled our different paths. We had buried our father three months ago. I knew my brother's loss was greater than mine could ever be. My father had mellowed a little in his old age. My brother would miss him dreadfully.

I squeezed his arm affectionately as the plane hit the runway. At last, our plans had materialised. Yet things had happened in my life since my father's death which made my visit to this country a far more serious venture; in my bag was an Irish property guide. Throwing caution to the wind, I was determined not to return to England until I had found a home in Co. Mayo for myself and the three children—though, at the age of twenty four, Marie could hardly be described as a child. Paul planned to stay in England and come over in the holidays.

Empty Promises

The most important thing to remember when fighting for a cause is not to lose sight of what one is fighting for. I eventually recovered from the shock of the kids being kicked out of school and tried to get on with our lives as best I could. A year passed in our new home, during which time I reluctantly approached the local Press, who immediately took up Marie's case. Weeks went by before any comment could be squeezed out of the Social Services, who finally promised the *Lincolnshire Echo* that when the new Day Centre opened in six months' time at Lincoln, Marie would be offered a place there.

'*Handicapped Marie's New Year Gift*' the caption read, but they were empty words. When the Day Centre was due to open, I waited in vain for the post every day. I then wrote and reminded them about Marie. No reply. I rang them. I was met with both surprise and astonishment that I could even contemplate Marie attending the new Lincoln Day Centre. I was told Marie's needs were too complex for the type of care and support they were offering.

Nothing shocked me anymore. I expected nothing from anybody and whether it was a healthy sign or not, I seemed incapable of being hurt. Never again would I buckle under as I did after the incident with the school. Concerned about the safety of the other children in the school, I had eventually contacted the NSPCC. Angry that the Headmistress was a law unto herself leaving young children unsupervised, but angrier that she had the audacity to put it in writing to me, they contacted the Department of Education and Science, who then sent one of their Inspectors to see her.

Passing the Buck

I had been wondering for some time about the possibility of approaching another county for help. I knew I had a moral obligation to see Marie's plight to the end. The Social Services were wrong to reject her and I was the only voice she had. In the meantime I would grab at anything for her to have some kind of life outside the home and for me to have a bit of freedom during the day. One afternoon I rang the Social Services in the next county and explained my *desperate* position. I told them that if I didn't get support for Marie soon that she would have to go into residential care. I felt like a long-playing record. I had recounted our story so many times. How often had I been about to have Marie admitted to hospital and been saved at the eleventh hour?

The gentleman who spoke to me listened patiently, occasionally interrupting with a question. Finally he said;

"If you can get Lincolnshire Social Services to pay your daughter's fees, then we'll be only too happy to look at your application."

There was no point in 'letting the grass grow' under my feet, so that afternoon I wrote to Lincolnshire Social Services, requesting they pay Marie's fees for a day care placement in the next county. I then took Marie out in her wheelchair to post it and hurried home to watch Oprah. I had done the donkey work for them; surely they would find it in their hearts to sign the stupid cheque. Just how long we were going to have to pay for *my* sins I did not know—forever, it seemed.

Months went by with no news. Tired of waiting and angry at being ignored *again*, I *again* brought the matter to the attention of the Press. As usual the Press had to chase and badger before anybody would confirm Marie's fees would be paid and that the application for day care could go ahead.

The Press were angry and pointed out that though this decision had been made three months ago, nobody had had the decency to tell me. I had learnt the good news through their newspaper. No moves had been made to implement this decision. It seemed that nobody would deal with me. The director apologised to me through the newspaper, stating that he wanted an inquiry as to why I had not been informed of this decision long ago. I thought they were all a load of hypocrites. While they were passing the buck and cutting each other's throats, I was busy making plans for my daughter's debut into the world once again.

After four years at home, in a taxi provided by the Social Services, Marie did a forty mile round trip every day for the next two years— two hundred miles a week, in all weathers.

Medusa

After Patrick left the private school, when the time came six months later, I sent him to the local state school. This was highly recommended by the parents in the area. It was the old, old story—they had gone there and now their children were following in their footsteps. What I hadn't realised then was that they accepted everything and questioned nothing. They had to say the school was wonderful because if it wasn't they would owe it to their children to do something about it.

The first thing that struck me was the overcrowded playground. Lonely children stood miserably in corners with nobody to play with, and harassed teachers who were too busy to notice them. All of this came under the description of education. By dumping our children in overcrowded schools every day, we were preparing them for life—weren't we?

Already I had been in to complain to Patrick's teacher after he was scared half out of his mind. On the second day of term, his class of four year-olds doubled with a class of eleven year-olds who were being given a lesson in Greek mythology. I found this out after Patrick was crying all night and shouting for me to move the bag with the head in from under his bed. The following morning at breakfast, he was trying to explain about the lady with the snake hair who turned people to stone. Her head was chopped off and thrown away—hence the dream that it was in the bag under his bed. The lady, of course, was Medusa.

Patrick's teacher, a lovely woman, was embarrassed when I had a word with her, and promised to speak to the teacher concerned.

Two weeks later, when it was raining, the children were left unsupervised in the school hall at playtime. Two boys from the top class started fighting and chasing each other and one of them ran past Patrick, and knocked the feet from under him. Patrick fell, banging his face very badly on the bench. When I collected him from school, I could have cried. One side of his face had almost doubled in size, pulling the corner of his mouth up. His poor teacher was white. As I stooped down to face Patrick, the fear in his eyes almost made my heart ache. His teacher explained what happened.

"I would have called you, only I knew you were due any minute. It's just getting bigger and bigger," she said anxiously. "I think you'll have to take him to hospital."

Sitting in the out-patients at the local hospital, my heart bled at the thoughts of him returning to that overcrowded crisis centre they called a school.

After Patrick had been examined by the doctor and no broken bones had been discovered, Paul drove us home.

"If this is school for you, then I'd do a better job myself," I said to him. My main fear was that Patrick would end up with such little faith when he was left in other people's care that he would be afraid to leave me.

Patrick returned to school a week later, his face still slightly swollen. I felt a wretch leaving him there. Though my son put on a brave face it was obvious he was very nervous.

I no longer understood the logic of sending a child to school. However, for the time being, I put that thought to the back of my mind. Two days later, armed with a list of schools from the Education Department, I set about trying to find a decent school for him. The first one I approached was full. I had walked the three miles to the little village school on the outskirts of the town one sunny April afternoon.

The second school was seven miles away, but with only thirty-two pupils and two teachers, I felt I had to go and see it. It was there that I met Pat Haddrell, the most amazing lady who had run the school for twenty-five years. I told her all about Patrick's school experience.

"He really needs to know he's safe when he's in other people's care," I told her. I could tell she cared. Had I not met this marvellous woman at that particular time, I don't know how Patrick would have ended up. I didn't know how long he'd be going to this little school, but for the time being it was worth travelling seven miles a day just to experience the warmth and exuberance this amazing lady generated.

"Is it Alright to Speak Now, Mum?"

"You can do anything if you put your mind to it." That was what my mother had drummed into me all my life, but in all honesty, I never even thought I would be able to drive. When I finally passed my test, she was the first to hear the good news. Of course, she was delighted—so was I. For days afterwards I kept pinching myself. I couldn't believe it.

Any observer would have been quite amused to see me taking the children out in the car. I had stressed the need for quiet in order for me to concentrate on my driving, so they hardly breathed as they sat in the back seat. Driving along, making sure I didn't get too near the kerb, gripping the wheel as though I was flying an aeroplane, I'd hear a quiet little voice from the back seat.

"Is it all right to speak now, Mum?"

When I became more confident, we had a stereo installed. Then it was the children's turn as the Beatles blasted out.

"Can you turn it down please, Mum?" they'd keep reminding me as I drove along without a care in the world. Often, I created more noise than they did.

With standards dropping in the town schools, more and more discontented parents sent their children to the little village school. The numbers of pupils started creeping up.

Travelling from so many different areas often denied the parents the opportunity of getting to know each other. It seemed such a shame, especially when the two teachers were so friendly.

One day I approached the Headmistress about the possibility of starting a parent's magazine. This would enable us to welcome new children and their families to the school, have features from parents, articles for sale, a birthday page and school work submitted by the children.

All for progress, she jumped at the idea and very kindly gave me the use of the photocopier. During the year I was Editor, I had great fun. Most of the parents made contributions of some kind. Their articles made very interesting and varied reading. Some parents looked the other way when they saw me coming, feeling they had nothing to contribute, but I usually managed to wangle something out of them (usually of great interest).

It was during this time I took myself off to stay with Cathy in Spain for two weeks. The children stayed with their dad so I didn't feel too bad about going alone. It was a healthy break for all of us, and besides it was school holidays and I knew the kids would have lots of fun.

Sitting on the London Underground on my way to Heathrow, I felt as though I'd been stuck in a convent for twenty years as I watched the various people travelling along the busy route. I could have gone up and down on that line all day.

When the plane took off, I sat back to drink in the experience—I had never flown before.

As time went on, the school became more and more popular and classrooms became more and more crowded. Almost doubling the number of pupils, the little school had finally outgrown itself and lost that special quality which had attracted so many people to it.

Armed with facts and information for when the education officials came to read me the riot act, I decided to deregister Anna and Patrick to educate them at home.

28

Speak When You're Spoken To

In 1989, shortly before the local hospital for the mentally handicapped was to close, one of the nurses opened a Home in our area for some fourteen profoundly mentally handicapped hospital patients. Imagine my utter astonishment when I learnt the local Day Centre found places for these people. People with disabilities and behaviour problems as severe as Marie's—not one, but fourteen! I certainly did not begrudge the patients a place at the Day Centre, but there was a principle involved. Marie was still banished from the county, and still travelling forty miles a day; no—it was unacceptable.

I wrote to the Social Services asking for confirmation of the news. As usual, the issue was dodged and the buck was passed, until finally, when it could no longer be avoided, a statement was given to assure me that Marie had not been forgotten about and they would have a fresh look at her case.

If those people start at the Day Centre and there is no word about Marie going there then I shall just take her there every day and leave her, I ranted, but I was kidding myself. Many, many times over the years, I had threatened to do the same thing but how can anybody leave her daughter in a place she isn't wanted? Yet I knew this was the final straw and drastic steps would have to be taken.

And then the letter I had waited nearly six years for finally arrived one morning a month later. I almost giggled when I read the first two paragraphs; their sense of urgency was touching.

> 'Dear Mrs Daly,
>
> The Director of Social Services has asked me to contact you regarding your recent comments relating to Marie's difficulties in obtaining a place at Gainsborough Enterprises. Having reconsidered the position I would

like to move speedily to agreeing satisfactory day care
provision for Marie.'

It was ironic that the meeting was arranged when we would be on holiday in Ireland. I wrote to cancel it. The next meeting, a month later, was the day of my father's funeral. I was able to keep the third appointment.

I was very nervous. I was also very frightened of my reaction to meeting these people. How could I even be civil to them? These people had caused such heartache and destruction, had sentenced Marie to four years at home and had almost deprived my little children of a normal home life. What beast would emerge from my being when I looked into their empty eyes? Shivers ran through me as I imagined being locked in a room full of dead bodies—that was how they seemed to me.

Yet at the end of the day they still held all the cards. I was that same person they had met and disliked six years ago. I still had strong views on peoples' rights and individuality. I would still not be dictated to and bullied. Could they now accept my views or would the meeting break down?

Unable to face them alone, I asked my friend, Jo, if she would accompany me. Jo worked as a councillor for both 'Rape Crisis' and 'Mind'. She was very good with people and very observant. She was also my witness.

Playing Their Game

Thanks to the open-mindedness of Colin Pitman, senior Social Worker, the meeting went very well. There were times we could have locked horns, but we compromised and heard each other out.

After much discussion, it was suggested that Marie be introduced slowly into the Unit because the staff did not want to cause her any upset. That was a logical attitude; the illogical one was for Marie to continue in her present Day Centre for half of the week and attend this new centre the other half. I told them I would not have Marie attending two day centres. Then the Manager, who had hardly looked my way, took the opportunity to enlighten me.

"We find if our trainees start straight away on a full time basis, it can cause them great upset. You really have to introduce them into a new environment very slowly."

"I wouldn't expect Marie to start full time straight away. Maybe at first I could bring her up to you for a few hours in the mornings and collect her at lunch time; then perhaps another week she could come in the afternoons."

"That's a good idea," Colin Pitman said cheerfully. "If Marie comes in the afternoons, she could travel home with the others on the bus. Save you from having to pick her up."

The Manager did not answer me. Her face remained cold and expressionless. She still did not like parents to have ideas. Thank goodness total decision making was no longer in her hands. What was noted as being difficult and awkward six years ago was now accepted as a relevant point of view.

Sitting around the table discussing Marie's day care in such a rational way seemed unreal to me. I thought I'd be dragged out of the meeting screaming obscenities at them all, yet I was sitting there as if it had all happened to someone else...I was playing their game.

"What about the contract?" the Manager asked Colin Pitman. He suggested she give me her copy to take home and read, telling me I would receive an official copy through the post with confirmation of Marie's placement. I stuck the document in my bag. The meeting ended and we left.

Jo linked her arm through mine affectionately as we hastily left the building and walked out into the blazing sun. It was over. At last we could get on with our lives.

Part Three

29

Caution to the Wind

I hated being on the motorway. I was such a dreadful back seat driver. Being sandwiched between two Lorries almost made my heart stop as they sped along, boldly flashing their lights to communicate messages to each other.

Having arranged an extended holiday for Marie from the Day Centre, (although deep down I knew she would not be returning), I was going with the three children to stay in our new cottage in Co Mayo for a few months. The furniture had gone on ahead and would be waiting for us when we arrived. Flying to Ireland from Manchester airport was a great day for us, not only because we had found an alternative lifestyle, it was the first time Marie had ever flown.

Naturally, Marie was unaware of the changes that were about to take place. I hoped this would be the beginning of a new life for her; she deserved the best and somehow I felt she'd find it in Ireland.

I knew I had reached the end of the road when I had eventually read over the Contract of Attendance I was asked to sign before Marie could take her new place at the Day Centre. No wonder they hadn't discussed it with me at the meeting. No wonder the Manager had made sure I had a copy. Designed to protect the staff and not the students (or trainees) or their parents, many rules and stipulations were laid down in the document. It stated that after two written warnings, Marie could be suspended for bad behaviour. *Were they having a laugh?*

I wrote to the Manager, stating that while I wished to co-operate with the staff in any way possible, I felt that the Contract of Attendance was a very narrow way to discuss a policy for future care for Marie. I didn't agree to her being suspended for bad behaviour, and said that in view of Marie's physical and mental disability, I regarded the Contract of Attendance as void whether a signature was on it or not. A suspension was a punishment and punishment was futile if the recipient had no comprehension of warnings leading up to and including suspension. *Oh, here we go again*, I thought. I refused to sign it.

Though there were many changes for the better since Marie had first attended six years previously, they had introduced certain policies which, I felt, took us back thirty years as far as attitudes towards the mentally disabled were concerned.

I was filled with sadness when I saw that all the staff wore uniforms. Dressed in navy blue skirts and cardigans with a white shirt, they resembled prison wardens. As nice as the staff were, having such a custodian image could only be damaging to the people they took out into the community. Having always taken such care over Marie's appearance, I deeply resented her being 'led' about by people in such drab attire. It was a great insult.

If Marie had remained at the Day Centre, these were issues I would have fought to change. But wouldn't there always be something to fight about? No, I decided, it was time to move on and have some peace in our lives.

Apart from a short spell in Liverpool we had lived in Lincolnshire for almost eighteen years.

Travelling in Style

We arrived at Manchester Airport in plenty of time. Paul parked the car while the children ran off to get the luggage trolleys. Laden with carrier bags, shoulder bags, four suitcases and Marie, I waited at the busy drop off for them to return.

We lay one of the suitcases flat on the trolley and sat Marie on top of it and then headed towards the check-in area to wait for their dad. We paused at the Ryanair information desk and enquired about our flight to Knock, in the west of Ireland. One eye was firmly fixed on Marie as I spoke with the lady behind the desk.

"Did you say you're on the one o'clock flight to Knock?" the young man standing next to her asked. I nodded. He came around the front of the desk to me.

"I'm sorry to have to tell you," he said, "But we changed our flights to summer schedule and we forgot to inform you. Your plane left at half-eleven this morning." I raised my eyebrows in disbelief. Some things did actually render me speechless and this was one of them. There wasn't another flight for two days.

"There is an Aer Lingus flight to Dublin due to leave shortly. We could put you on that and then pay for a taxi to take you to your destination at the other end." The more he tried to help the worse he made it. Oh God…the thought of a four hour drive across Ireland with a car full of luggage, two kids and a young disabled woman— and a strange driver… I thanked him but said his offer was out of the question. "I'll tell you what, if we let your husband go with you, he can drive the car at the other end." At least that was feasible but, after negotiating, the car hire firm needed Paul's driving licence and he didn't have it on him. By this time, the children were looking really fed-up and Marie was pulling ugly faces, trying to force herself to cry. The steward kept looking at his watch.

"Okay, how about if we lay a coach on for you from Dublin to Knock?" Now he was talking. At least there'd be plenty of space!

"That would be fantastic," I told him.

I've never seen anybody move so fast.

"Right then," he said, "you're going to have to dash. You've only got four minutes." Shouting to the Ryanair staff that we would be boarding the flight, there was a mad panic as they ran to the Aer Lingus desk to get our tickets. With no time to check the cases into Ryanair, the stewardess told us to run as she pushed one of our trolleys.

Poor Marie, I knew I should have brought her wheelchair but at the last minute I sent it with the removal men, not really thinking she'd need it at the airport. She wasn't able to walk for long, let alone run. Forcing her to run when she wasn't able, I knew, could bring on an epileptic fit. That was all we needed.

Arriving at Customs, we still had to go through all the usual procedures. Paul walked Marie slowly on ahead while I put the cases through the barrier. One of them set off the alarm.

"Can you open this case, please?" I was asked.

I had gone around the house at the last minute, throwing odds and ends into the case. I didn't know what was in it. Then I searched frantically for my key until I remembered Paul had them in his pocket. I ran to catch him, got the keys and hurried back to the security desk. I was shaking so much I could hardly turn the key. One of the staff who'd been standing staring at me suddenly came to life and unlocked the case. I watched him rummage through my belongings and pick out my metal stapler; deciding that had been the culprit he held it in the air to satisfy the other security guards.

I locked the case, threw it back on the trolley and ran like mad with Anna and Patrick at my side. We caught up with their dad as he was crossing the departure lounge. I took Marie by the hand and encouraged her to run.

"You're going to miss this flight if you don't hurry," the steward warned. We reached gate number two and ran down the stairs as fast as we could, all things considered, only to be told when we reached the bottom that we were too late—the doors were now locked and the flight was taking off. Sure enough, as we looked through the glass doors the plane was reversing.

My eyes returned to the officials with their walkie-talkies before resting on two sad little faces looking wistfully out of the window. 'Now, Michelle,' I thought, 'Get out of this one.'

"Don't worry," I said. I was about to promise them the earth when the doors to the runway slid open. The signal man was waving to the pilot. The plane stopped and he was bringing the steps for us to climb aboard.

There was a burst of excitement as we scrambled to pick up our bags and run out onto the tarmac to the plane.

Stepping inside the doorway to an aircraft full of curious people, relieved but exhausted, we flopped into our seats. With hands that still shook, I strapped Marie into the seat beside me as the engines once again roared and the plane cruised towards the runway. Anna and Patrick were giggling with excitement and the smile on Marie's face showed the unexpected pleasure as the plane gathered speed and soared into the sky.

Have I Died and Gone to Heaven

Connaught Airport is situated midway between Kilkelly and Charlestown and was officially opened in May 1986. Building the airport at Knock must have made a tremendous difference to the people of Mayo. I, for one, would certainly have had second thoughts about living in Ireland had I not been able to fly back to England in an emergency.

The route from the airport to Ballyhaunis is very picturesque. Green sloping fields are scattered with cattle and sheep, with men in the distance busy working on the land. Every so often we see a tractor crawling along the road, almost stopping as we let it pass. What is so surprising, apart from the scenery, is the friendliness of the people. Drivers put up their hands to greet us as they pass by. Driving through the busy market town of Ballyhaunis, there are numerous shops and pubs, banks and a railway station (with a main line from Dublin to Westport!) but what impressed me most of all was the cinema!

Living only one mile from the town meant we were able to benefit from the local amenities and still enjoy village life. We had a lot to look forward to!

Home From Home

Bikes, scooters, skates, filing cabinets, photocopier, computer, word processor, desks, TV and video recorder, deep freeze, fridge and many other items were all waiting to be unpacked when we arrived.

In England we'd had no garden, and with the streets no longer safe for children to play alone they spent most of their time indoors. In Ireland they could play outside all day and in all weathers.

So we arrived in our new home and I felt like the world had been lifted off my shoulders. Most people thought my moving to Ireland with three children was a brave step, but I'd faced far more challenging situations over the years.

I could hear the children laughing outside. They were running through the long grass shrieking every time they saw a frog. I took Marie out to join them. Life was going to be good.

The rooms were so crammed with furniture that we could hardly move. I got the children to put their bikes and scooters against an old white-washed shed at the side of our cottage and began to organise what was going where and then put up the beds. I found the container with my books in and stacked them on the shelves in my heavy wooden sideboard. We had so much fun unpacking and finding a place for everything. I had cushion floor fitted throughout so the children could run in and out in their wellies without worrying about making a mess.

Our cottage lacked many mod cons we were used to in England but I didn't care. The move had been worth the sacrifice. Normally, when people move into a new house, there are squabbles over who is having what bedroom. We didn't have that problem. With only one bedroom between us, Marie, Patrick and Anna had to share for the time being. I slept on the sofa in the living room.

In those first few weeks I'd have slept standing up. The highlight of our day was the mile walk into town and, as a result of this care-free way of life, the weight began to fall off me. Rain or sunshine, we went into town every day and became a familiar sight around the shops where people would stop to greet us, or wave from the other side of the road.

The shop assistants were always pleasant. Nothing was too much trouble for them. I'd go to buy one of the children a pair of shoes and the staff would have half the boxes out from the back of the store.

I bought a red plastic bath in the local hardware store and filled it up every night enabling my grubby children to go to bed lovely and clean. Hot water was no problem; I had an electric emersion heater put into the cupboard beside the hearth and the water was also heated by the turf fire.

When I awoke in the mornings, the first thing I did was rake the two fires. Our living room had an original fire-crane with hooks for the pots and pans. When the grates were done, if all remained quiet in the bedroom, I would empty the ash bucket behind the shed and stroll around the garden for a while on my own, enjoying the peace and quiet.

When I listened to my neighbours' cattle lowing in the field and the birds chirping in the trees, it often seemed like I was dreaming. My life had altered so dramatically.

On my way into the cottage, I'd gather bits of wood from the garden and if it was chilly, I lit the fire in the living-room and kitchen. The rooms were usually lovely and warm when the children woke.

The three of them were always awake early, often reading for an hour in bed before they decided to get dressed. If Marie was in a good mood, she would get up and go and sit on the end of Anna's bottom bunk with an open book and pretend to read to her and Patrick. With both hands holding the book in the air, Marie would proceed with her story.

"On day!" she'd say in an authoritative tone as she turned each page respectfully, imitating Patrick. She soon had them both laughing and the more they laughed, the more she performed.

Our neighbours told me (with great pride) about a 'beautiful' new village complex, 17 miles away, for people with learning difficulties. It was supposed to be the most modern in Ireland and had opened the previous year. Wow, how fortunate were we? A residential village almost on our doorstep was the icing on the cake.

Making New Friends

Being up so early in the mornings meant the days were very long. Some nights the library was open until eight in the evening, so we'd go down there and have a cup of tea with Anne, the librarian. We were the same age and had much in common. Anne was a busy housewife with four school-age children, and had made the daily seventeen-mile journey from her home in Ballyglass for the past seven years.

The first time I took the children to the library, we sat in a little room at a long table with Marie close by in her wheelchair. We all nearly jumped out of our skins when a fire alarm rang out through the building—I hadn't realised that the Fire Station was next door! I laughed until I almost cried.

Anne, on seeing our surprise, attempted to explain until, infected by our hysterical laughter, she finally gave up. The fire engine came charging out and parked outside the building, causing us further fascination as local businessmen, and some we recognised, ran from all directions to form a fire fighting team.

The library turned out to be our second home. When things

became too much for me, that's the place I would head for, especially in those early days. It was a distraction from my thoughts. As soon as I went into the library Anne would put the kettle on for a cuppa.

And then Anne introduced me to Maureen, a local woman who'd recently returned home after years in England. Maureen took me under her wing, especially when she found out I had no social life. She was a beautiful singer and later on in the year, she arranged for her auntie to look after Patrick and Anna so she could take me to the Irish music sessions every week.

Mary Durr was another favourite of mine. Mary was in her seventies and lived nearby on the land her grandfather had been born and bred, accompanied by twelve hens, four cats, two dogs and twelve cows!

Mary was the first person Paul and I met when we looked at properties on our first visit to Ireland. We drove from Sligo to Ballyhaunis, but despite following directions the townspeople had given, there was no sign of the cottage advertised in the property magazine. Up and down, up and down we drove along the Irishtown road and still we could not see a sign for Drimbane.

There was a short elderly woman walking along the road wearing a blue headscarf and accompanied by two dogs. We pulled up alongside her and on seeing the English car I guess she realised we were lost.

"Can I help you?" she asked, sticking her head in my window. I smiled at this tiny, plump, rosy cheeked Irishwoman, the strands of white hair peeping from under her scarf.

"Oh, I hope so!" I said, passing the property brochure through the window. For a moment I thought she couldn't see the photo. I leaned over to point the house out to her before I realised, with some amusement that she was standing on the roadside scanning the information below the picture, obviously looking for the price!

Mary looked up from the brochure and smiled at us. She knew the house well and told us we only had to drive a couple of hundred yards then turn right into a cul-de-sac.

From the day I first came to the village, Mary's door was always open to me.

Not long after we moved to Ireland, my mother came over for a holiday. It was the first time she had ever flown and I hoped travelling alone hadn't been too stressful for her. When we were driving out of the village on that beautiful May morning we could see Mary resting against the hedge at the side of her lane. On seeing us approach she pulled herself up with the support of her cattle stick and together with her dog Arnie, she came onto the road as I stopped and wound down the window.

"Hiya, Mary," I said as she leaned on the car door. "And how are you today?" Mary typically answered a question with a question.

"Is your Mammy coming?" she asked me eagerly. I nodded.

"We're just going to fetch her, Mary," I replied.

"Awe," she whispered. Her blue eyes filled with tears. "Well, I'm happy for you!"

"You'll have to come over for your tea, Mary," I told her. Her face broke into smile.

"Aye, I'd be very happy to," she answered as she slowly made her way across the road towards home. "And good luck to you," she shouted as I started the engine and began to wind up the window. Suddenly Arnie left Mary's side and ran in front of my car. With her stick waving madly in the air Mary called to her dog;

"Come here, you little cunt!"

From the back of the car the children giggled. Unfortunately, I lacked their diplomacy and burst out laughing. Arnie immediately obeyed and was soon at Mary's side heading towards her house.

"See you, Mary," I shouted as we moved off.

"Aye," she answered, "with the help of God."

I laughed all the way to the airport. She was such a colourful character; I couldn't wait for my mother to meet her.

"But What If?"

My mother was thrilled with the cottage. She scrubbed and cleaned from when she got up in the morning until she went to bed (on the couch) at night. The windows gleamed, showing off the new cream nets she brought over from England. The tiny toilet and hallway was transformed from a dull yellow to a brilliant white.

I felt guilty. I should have had the decorating done before she came but it took me all my time to look after the children, let alone decorate the house. I just didn't have the energy.

When I introduced Mary to my mother, Mary shook my mother's

hand as if she were a long lost friend. It was then I realised that special Irish—it was their warmth and affection that made everybody they met feel special.

Having my mother around had been a welcome distraction but those few days flew by and it was nearly time to say goodbye. In that short time I was ashamed to admit that as much as I made the effort, I was often depressed. Painfully aware of the difficulties Marie's handicap presented, I was trying to come to terms with her going into residential care. My mother was very supportive and constantly reminded me of the wonderful life Marie had been able to live through being at home, but she was also aware of the heartache her departure would bring.

I have always made it clear to the children that Marie would one day be leaving home, letting them know it was out of the question that they would ever be allowed to take over her care in their adult life. Marie was my responsibility, not theirs. But I noticed that the older they got, the more they questioned, and they raised some logical points.

"Ah yes, but what if?" was constantly put to me.

"What if she cries for us?"

"What if nobody understands what she's saying?"

I'd tell the children most people left home when they reached a certain age. I explained how Marie would benefit from the social interaction life in the new village complex would bring. It helped, but they weren't convinced.

But how desperate did I need to feel before I took such a drastic step and requested residential care for my twenty-six year old daughter? I wondered if people realised that parents only apply for residential care when they reach the end of the road. I had been Marie's mother for almost twenty years, but I had grown tired. Not the kind of tired a good sleep would cure, or two weeks holiday. I mean I was burnt-out; had given all I had to give. I no longer had the bounce and energy to deal with situations Marie's unpredictable behaviour created. As much as I loved her and wanted to look after her forever, I had to be realistic. If I kept Marie at home wouldn't I be imprisoning the person I fought to free so many years before?

I knew there was only one thing to do and I had to get on and do it! Emotionally isolated, I was my own worst enemy. So used to shutting myself away and dealing with my own problems, it was difficult for me to open up and ask for help. Feeling sick with anxiety, I picked up the phone with my clammy hand and dialled a contact number a friend had given me. From somewhere, I had to find the courage to see this through.

31

A Special Place

Aras Attracta was the name of the village complex where Marie was offered a place—only 20 miles from where we lived. It was built on a twenty acre site, providing residential care for some of the moderate, severe and profoundly handicapped people in the community.

The 140 bed complex was the biggest building project undertaken by the Western Health Board at the time. The accommodation comprises sixteen bungalows, enabling the residents to live in small family groups under the care of learning disability trained nurses. There was also a thirty-bed unit for the multiply handicapped and an eighteen-bed unit for the older retirement group; and four short-term beds offering both clients and their families a welcome break.

The Day Centre offered varied activities with a pool of professional services at hand—physiotherapy department, central assessment clinic, workshop, vocational training unit, and day centre workshop. Adjoining these facilities was the Recreation Centre with a swimming pool, gymnasium and weight training room.

It was a relief that Marie would be under the care of people with the professional skills to look after her. I am very aware that in this day and age the title of 'nurse' sets off alarm bells, implying that disabled people are sick and need nursing care. As a parent, I believe the three years' training, covering many aspects of the world of people with special needs, more than equips them for the job. It's the title that needs doing away with, not the nurses.

For me, it was a dream-come-true. To set up home only twenty miles from the most modern centre in Ireland without even knowing of its existence was quite astonishing.

It was arranged for Marie to travel to Swinford on a daily basis for two weeks prior to taking up her residential place. This slow introduction would help to familiarise her with staff and give her a taste of what was to come. With the use of her diary, there was frequent communication between the unit and home.

The plan was for Marie to arrive at the bungalow where she would eventually be living, have some lunch with the other clients, and together with the nurses she would spend a couple of hours in the recreational building before coming home just in time for tea.

In England we'd had a taste of Marie leaving home when she spent Monday to Friday in the hospital. I was hoping this parting wouldn't be so traumatic. She wasn't too far away and could come home anytime.

I felt sad because I could not sit down with Marie to explain the forthcoming changes in her life. I was thirty-seven; we'd been together since I was a teenager. My life was going to be so different and so was hers.

I had days full of doubt when I almost cancelled Marie's placement, and other days, where I was filled with hope for our future.

Mixed emotions are common when any child grows up and leaves home but they're more profound when the child is disabled. Marie wasn't making these decisions about her future – I was, and I was painfully aware that her life would always be in someone else' hands.

In September 1990, five months after we moved to Ireland, Marie went to start her new life in Aras Attracta where she would live for the next seventeen years.

Part Four

32

Opening up Old Wounds

After Marie left home, I began to work on the manuscript that I'd written a few years earlier. In the weeks that followed, I would sit at my typewriter with great determination as I struggled to put our past into words. So much had happened since writing the first draft. Sometimes it was too painful to face. I missed Marie so much and prayed I'd done the right thing letting her go. It was at times like these I would take myself off to the library. Not wanting to burden Anne with my troubles, I would casually mention doubts about my writing ability. She would have none of it and said I had no choice in the matter; the book had to be written and the story told.

So I worked hard for the next few months, writing, writing, writing, often during the night when the children were sleeping. The silence was perfect and allowed my mind to travel back, uninterrupted, to places and times I had desperately tried to run away from in the past.

The only sound was from Sally, a donkey I rescued from an over-zealous owner. I'd seen him hit the poor thing with a stick once too often when he walked her through town. I stopped him one day and asked if he would sell her to me. He looked aghast and shook his head as if I had asked to buy one of his children. However he must have had a change of mind (like you do about your children) because when I saw him again a few days later he said I could have her for a blue. A blue? I repeated. Twenty pounds, he replied.

Sally must have thought she'd died and gone to heaven when she moved in with us. She roamed freely day and night on the huge garden around the house.

In the dead of night, she came hee-hawing at the door and in she shuffled to stand behind the settee watching me get her marshmallows biscuits out of the cupboard. She munched on a couple of them then backed herself out of the room through the front door. I stood and watched her turn around on the step and off she would go into the night.

When November came, the village seemed to fall asleep. The birds flew away, the trees were bare and the cows went into the sheds for the winter.

Not only did the children and I spend weekends at Anne's, she also took me to meet her parents who lived in the next village. I loved seeing Anne's mum, Winnie, who always made a fuss of me. She was tall and slim and smartly dressed in layers of cardigans and jumpers, with a thick tweed skirt to protect her from the cold she so fiercely felt. Winnie laughed and joked pretending to envy my single status. Anne and Winnie made me feel like one of the family as we sat by the range sipping hot whiskey.

"And how are things beyond?" Winnie asked if I had recently returned from England. She was one of 16 children with brothers and sisters scattered all over the world. Head teachers, priests, doctors, they followed many different professions.

She loved to hear news of Marie—how she was settling in and if she was happy; did I like the Unit and were the staff nice? It was painful to admit that I did not visit Marie as often as I should but Winnie would have none of it and said Marie needed time to settle down.

Marie had settled down and seemed happy, but it was so upsetting when the children and I took her back to the Unit after a day at home that it was sometimes easier not to visit her.

Those weekends at Anne's and visits to Winnie did us the world of good. When I arrived home late Sunday afternoon with Patrick and Anna, our house would be freezing so I hurriedly lit the fires and then we went over to Mary's for a cuppa while the place warmed up. When we walked into her kitchen she'd be dozing in the chair near the range, having recently come in from seeing to the cattle. Even though she was probably tired she had a great welcome for us. She would instruct Patrick to get the biscuits out of the press and Anna to set out the cups and then she got two glasses and poured us both a Whiskey. I loved chatting with Mary. Once I was so engrossed chatting with her that by the time I got back home the fire had gone out.

Done and Dusted

It was snowing that Christmas Eve as I handed the heavy manila envelope over the Post Office counter with my completed manuscript inside. I think the children were not only excited for me but also glad to see the back of something that had consumed me for months.

How did I pick the publisher? One of my favourite books of all time is The Famine by Liam O' Flaherty and I cheekily chanced his publisher for luck. I didn't hold my breath. In the past, lots of editors had enjoyed reading our story but nobody was able to publish it.

Ten months later, I had a phone call I never thought I would get. The publishers invited me to Dublin to meet with them. I was ecstatic.

33

What to Wear to the Publisher's

Just what do you wear for an interview with a publisher? Oh my goodness, I was stumped! Within hours of arriving home from my friend Anne's where I had left the children overnight, I had the contents of my wardrobe strewn across the bed. Blue and black—black and blue—were the only colours I ever wore. Should I look smart? Casual? Smart-casual? Then again, did it really matter? Yes, I decided, it did, but I needed to wear clothes I felt comfortable in so I could relax and be myself. Not too relaxed though, because I had to try and convince this publisher that my story deserved to be published. Yikes, it was a scary thought.

I settled on a light-blue top and gypsy skirt with navy sandals to match. I thought 'bright and breezy' was the best option and reminded myself the most important thing to wear was a smile.

I couldn't sleep that night. I hoped the weather remained dry. Rain would be disastrous for my curly hair. I only had to go near a boiling kettle and it frizzed up. My biggest nightmare would be arriving at the publisher's office like a drowned rat or worse still, like I'd had an electric shock.

I arrived in Dublin in plenty of time and strolled up O'Connell Street, weaving in and out of the lunchtime crowd, up past the famous Floozy in the Jacuzzi and the Gresham Hotel.

I was excited about meeting the publisher, and pleased too, that the sun was shining. So far so good; all was going to plan.

I stopped a passer-by for directions and as instructed, I kept walking until I reached the Gate Theatre, and turned right. I found myself in a street full of hotels. When a cheerful Irish person says, 'it's just up the road' I'd learnt their 'just up the road' could be a mile—or two—or three, away. How awful would it be if I arrived at the publisher's office late? So I asked another passer-by for directions, just to make sure I was on the right track. I was.

I continued on past the hotels to the end of the street, turned a corner and found myself standing in Mountjoy Square, one of the five Georgian squares in Dublin, and where the publisher was based.

I took a deep breath. It still hadn't sunk in—Me—going to meet a publisher?

I stood for a moment admiring the elegant houses that had been converted into offices. I was an hour early, but that was me. I hated to be late for anything. The plaque on the wall a few houses along told me Wolfhound Press was on the top floor. Now that I had my bearings I about turned and walked down the street to find a café or pub to kill time, and freshen up.

Crossing the busy road, I tried to imagine the kind of questions the publisher might ask:

Publisher: *"Tell me a little about yourself?"*

Me: *(Thinking) Yikes! Where do I begin? "I was born in Liverpool on Hitler's birthday, a day before Queen Elizabeth's coronation. I was the only child of eight to be born at home. I cut my first tooth when I was seven months…"*

Publisher: *"What inspired you to write your book?"*

Me: *Ooooh, myyyyy Gooooood, don't get me started! (But what kind of an answer is that?)*

Publisher: *"What books are you reading at the moment?"*

Me: *'Feel the Fear and Do it Anyway'—'How to Win Friends and Influence People'—'The Power of Positive Thinking'. " Erm, 'War and Peace'."*

Publisher: *"When did you first consider yourself a writer?"*

Me: *Me? A writer? Okay—okay, I hold my hands up—I'm a fraud. I shouldn't even be here. My book was* *an accident. You see I was typing myself out of a nervous breakdown and the words just kept pouring out and the pages piling up and before I knew it...* "When I finished writing my story and held the manuscript in my hands."

Publisher*: "Did you learn anything from writing your book?"*

Me*: Yes, I'm not as crazy as I thought I was.* "Oh yes, it was an interesting journey."

Publisher*: "Who or what has been your biggest inspiration in life."*

Me*: Well, for the last few years I haven't had much adult company, but one of my best friends, is Oprah Winfrey, although she doesn't know it. Oprah Winfrey, is the mother of all mothers; a woman that helped half the world raise their children; she certainly helped me raise mine. Oprah is the sister everyone would love to have and...* "Oprah Winfrey."

I blamed my undisciplined hair for my undisciplined thoughts. I looked at my watch. This time in two hours the meeting would be over. I pushed open the pub door and went inside.

The room was dark and dreary, making it difficult to tell if it was day or night. Maybe that was the idea; to remove all sense of time. There were three elderly men at the bar so I said "Hello" and ordered a coffee. Then I went to the Ladies.

When I returned to the bar, my English accent aroused curiosity, and I was soon deep in conversation with three Dubliners. They asked if I was on holiday and were surprised to learn I lived in County Mayo. When I told them the reason I was in Dublin, and how nervous I was, they wanted to buy me a drink, but I graciously declined. "Oh, no, I'm fine, thanks!" I told them. I daren't touch any alcohol—there would be plenty of that later when I met friends in my home-town that night.

"What'll ye have to drink?" I was asked again when one of the men ordered a round of drinks. "Give the woman a brandy." He instructed the barman. "It'll calm her nerves." I didn't suppose one could do much harm. The barman smiled as he placed the glass in front of me. I picked it up and we toasted. "I'll not be wishing you luck," he stated 'cause ye won't need it. 'Tis yer success we'll be toastin' to. Isn't that right, lads?"

"It is!" they chorused.

I'd never tasted brandy before and fixed a smile as the liquid nearly took the lining off my tongue. The next thing two more drinks are placed in front of me. With all the excitement I'd forgotten to eat so there was no way I could drink those shots.

"Oh, that's awful kind of you but I can't drink that. Honestly, I will just…"

"Get it down ye! Go on!"

So I did.

I left the pub with a great send-off and headed towards the publishers. Now I understood the meaning of that Irish Blessing, 'May the road rise up to meet you…' haha, only joking. The road stayed where it was and the medicinal liquid did the trick. I was no longer nervous as I hurried on up to the publisher's office—I couldn't wait to meet him.

Bernie, one of the editors opened the front door and smiled brightly, inviting me to follow her. Oh, was I glad the publisher's office was on the top floor and not in the basement – it's less damaging to trip up one step on a gypsy skirt than to stumble and fall down the lot. I laughed with Bernie, as I followed her up the stairs. When she showed me into the publisher's office I smiled as he crossed to room the greet me. I shook his outstretched hand, accepted his invitation to sit down, and the interview began.

34

Marie's Voice

My hard work paid off, and there was great excitement when my book was published. The publisher had selected the cover and changed the title from *Swimming Against the Tide* to *Marie's Voice*, but did I care? Good God, no! No title is set in stone. My original title had been *With a Little Help From My Friends*.

Due to a national postal strike, the publisher Seamus Cashman, very kindly sent my book down by train. It was a gorgeous summer's day and I was sitting on a bench with Patrick and Anna, in the railway station in Ballyhaunis. I smiled when I heard the Dublin train in the distance, knowing it had my freshly printed book on board. What a feeling when I opened the box on the platform to see Marie smiling on the cover! It seemed so unreal. This wasn't supposed to happen to someone like me; someone with no education.

It had been a long journey since I first spread my pages across the pasting table and tapped away on my Brother typewriter. It proved to me that anything is possible.

I couldn't wait to take the book to Swinford to show Marie and the nurses. The nursing staff didn't get much feedback, and seeing the book with a special mention to Aras Attracta inside the cover, let them know how much they are appreciated. I rang on ahead so the nurses were expecting me. With Marie having no sense of time and to avoid confusing her, she was unaware of my impending visit.

She'd been in the unit for 18 months and I still got a lump in my throat whenever I saw her. She was often sitting alone watching the activity around her. As soon as she spotted me she came to life and her eyes watered, just like mine did. Some things you just never get used to and Marie leaving home was one of them.

Some days I could tell there was a staff shortage in the unit and I did feel sorry for the nurses. Routines have to be followed which makes their job twice as hard.

I didn't always take Marie back home. If I was only visiting for a few hours we'd go for a drive in the car, accompanied by tape recordings of her favourite songs compiled from our vinyl record selection. Then we would go for a meal which she always enjoyed, and then back to the unit.

I kissed her and gave her a hug and then I said, "Wait until you see what I've got?" I reached into my bag for the book and knelt in front of her. As expected there wasn't much of a response, so I carried on dipping into my bag and brought out her usual treats. The nurse who came over to greet me gasped when she saw Marie on the cover. Her reaction brought the other nurses over to investigate. The three nurses stood close together and flicked through the pages, pausing to admire the photos. Included in the selection was the photo of Marie and me, taken by 7 year-old Morgan outside the hospital in Bristol. When I told the nurses they couldn't believe it. I wished I had more than one copy to spare so I could give one to each of them.

My family were anxious to get copies of my book, too, but I didn't know how long the postal strike was going to last. Then I had an idea. I drove to Knock Airport and asked some passengers who were travelling on the Liverpool flight if they would carry the small box of books and deliver them to my sister who would meet them at the other end. A woman I approached refused to carry the box, but the group of golfers that were returning home to Liverpool were only too happy to oblige.

The box contained a copy of *Marie's Voice* for my mother and six brothers and sisters and also in the box was a copy for Dr. Kidd, which Maureen promised to post on to her.

Then I had to get out into the world and promote the book. Overnight I switch from amateur writer to actress; from introvert to extrovert. Unless you're a celebrity who wallows in the limelight, I think most writers feel a bit overwhelmed at what's ahead of them. It was important to tell our story, and I owed it to the publishers to do as much promotion as I could.

Unfortunately two weeks after my book was published my lovely sister, Cathy died. It was ironic; she'd been so instrumental in bringing Marie home all those years ago. I cancelled my bookings and after she was buried I had to pick up where I had left off. I was so devastated; I don't know how I did it.

The strange thing was that Iris Brown rang me to do a piece on the book. She'd moved up from feature writer for Woman's Own to

Editor of Woman's Weekly. I thought back to 1972, when Cathy had been frantically polishing the schoolroom furniture in preparation for her visit...I couldn't believe Cathy had died.

35

Feedback

One of the perks of the publicity over the years was the set of professional photographs we were given after the magazine and newspaper shoots. I was always bowled over by the letters and cards I received from all over the world. I remember when I collected the post from the wooden box on my gate and opened a letter from Australia. It contained a photo of me from when I was about 16, but I didn't recognise the clothes I was wearing. I read the letter as I strolled up the path towards the cottage. It was from a lady named Catherine O' Loughlin. She was sitting in the doctor's surgery in Australia browsing through Woman's Weekly when she came across the article about my book. She said she nearly fainted because for a moment she thought the photo was of her. The penny dropped and I knew exactly what she meant because I thought her photo was of me. When she arrived home that day she rung the local Ballyhaunis Police to see if I still lived at the cottage (that's just the kind of thing I would have done!), and then wrote to tell me how incredibly alike we were. I am so glad that she did. I am still in touch with Catherine and we refer to each other as twins.

Erna Naughton

Erna Naughton is another wonderful person I met through the publication of my book. After reading our story, Erna sent me an invitation from the Isle of Man to give a talk at The Kenny/Naughton School in Co Mayo. The School commemorates the lives, works and times of two very distinguished Irish writers, Bill Naughton (Erna's late husband) being one of them. Bill was born in Ballyhaunis and his family moved to Bolton in the north of England when he was four years-old. He was the creator of *Alfie* and *The Family Way*, to name but a few. The school, which takes place over the October bank holiday weekend, consists of lectures, readings, local tours, workshops, new publications, drama and entertainment.

Erna is Austrian and did her State Registered Nurse training in London. She is such a kind, dignified lady; I'm so lucky to have met her that day. Always wanting to do good in the world, Erna is generous to a fault and has helped many charities in both England and Ireland.

For example a friend of mine had a nervous breakdown and spent eight months on a locked hospital ward. I remember the first time I visited, dragging my feet up those stone steps and ringing the bell, wondering what I was about to encounter. I visited often and came to realise that doors are not always locked to keep people in; sometimes too, they are locked to keep people out.

I used to tell Erna about the psychiatric nurses and how they always made me so welcome and did all they could to help my friend recover. I asked her if we could introduce a 'Certificate of Achievement' to the Kenny/Naughton School and present it to a community-based project each year. The next year we had it up and running. The nurses at St Mary's Hospital were presented with the first certificate along with a video recorder for the patients. Another time Erna sent me a cheque for a newly built domestic violence hostel, a cause always close to my heart ever since I'd read Erin Pizzy's book in the 70s, *Scream Quietly or the Neighbours Will Hear*.

I went to stay with Erna in the Isle of Man the following year and have done so almost every year since. She's so entertaining. We laugh and laugh and talk about everything. She bakes gorgeous cakes and there's always one in my bag to bring back on the plane.

36

Just in Case the Worst Happens...

And so the years passed by. The children had always talked about entering higher education, which meant that Patrick was the first to leave the nest.

In August 1997, when he was almost 16, Patrick flew from the West of Ireland to England for a college interview to study for his GCSEs (General Certificate of Secondary Education). I knew he'd have no trouble adjusting to such a change of environment; besides, country life is not for teenagers!

When Patrick rang to say he'd been accepted, I was delighted and arranged to meet him off the plane the following day. I was sad for myself, but he was very bright and a bit of a pack animal and a cheerful soul at that.

I waited with Anna the next day at the airport, occasionally glancing out of the window, expecting the plane to burst through the clouds at any moment. An hour later, when there was still no sign of the aircraft, I began to feel uneasy.

There seemed to be a lot of to-ing and fro-ing at the information desk but no explanations as to why the plane was so late. Then an announcement came over the loudspeaker that due to technical difficulties BA7725 had returned to Manchester Airport, but it hadn't!

A man sitting on the table beside us phoned his sister in Manchester to inform her of the delay. Thanks (or no thanks) to technology, the sister told him Sky News was reporting the real reason the aircraft was late. The plane, with my precious son on board, was circling over the north west of England and had been for almost three hours as it tried to burn off a tank full of fuel in preparation for a crash landing on two wheels because the third wheel had jammed on take-off. Firemen were spraying the runway at Manchester Airport with foam in preparation for a crash landing.

Patrick—on a plane—preparing for a crash landing!

I couldn't imagine what my son was going through. He must have been so scared! Was he sitting beside another passenger or in a seat all alone? Oh, the agony for me, and I was safe on the ground. I also had Anna to consider; she was bewildered.

Doctors I recognised began arriving at the airport, I suppose to be on hand in case we received news of a crash. I started to berate myself. If I'd sent Patrick to school he might not have flown to England looking for an education. Why had I encouraged him to go to college in England when he was so young?

After what seemed like an age, the news broke that the plane had landed in one piece and passengers had been evacuated down the emergency chute. They were booked into a hotel near Manchester airport and would be flying home to Ireland the next day.

My son got the longest hug when he arrived home. He later told us that many attempts were made to loosen the wheel during the flight and at one point the co-pilot came out of the cock-pit and lifted a carpet in an effort to loosen it manually. That didn't work and as time went on the atmosphere became very tense.

The stewards started moving the elderly people to the back of the plane, then told everybody to sit on the floor. The lights were turned out and Patrick said he then realised he was probably going to either be burnt alive or die from a broken neck. He said he wasn't scared, but was concerned we would think he'd died in agony and wanted to get some kind of message to us. He found a 2-inch scrap of paper in his pocket, borrowed a pen from his fellow passenger and scribbled the following message:

'*The Plane 3/8/97*

Just in case the worst happens I want everyone to know I've had a cool life and regret nothing...I owe you all so much. No-one's panicking. Don't worry.

Love Patrick.'

I was so proud of my son. After the way he'd coped when staring death in the face, I felt he was going to be okay in life. Patrick took his place at college and went to Preston University.

Anna followed Patrick's footsteps shortly after, attending the same

Blackpool & Fylde College with the same wonderful English teacher, Linda Dodd. We rented a large apartment in St Anne's on Sea, only a few miles from Blackpool, and which served as a base between England and Ireland for the next few years.

37

Empty Nest

The danger of being an eternal optimist is that I never worried about the future and lived from day to day. Now I was taking a good long look at my life. I had been in Ireland for over ten years and something began to tell me I needed to get out into the world again and do something useful. Lots of Irish people lived in Dublin during the week and travelled home to the country-side at weekends. Even the elderly ladies who used to own my cottage had worked in Dublin all week. It made sense.

I hadn't been very well but I was determined to pick myself up again. After mulling it over, I decided to bite the bullet. What did I have to lose? On Monday morning, I got the coach up to Dublin for the day. I registered for work with a care agency and travelled back home that evening to collect some documents and pack some things.

I loved being on my own and was never lonely. Living in Dublin was going to take some adjusting but I like to think I was an adaptable kind of person who would make the most of things.

I booked a taxi to collect me early Wednesday morning for the 8 o'clock train. I woke to a heavy snowfall and stood admiring the Christmas card scene through the window. The conifers Patrick had planted as a little boy now stood like 20ft ice cream cones. Where have the years gone? I wondered. I secretly hoped the taxi wouldn't be able to get through the roads to my cottage, but this particular driver was kind and reliable and would have dug his way through if he had to. So it was no surprise when I saw him crawl through the gate and up the path to collect me.

The Ticket Collector

George, the ticket collector, was on the train and I smiled at him shyly when he asked how I was. "Don't forget your bag now." He grinned over his shoulder as he moved down the aisle. I laughed softly. George was someone I would never ever forget. I thought back to that lovely summer's day, a few years earlier when I took Patrick and Anna to Westport for the day on the train. It was about an hour away, near where the famous Croagh Patrick stands. I loved this train journey and as soon as we arrived we went into the town. We strolled down the Mall, met up with a friend, had lunch in the Railway Hotel, bought some Irish books and gorgeous hand-knitted sweaters, lit a candle in the local church, and before we knew it was almost time to head home.

I booked a taxi to take us to the railway station and with half an hour to spare, we left our bags in the taxi office and sat on a bench in the afternoon sun.

When we returned, the driver was ready and waiting with our belongings already in the taxi. It wasn't until George, the ticket collector, boarded the train (he was very popular on the Dublin to Westport line) and we were about to depart that I realised my black document case was missing. I was panicking because it contained my land map.

I jumped up and told George that I may have left my case on the platform and quickly followed him off the train to have a look. My eyes scanned the benches but it was nowhere to be seen. I then realised it must still be at the taxi office. I sighed and told George I'd ring the taxi driver when I arrived home. I would ask him if he'd drop my case off at station to be put on the train the next day for me to collect.

"Ah, just hang on now. Don't you be worryin'," he said in that laid back Irish way. "What does the taxi driver look like?"

"Erm, all I know is that he has a beard," I told him, feeling rather foolish. I watched George go into the ticket office and look through the phone book. I glanced at the train which should have been whistling down the track by now and when I turned back to George he was on the phone. Next thing he came out of the ticket office and suggested I go and sit on the train, telling me he wouldn't be long. I could not believe my eyes when he turned and walked out of the station.

The children, with the other passengers, were looking out of the carriage window. I climbed up the steps onto the train and was immediately bombarded with questions. Everybody wanted to know the reason for the delay.

I could see beyond the station wall. I watched George standing at the edge of the road when a few minutes later the taxi pulled up beside him and handed something out of the window. I couldn't believe it.

I was awestruck a minute later when George boarded the train with my black case under his arm and made his way down the aisle towards me, just like the man in the Milk Tray advert. I could hardly speak as I reached out and took the case from him.

The train pulled away and so ended our lovely day in Westport. I couldn't stop smiling. Just couldn't get over what George had done. That was one of those days were you have to pinch yourself and ask, Did that really just happen? And now here was George still collecting tickets on the Dublin train.

The Good Samaritan

I arrived in the city at lunchtime and off I went through the slush up to the agency near O'Connell Street. There was no turning back now; I had to resist the urge to go rushing home to my comfort zone.

I had booked a room in a B&B so it was just a matter of signing in and dropping off my bags before I went to catch the Dart to Blackrock, just a few miles away.

I was on my way to a convent/residential home to look after elderly people. Though I've nothing against the elderly, I wasn't looking forward to the heavy lifting as I still felt weak from having shingles on my head.

Unfortunately, I got off the Dart a stop too soon. When the rain came down in torrents, I sheltered in a shop doorway for a few minutes until I glanced at my watch and realised time was getting on. I stepped out into the pouring rain and asked directions to the convent.

My head felt like it was covered with an ice pack, and it rained so heavily that water was dripping off the bottom of my coat. From since I can remember I cannot bear being cold. When I was little, I used to lie in bed crying as I tore at my chilblained feet. To me, cold is pain.

I walked for a few minutes before I spotted the convent in the distance. I hurried on through the gates and stood there like a drowned rat as I rang the doorbell. The nun who answered the door took me down to the staff room in the basement where I hung up my coat to dry. I was working until nine that night so it had a good eight hours.

I was shown over to one of the three units and introduced to staff I was to work with. They brought towels to rub my soaking hair but I couldn't seem to get warm. Even when my hair dried, my head was still freezing.

My charges were not elderly; they were young women with a learning disability, and I could feel the tears welling up in my eyes. How awful to be looking after these women when my own daughter was in a home.

The staff had learning disability nurses training, (LDN) and it showed. The staff/client ratio added a personal touch and there was a homely atmosphere about the place. I'd never seen such lovely bedrooms and so many possessions. Individuality was stamped on every door. Poor Marie could never live in a place like this. Her screaming and screeching would echo through the building and spoil it for the other residents.

We finished the shift and as typical Irish, they all wanted to make sure I got the Dart into Dublin from the correct stop. I went downstairs for my coat. The room was cold and my coat was still soaking wet.

The staff were waiting on the path for me when I went outside. My coat weighed me down, but I tried to put on a happy face. You would have thought these people had known me for years the way they looked out for me when I was really only a stranger.

We made our way to the station amidst cheerful, chirpy conversation. Two of the group had a two-hour coach ride to and from work and had become avid readers. One of them was reading Maeve Binchy's Tara Road, a book I absolutely loved.

Six of us travelled into Dublin together. We were chatting away and for a moment my thoughts took me to the window. I remember looking beyond the sea of faces reflected in the glass and up towards the heavens. I said a silent prayer. My blood felt like cold water and I wasn't really looking forward to staying at the B&B. It sounds like self-pity but it wasn't. A B&B was going to be so different to my cosy cottage.

Dara, who was sitting beside me, and the only male to work at the convent, brought me out of my trance when he asked where I was staying and I told him.

His face registered surprise as if he suddenly had an idea. "Hey listen," he said, "I'm going to India for six weeks on Sunday so you can stay in my flat if you like."

If I like? If I like?

I looked out of the window and smiled up at the heavens.

38

An Unexpected Pleasure

The job was fantastic. It was such a lovely place to work in. As time went on, the nuns asked me if I would take a permanent post with them. I was tempted but accepting their offer would have meant giving up my weekends in Mayo and I couldn't do that.

I was preparing to go to work one morning when the agency rang me and asked if I would go to a home for retired nuns. I obliged but felt peeved to be at the beck and call of these elderly religious ladies. I was arguing with myself all the way to the home about what I would and wouldn't put up with from them.

I arrived at the home to find a mixture of elderly and middle-aged women. I couldn't help noticing how maternal they were, wanting to know all about my life, my children, if I had any breakfast or not before I left home that morning. They were so kind and caring that all the tension left me. I was happy to be there after all.

One of the staff gave me a cup of coffee. I glanced out of the window as I sipped the hot liquid appreciatively. I remarked to her about the unusual architecture of the buildings with their funnels and high walls.

"Don't you know where you are?" she whispered. I shook my head, "You're in the Magdalene Laundries."

I loved doing night duty at the laundries. I used to sit and talk to some of the women in the dead of night if they couldn't sleep. I would imagine most people reading this are familiar with the well documented stories about the women and how they became virtual prisoners for years. However, when I worked there, the laundries was no longer run by the church but the Eastern Health Board with lay people in senior managerial posts although the nuns from the adjoining convent were very much involved, and lovely nuns they were too! The women were very well looked after but now they were free to go they were too old and institutionalised to venture out into a world they'd spent years being imprisoned from.

I went back to Mayo after I finished my shift that first weekend. I didn't get home until 9.30 in the evening. The cottage was freezing.

I'd left enough turf beside the hearth to get the fire going, so I quickly lit it and the room slowly warmed up. It was heaven getting into my own bed to the soothing sound of silence.

Early the next morning I slipped into my wellies, put my blue duffle on and bagged the turf in the shed. There was a nest in the rafters above, and I could hear weak cries from tiny birds as they huddled close together. The cattle congregated at my back fence as if to say, "Where the bloody hell, have you been?"

There was one person at home who held the threads of my life together and that was Sam. He lived about five miles from me and I met him in a pub one day when I bought our second donkey off him for £10. Over the years he became a kind of father figure to me. As soon as I went back to Mayo, if it wasn't too late, I'd get changed and go straight over to Sam's. We'd sit beside his roaring fire, and I'd tell him all about my days in Dublin. He was always there for me, especially when he heard my sister Cathy had died, and whenever my stack of turf began to dwindle in the shed, there was Sam with his horse and cart stacked with bags of turf to replenish my stock. He always told me I was welcome as the flowers in May. I knew he meant it too.

Stoppin' and Startin'

When I think of all those years I lived in Mayo, always owning a car yet had never driven to Dublin. So even when I bought a new car, I parked it in the nearby town and travelled up and down to Dublin on the train or coach. The journey was long and tiring and working around the bus or train schedules was a pain.

The women in the laundries couldn't understand me travelling all the way to Dublin on public transport when I had a new car. 'Sure can't ye keep stoppin' an' startin'? They asked when I told them I was too nervous to drive all that way. People like that can really put your life into perspective. There was I worrying about the trials and errors of a three hour car journey after all they had been through.

So that's what I did. I followed the ladies' advice and kept stoppin' an' startin' when I felt stressed. Within a few weeks I was not only driving up and down to work, but when Anna came to stay I had the confidence to take her back to England on the ferry. Soon I was doing agency work in England, too.

39

Touched by Love

I kept in touch with Marie, but I hated taking her back after a home visit. It didn't seem right, and deep down I thought she should have been at home. But her future was secure. What did I have to offer her? With my children now so far away, I had the feeling I would eventually settle back in England. I mentioned my future plans to the nurses once or twice and asked them what they thought about me taking Marie back to the UK. I was relieved to see their faces light up. It was in the distant future, of course, but when one of the nurses said they would miss her, that they were her family now, I decided to think long and hard about it. If Marie was happy where she was, then why on earth would I want to uproot her?

Free Spirit

Two years passed, and I seemed to be spending most of my time doing agency work in England. It was such a contrast to the idyllic life of Mayo. Night duty throws your social life out of the window. The phone goes straight to messaging service. The only dressing up I did at night was to put my uniform on for work. The job was not miserable; far from it. One thing I had noticed on nights is the camaraderie amongst the staff. We worked all night and talked with each other for most of it. If a member of staff had a problem, it was shared and for example, if one of us had a doctor's or hospital appointment, we'd all be dying to get to work to find out how they got on.

The nurses used to ask why I hadn't done my nurses training and there were two reasons for that:

1. I liked the hands on approach on the floor. When I started my shift, I would go to each bedroom and check the residents were all warm enough, especially those who couldn't talk. When I found a patient with freezing feet, if they didn't have any bed socks I'd pinch them from someone else's room to put on them.

2. I was too much of a free spirit and didn't think I had the

personality to comply with the rules and regulations set down by the home (or any other place).

At first, some of the staff thought I was an undercover inspector because I was always asking questions about the way things were run. I didn't tell them I wrote a book; judging from reactions over the years, I learnt I might as well have said I was an investigative journalist for 24 Hours or Panorama.

I missed Ireland; it was a country that had been good to me; a country where I'd had the luxury of home educating my children and a country that accepted and cared for Marie.

One night I had just finished reading Jane Eyre (again) and it reminded me so much of my sister Cathy. When I was little, my four sisters and I would top and tail bunk beds: Liz, the baby, slept in a cot. When all was quiet, Cathy would open the bedroom curtain slightly and move the book strategically across her pillow until it caught the light from the street lamp. I lay in the dark shadow-filled room, safe and secure with my sisters, listening to the terrifying ordeal of Jane Eyre, a child not much older than myself, being locked up alone in the red room. The novel remained etched in my mind.

I began to sit near the radiator on my break during the night and would scribble ideas into my notepad. Most of what I read about the Brontë's was written by academics, so I decided to write a book through the eyes of a working class woman, with Jane Eyre as the thread running through the story. Since the Victorian novelist was half Irish, I would set the scene between Liverpool and Ireland. I would make the heroine a care worker who loved Jane Eyre and was inspired by the author. I decided I would call it I Love Charlotte Brontë and dedicate it to my sister, Cathy.

People Who DON'T Judge

I was firmly settled in England in 2005. I rarely visited Marie, yet a day never passed without me thinking about her and wondering how she was. I used to ask myself if the staff realised how much I loved and missed her. One day I received a letter out of the blue.

The letter was from a nurse at Aras Attracta and was filled with news of Marie. She had also enquired after my health. There was not the least hint of the judgement I'd expected, and I found it so moving.

Today I wonder had the nurse not written the letter would I have completely severed my ties with Marie. It had been so long since I'd visited that I was too overwhelmed with guilt and shame to show my face on the unit. The letter let me know I was still welcome and it warmed my heart.

I immediately wrote back to the nurse and thanked her for her very welcome letter. I also told her how aware I was at the lack of contact and thanked her for not pointing this out. I told her I still had Marie's possessions and that I planned on bringing her over for a holiday.

In the back of my mind, I wanted to bring Marie home. She must have felt so abandoned, but bringing her home was such a big operation. Apart from the journey from Ireland, it was finding a suitable place to live. I rented a small house with steep stairs and I had neighbours on either side of me and I wouldn't have expected them to put up with the noise Marie created. There was a lot to think about.

40

The Visit

My friend Sam had died and left me a legacy. That gentle, man who'd been there for me through thick and thin, was still reaching out to me from beyond his grave. I was overwhelmed by his generosity. His inheritance gave me many choices. One of them being that Marie could come home. When I flew to Ireland again to see my solicitor, I also visited Marie. The staff had tears in their eyes when they saw how happy she was to see me. I hugged her hard. She knew how much I loved her. We went out for a few hours and when I took her back to the unit, I told the nurses I would return to Ireland in a few months when the weather was warmer, to take Marie on a holiday. I couldn't wait.

Quality Time Together

On my next visit to Ireland I loaded the car with Marie's favourite things: Joey, the monkey, the baby's buggy that she loved to push, our music videos and DVDs, catalogue, colouring books and pencils. I also took her big container of Duplo bricks, that she spent hours putting together in her own fashion—a house with no roof, a 'twain' with no wheels. I'd rented a holiday cottage near Balla on the west coast for two weeks. Marie and I were going to have some quality time together.

She was always pleased to see me, and no matter how far apart my visits were, she never forgot how to interact with me in a way she did with nobody else. We developed a language and understanding that never faded with time.

Marie and I met the owner of the bungalow in town and trailed him through the countryside to our destination. We weaved around a thousand bends, passing a million cows and sheep on the way. Thank goodness the owner had arranged to meet us because I knew I'd never have found it on my own.

The bungalow accommodated eight people, and we were spoilt for choice; so much room and a long hallway for Marie to push her pram up and down. They even had a baby room with a cot. Marie was going to have a great time.

I unloaded the car, and put on the kettle, the CD player was plugged in and Abba rang through the bungalow. After a cup of tea, I put our clothes away and off we went to do some shopping, tying a carrier bag to gate posts or trees at every bend we came to so we'd be able to find our way back. Marie laughed as I jumped in and out of the car and so did I.

Decisions—Decisions

The next time I saw Marie, I couldn't help noticing how thin she was. She was a slow, finicky eater and must have also missed out on some of her meals when she caught up on her sleep on a chair in the day-room. That morning the staff said she knew I was coming and had kicked off with her screaming, sitting on the floor crashing her head into the door.

This is where the one-to-one staff member is essential for people like Marie, with such severe challenging behaviour. Most of her frustration was due to lack of speech and inability to express herself. I felt sorry for the staff. They wanted my visit to be as pleasant as possible, and they ended up having to sedate Marie to calm her down and stop her from injuring herself. A one-to-one staff member could have distracted Marie and nipped her behaviour in the bud before she got out of control. Their job was almost impossible, and Marie's needs were no longer being met.

We went to Knock Shrine, which was only about eight miles away. It was a place visited by pilgrims and tourists throughout the year. People came from all over the world to see where Our Lady was supposed to have appeared in 1879.

The car park was full of coaches. Different accents drifted our way as groups of people strolled towards the churches. I lifted Marie's wheelchair out of the back of the car, strapped her into it, and off we went. She loved being on the move, but this day she seemed quite sad and unresponsive.

We went into the church and I lit some candles. I loved engaging in this ritual since I was little. I considered myself a Christian, not a Catholic. The masses were meaningless to me and I never attended them, but give me an empty Catholic church and it's my kind of heaven. I put coins in Marie's hand and held it over the slot in the metal box so she could drop them in. A slow smile spread across her face as the coins clanged on top of each other.

I must have lit ten candles that day. The first one was always for my sister, Cathy. I said a special prayer for the rest of the people in my life. I also said a prayer for Marie's future, that I would make the right decision.

We walked around the souvenir shops. I took Marie out of the wheelchair and encouraged her to push it with me. We did a slow walk back into the church grounds and sat on the wall to have something to eat. I was looking in the bag on my knee for the sandwiches. Marie was trying to peer in, making oo and ahh sounds, waiting expectantly to see what I have got when I noticed two cuts on her head. They were nasty gashes; although the bleeding had stopped, they were red raw. I knew it was from bashing her head into the door. Even today the scars remain, leaving tiny bald patches.

I broke the crust from the sandwiches and gave Marie small pieces at a time, making them easy for her to hold. If I gave her the whole sandwich, she would have had difficulty holding the bread together and the filling would have fallen out onto the ground. I chatted away to her, but she stared beyond me into the distance. I wondered what she was thinking. She looked so sad at times. I could feel my eyes welling up. I felt I'd let her down.

I knew she rarely went out because her behaviour was so disruptive and unmanageable, and yet she sat with me as good as gold. Just like always, she liked to be close by. That day, it was as if all the hope had gone from her.

So there we were, lost in our own thoughts, sitting together on the wall. Suddenly her little hand reaches out and touches mine. She took it to her lips and kissed it before putting it back on my leg. I felt overwhelmed at such a show of love. That kiss told me she knows— that she's always known—deep down I will always be there for her. These are precious moments nobody else sees. I turned to meet her eyes, and for a fleeting moment, I felt God looking back at me.

I looked around me and it felt as if I had become one of those visiting mothers I'd seen sitting on benches in the hospital grounds at Taunton all those years ago. Those mothers I'd witnessed visiting their son or daughter, whiling away the time with no particular place to go, maybe trying to accept the impossibility of ever being able to bring them home again. But it wasn't impossible for me.

I didn't feel the sorrow or heartache of giving birth to a disabled child that I was unable to look after the way they did. My heart would never ache as much as theirs. However, I was weighed down with trying to make one of the biggest decisions of my life. I knew it was time; I had to seriously think about bringing Marie home.

Age Appropriate

I had been scouting around for a decent residential place in the UK where Marie could live close by and have lots of family contact. I took a job in one of them to see how it was really run. I was shocked at the poor level of training and the exaggerated status an NVQ 2 (National Vocation Qualification) gave to some very unsuitable people. And staff who, after holding the same position for years, were too set in their ways to welcome ideas from new staff. Intuition and initiatives had been replaced with policies, and most of their personalities had been submerged in the box ticking, chart filling paperwork. On one occasion, the NVQ tutor popped in to do assessments and asked if I'd like to do the Course. "No thanks" I told her blankly. She said if I had problems with writing or spelling, she could audio tape my answers. This surprised me. Surely a decent standard of writing and spelling would be a basic requirement for the course?

Before my NVQ friends start letting my tyres down, I am not talking about people who have a feel for the job. I am talking about people who take jobs as support workers because they can't get work anywhere else; people who are not clever enough to realise how little they know and how much they have to learn. People who are quite unsuitable for that particular kind of work yet do it because there is nothing else.

After several weeks I discovered one of the residents could read. I had seen her sitting in one of the two large lounges holding her handbag and reciting our birthdays with great accuracy. I saw her reading the names on a birthday card and thought she might enjoy visiting the children's library. I never saw her with a book or magazine and offered to buy her some reading material. "What's your favourite book?" I asked and her face immediately lit up and without a moment's hesitation she said, "Goldilocks!"

"Okay!" I said. "I'll..."

"I'm sorry," the support worker beside me interrupted, "but you can't bring that in for her because it's not age appropriate."

Bloody age appropriate! I'd like to know which bright spark invented that outrageous policy. Is it age appropriate to tell her when to go to bed and when to get up? Is it age appropriate to tell her when to have her meals and what to eat? Is it age appropriate to tell her what she can and cannot read?

I visited another home where a young woman had recently been admitted with her collection of dolls. She was given a separate room to her bedroom to store her dolls because collecting dolls at her age was not classed as age appropriate. At least this home, though not able to challenge the policy, had staff that were intelligent enough, confident enough, and caring enough to find a way around it.

Thanks but no thanks.

The only alternative was to look after Marie at home, but did I still have what it took? It seemed a long uncertain road, yet I had to be positive! Didn't things always turn out ok?

I took Marie's hand and squeezed it. She looked at me, and I smiled at her. I told her that one day I was going to bring her back home. I didn't know when, but I knew it wouldn't be too far away. I knew she didn't understand.

Starting the Ball Rolling

I returned to Ireland a few months later and collected the last of my things from storage.

When I visited Marie the nurses told me her behaviour was so unmanageable when she went out, sitting on the ground in the road, screeching, etc., that they no longer took her anywhere. I suspected she sat down in the road because her left leg had gone into spasm and she could no longer walk. Some days she walked better than others, but she could never walk very far.

I made up my mind and took her to the chemist to have her passport photo taken. Passports were now compulsory on all flights in and out of Ireland. After much face pulling and clowning about, I managed to get her to look at the camera.

When I left Marie back on the unit that day, I asked the nurses if I could leave her wheelchair with them because I'd need it for her transport home.

I think they finally believed that Marie was going to be near her family.

41

Taking the Leap

I have to confess: I cried the night before I brought Marie home. I was scared. I knew I had to put my trust in God, and take one day at a time.

It was snowing when I met Anna at Manchester Airport the next morning. I travelled from Liverpool and we met up two hours before the flight. Anna lived quite near the airport. When she finished her degree in English Literature and Language at Manchester University she became so attached to the city she made it her home.

Anna's expression when she laid eyes on Marie's new bright pink luggage set was priceless. I was nervous. After all the trouble I'd gone through to obtain a passport for Marie, filling out the forms, presenting the correct documents at the Post Office counter, even paying the express fee, the post office clerk looked at the photo and deemed it unsuitable. Marie was only showing one ear instead of two. My heart sunk. She lives in Ireland, I told them, but rules were rules and they didn't make them. And now, with no passport, I wasn't sure if Marie would be on the return flight with us.

The nurses had taken Marie back to the chemist to have her photo taken again, without success. What the image showed was a snarling, anti-social woman totally unaware of the effort those around her were making to enable her to return home to her family.

Out of desperation, I asked the nurses to obtain a letter of identity from the   Irish Police and also to get the police to sign the back of Marie's photo. Had it been any other country, my request would have been futile, but the Irish will find a way around anything. I felt the nurses and police and anybody else involved, would do all they could to help us.

The Director of Services rang me a week later to let me know that, two nurses had obtained the signed letter and photo and these items were locked away in the safe. I was so appreciative. I asked her if they'd obtained many letters like that from the Police. "It's never been done before" she answered. Oh my God, I'd thought, I hope it works.

We spent the night in a local hotel and collected Marie at two o'clock the next day. How could I thank the people who gave her a home for all those years; gave her the birthday and Christmas presents and the parties? One thing was for sure—they were delighted Marie was going home.

I was gently warned how much Marie had deteriorated and how difficult her behaviour had become. The nursing officer doubted I'd get her up the steps of the plane. He suggested if she started her screeching at the airport to get her a cup of tea and a plain biscuit.

I signed the discharge papers and Marie slipped her hand into mine and Anna's. We said goodbye and left.

We stayed another night in the hotel and left for the airport very early the next morning. The nurses had given me the official letter and signed photo from the Irish Police, and I just had to keep my fingers crossed they would accept it when we arrived at the airport. If they refused, we'd have a long trek on the coach up to Dublin to travel as foot passengers on the overnight ferry. I shivered at the thought.

The ground was still covered in snow. We left the hired car in front of the airport entrance as arranged and hurried in through the doors.

Standing in the airport with my two daughters was surreal.

I hovered around the check-in desk waiting to get this final ordeal over with. As soon as it opened, I put the luggage on the conveyor belt. Anna and I handed over our passports. The operator checked them over and handed them back. Then I took Marie's letter out of the envelope and acted as though it was the most natural thing in the world when I handed it over for her to read. I bit the inside of my cheek as I stood watching the operator scan the letter, searching her face for a sign of disapproval. She looked up at me.

"Oh, that's fine!" she smiled and handed it back. "Have a good flight."

I turned to Anna and sighed with relief. At last I could relax.

We were starving, so we went to the café for some breakfast, the three of us sitting together. It felt good.

We left the departure lounge earlier than the other passengers and wheeled Marie out to the plane. She was a little angel and took everything in her stride. I must have been beaming like a Cheshire cat when we reached the aircraft and the steward took her wheelchair to put in the hold. Marie was definitely coming home.

I watched her hold onto Anna's hand and climb one slow step at a time...up...up...up...and through the narrow doorway for our journey home.

The propeller swished and we held hands as the stewards went around slamming the overhead lockers closed. There was something quite final about this journey in December 2007; so many of my Irish friends had died. I looked out across the snowy fields and thought about Sam and how good he'd been to me and how he'd made all this possible. There'd be no more chats around the turf fire with him on those cold winter nights. No more trips into town for a meal on market day. I had very mixed emotions as we flew into the clouds leaving the bogs of Mayo behind—so much sadness, but there was also plenty to look forward to.

Part Five

42

Home Sweet Home

When we arrived in Manchester, Patrick was there to meet us off the plane and we all drove home in his van.

Marie, Patrick, Anna and I spent Christmas together just like old times. She was the same old Marie, and now that I'd taken the leap, having her at home was the most natural thing in the world.

The first practicality was our sleeping arrangements. Marie had always hated being alone. After all those years of living on the unit, she had never settled at night. She still screamed and screeched at the least thing. Marie's notes stated that she woke at 5 a.m., screeched if she wasn't seen to immediately, and then caught up on sleep on chair in day-room during the day.

There was no way I could leave Marie to sleep in a room on her own, at least until she became accustomed to her new environment. She couldn't bear having the door closed, nor could I place a nursery gate in the doorway—she'd have panicked and ripped it off its hinges. I couldn't risk her wandering out of her room at night and falling down the stairs. If I was going to look after her at home, I needed to make sure I had a decent night's sleep. There was nothing for it but to let her sleep with me until she developed a sleeping pattern.

She lapped up my attention. We'd go to bed at ten o' clock and she would lie beside me as I read, and pretty soon she would be fast asleep and not wake up until eight the next morning. I imagined that uninterrupted sleep had to be doing her some good.

Marie was 5 foot-tall and weighed seven stone. Her appetite was so poor, a nurse had handed me vitamin medicine and drinks to supplement her meals, which she hated. She always had trouble swallowing and choked easily, so I had to make sure her food was chopped up. I gradually introduced new foods, and Marie seemed to have difficulty with the texture rather than the taste, however, pretty soon she was eating everything.

She loved egg custards but couldn't hold them, and like most crumbly food, she ate from a dish, with a spoon. On a Saturday night she had fish & chips on her special beany lap-tray, in front of the

TV. She was so pleased and grateful, repeatedly saying, "Banchyou" whenever I gave her a meal or a treat, but the pleasure was all mine. She was a joy to be with.

When I took her for new clothes, I bought her seven beautifully coloured velvet tracksuits, one for each day. The suits were too long in the leg, so I took them to a dressmaker to have them shortened. She looked lovely in the outfits, but outgrew them within two months as she slowly gained weight.

Noo Soos

People complain about our NHS, (National Health Service) but I have no complaints. In those first few months we tapped into many of their services. Almost immediately Marie came home, I requested a fitting for support boots to be specially made. When the appointment came through, I took Marie to the local hospital for a foot measurement and to select the boots we liked. I flicked through the catalogue, spoilt for choice with so many different styles. When I showed the shoes to Marie she was unable to show any preference. Any "noo-soos" would bring a smile to her face. She is allowed two pairs a year and up to date, she's had blue and black leather boots, white trainer-boots, and oh, eat your hearts out, my very tentative suggestion of black patent leather was met with approval and there were lots of oos and ahhs the day the box arrived with the gorgeous black patent boots inside.

We moved to a bigger house which had three floors and three bathrooms and plenty of room for support workers to stay. Marie had a huge bedroom, which I temporarily slept in (again) but this time she had two single beds in her room. I slept in there for about a month until she got her bearings, and then I moved next door into my own gorgeous room.

One of the reasons Marie settled in bed was because I used blankets and sheets to tuck her in. If she had a quilt that fell off during the night, she wouldn't be able to retrieve it and cover herself up properly. The blankets made her feel safe and snug.

I was quite strict with the bedtime routine and encouraged Marie to stay in her bedroom after I put her to bed. Had she refused to stay in bed, she could sit on her bedside chair, but Marie liked her comforts too much, and preferred her warm cosy bed.

Each morning, she would wake at about seven and come looking for me. I would ask her to go back to bed, which she usually did and when I was ready I went into her bedroom and lavished her with praise for waiting so patiently.

Direct Payments

I thought the only day-care facility for people with a learning disability was the traditional adult day centre, but there was now another option, introduced in 1996, called Direct Payments. This Direct Payment option allowed disabled people to employ their own support worker for the amount of hours they would normally spend at the day centre. It also gave disabled people control over how and where they spend their time. Marie's needs were assessed and she was given the finances for 18 hours support a week.

We were also offered 21 days' annual respite, which would allow me to have three weeks break every year, again with the option of Direct Payments. This meant I could either employ someone to stay at home with Marie, or opt for 21 days residential care provided by the Social Services. Then Jan, our social worker, put in a request for an extra seven days and we got it.

I opted for respite at home for the foreseeable future to give Marie time to settle down. Respite is such a valuable support system. For anybody reading this who feels guilty about using respite, you mustn't. If you don't have these breaks and take care of yourself how can you take care of the rest of the family? Your family rely on you. The person you care for is able to remain at home because of you. Be good to yourself and don't let anybody make you feel bad about something they don't understand.

Up until this time, I had paid privately for agency support workers. The support enabled me to catch up on my social life. Now, with the allocated Direct Payment funds, I spread the 18 hours a week over three six-hour days on a Monday, Wednesday and Friday, and I employed a young woman named Melanie to be Marie's support worker.

Contentment

We settled down to a pleasant life and Marie came on leaps and bounds. She loved being at home, and everybody who came to our house fell in love with her. We all worked together and managed her challenging behaviour in the same way. The screeching and screaming stopped, because of the one-to-one relationship she had with an adult.

I took her out in her wheelchair every morning and usually spent the afternoons at home. I left my book, *I Love Charlotte Brontë*, to ferment in the drawer for a few years. Now that Marie was settled at home, I began to rewrite it.

My office was a peaceful place. I didn't answer the door and I didn't read much because when I wasn't writing on my computer or scribbling in my pad, I was writing in my head.

Marie and I sat in the attic listening to Enya—she with her colouring book and pencils and me with a million ideas running through my head. I lost myself in *I Love Charlotte Brontë* and even though the book was fictional, I brought snippets of the friends I'd loved and lost back to life.

I was far more confident and familiar with the publishing world when I wrote, *I Love Charlotte Bronte*. I knew exactly what I wanted even down to the cover. But it was also a different publishing world. The market was saturated with writers. Nowadays so many people work from home and there are more opportunities to work on that novel. Publishers no longer had in-house readers and were far more unreachable. I realised the only way I'd have full control over my work would be to publish it myself. I had to work twice as hard because I didn't have a team of professionals behind me but I'm glad I went down that route. There used to be a lot of snobbery towards self publishing but it's becoming more acceptable as people are taking control over their own work. One of my proudest moments was visiting Haworth and seeing *I Love Charlotte Brontë* on the shelf in the Bronte Parsonage Museum Bookshop. You should have seen the smile on my face.

43

In the Event of an Emergency, Don't Ring Us

Marie had been living happily at home for about two years when I went to bed on this particular night at around eleven-thirty and woke at one in the morning with pains in my chest. I lay there for an hour thinking I had indigestion and although it didn't get any worse, it didn't get any better. Half an hour later I decided to go downstairs and take my blood pressure. It was extremely high and by this time my mouth was starting to fill with saliva, so much so that I had to sit holding a bowl so I could keep emptying my bloated cheeks every few seconds. I didn't know what was wrong. I began to feel scared and thought I should go to the hospital.

Marie was sleeping soundly. I sat in the sitting-room for a few minutes trying to think of the best way to handle the situation. If I rung for an ambulance, they'd never let Marie go with me—and she would be taken into emergency care. I couldn't let that happen.

I slowly walked upstairs, got dressed and then woke Marie out of her deep sleep. Almost three in the morning on the last week of November is not the time to put on your clothes to go out. Marie will do anything for me and sat quietly whilst I dressed her.

Part of me was in shock. How much easier if this was happening during the day. I could have picked up the phone and rung a number of people? That night I felt we were the only two people in the world.

We slowly walked downstairs and I wrapped Marie in my three quarter padded coat which hung well below her knee, and then rang for a taxi. The taxi came almost immediately, and I was still emptying my mouth into the bowl when we went out into the cold. Marie linked her arm through mine as we carefully walked down the steps and got into the cab. I had my cash card and two mobile phones in my pocket. I asked the driver to stop at a cash point. Although I had a little money on me, I wanted to withdraw more cash to give to the agency staff when they came to collect Marie from the hospital.

We must have looked pathetic when we stepped out of the taxi and crossed the forecourt slowly making our way into A & E. Marie, in a coat three sizes too big and me holding the bowl to my mouth.

The nurses quickly escorted us to a side-room where I lay down on a trolley and Marie sat on a chair beside me. I apologised for bringing her, explaining that I was about to contact the agency to come and take her back home. Melanie, our eighteen-hour-a week Godsend, was off duty, enjoying time with her own children.

In between tests, I rang the agency I used for Marie's respite but the weekend on-call was not answering the phone. Half an hour passed, then one hour, then two, and still no answer. The nurse gave me aspirin and an injection in my stomach. My blood was then taken to see if I'd had a heart attack. A doctor told me I would have to remain in hospital until the results came back early evening.

The A & E sister asked several times if she could contact my son or daughter, but I told her "Only if I died." Anna was on a weekend course in a hotel with her counsellor colleagues. She had rung me the previous day to let me know her phone would be switched off and left in her room, just in case I was worried if I tried to ring her and got no answer. Patrick was working in Bristol and there was no way I wanted him jumping in a car and dashing up the motorway.

By ten o' clock the agency was still not answering the phone and I had to go for an x-ray. The emergency ward sister approached me again asking if I'd like her to ring the duty social worker. I knew she meant to take Marie into emergency-care so I said no, that I was sorting Marie's care out myself.

The staff treated us with such kindness. They knew I was doing my best to arrange cover for Marie and didn't put any pressure on me.

The nurse accompanied us to the x-ray Dept. I was attached to a mobile drip and the wonderful radiographer stood holding Marie's hand behind the screen as my chest was x-rayed.

My symptoms were beginning to clear. My blood pressure was down, and I no longer needed a bowl, but I couldn't relax because I was still trying to get through to the agency. By eleven, a nurse came to admit me to the day-ward and told me it was illegal to take Marie in with me. I looked at poor Marie and realised, with still no sign of any agency support for her, I had no choice but to ring Melanie.

When I was admitted to the day-ward, I assured the ward-sister Marie's support worker was on her way to collect her, so she broke the hospital rule and let me take Marie into the ward with me. Melanie arrived soon after with her son and daughter, Aaron and Becky, and took Marie home in a taxi.

Melanie continued to ring the agency, and when the phone was eventually picked up, (after ringing for eleven hours) the on-call staff member told Melanie they had no staff-cover for Marie and that because Marie was not contracted to their agency they were not responsible for her.

My results came back clear at six o' clock. I was free to go. The nurse gave me a spray to use under my tongue just in case the symptoms reoccurred. They never did.

When I arrived at the house, Melanie stepped into the taxi that I stepped out of. It had been a long eventful day and I was glad to be home again.

My experience that day demonstrated how the best laid plans can go astray. I had opted for respite care at home. It had been so successful that my annual weekend visit to Erna had continued— I'd been to the Isle of Man twice since Marie had come home. The agency staff (usually the same woman) had slept in the spare bed in Marie's room, which enabled her (agency staff) to have a good night's sleep, knowing that Marie was nearby and safe.

No matter how much you scrutinise an agency, their strength and reputation is built on how supportive they are in a crisis. The time and energy I spent building up a support system with this particular agency, was disheartening. I had to start the whole process all over again.

After the dust settled I wrote to the Director of Nursing at the Royal Liverpool Hospital and told him about my emergency visit. I don't know how often a parent turns up at A & E in the early hours of the morning with a severely disabled daughter in tow. I told the Director how appreciative I was of the treatment Marie and I received from the hospital staff, and asked him to thank them. When I received a reply a few weeks later, I discovered the letter I wrote to him had been copied and sent to 12 different departments in the hospital.

44

Footloose and Fancy-Free

I let Christmas come and go, and in early January, 2009 after much searching, I phoned another agency that specialised with clients with learning disability. I told them what had happened at the hospital and how let down I felt by the previous agency I had used. I explained how I needed backup in an emergency and that I never wanted a repeat of our hospital experience. They were aghast that such a thing could have happened and assured me they'd never let me down. That was good enough for me.

The respite girl—we'll call her Agency Girl—was introduced and shown around the house. She then came to spend time with Marie and me, Marie and Melanie, and Marie alone. She spent the night, and I showed her the routine, and the following morning she got Marie up and dressed without any problem. I felt so happy to have found this agency and I crossed my fingers for the future.

I was aiming to spend two nights in Manchester on Anna's birthday. Melanie would cover the one day I was away. Agency girl would arrive at four in the afternoon to relieve Melanie, stay the night and swap over at ten in the morning.

Juggle Juggle, Toil, and Trouble

As my short break approached, Agency Girl was quite familiar with the routine. She sat with Marie when I visited Linda McDermott's BBC Radio Merseyside's Late Night Live radio programme to talk about my book, *I Love Charlotte Brontë*. Linda McDermott is a brilliant broadcaster and an exceptionally gifted journalist. She's one of the cleverest people I have ever had the pleasure of meeting. It came as no surprise last year when she was the second—ever female president of the Liverpool Press Club in its 128 year history. I very rarely went out at night and to be in her company was a privilege.

So the day came for me to set off for Manchester. I'd wanted to avoid the heavy traffic, but Agency Girl arrived half an hour late, just as a snow storm descended in the North West. By the time I reached the motorway, I was driving through a blizzard that almost stopped the traffic as it covered the lane markings.

I was happy to leave Marie in her comfort zone with a woman she'd taken to without any hesitation. Marie's file, which I painstakingly put together, covered anything and everything that could possibly go wrong and how we responded to any challenging behaviour Marie might present. Patrick and Anna's cell numbers were also included with mine in case of an emergency.

I rang Agency Girl from Anna's to check that all was well. I rang the next morning as Melanie was about to relieve Agency Girl so I could speak to them both. Everything was fine.

At last I could relax with the satisfaction I had achieved a balance. The future looked good. These breaks were important to my health and well being, and would give me a lot to look forward to.

I am a home bird at heart. There's nothing I like more than curling up with a good book, but I knew it was important to get out of the house and mix with people. The success of Agency Girl would now afford me special time to go places with Anna and Patrick or friends—places Marie would not enjoy visiting.

The next morning, just after nine, Anna set off for work. I was gathering my things together and looking forward to seeing Marie. I arranged to ring Anna when I was about to leave her flat and was brewing a coffee when my phone rang. It was Melanie.

"Hello Melanie! You're at the house very early" I said, "is everything ok?"

And she said, "Michelle, you need to come home right away, the police have been at the house and there was a different agency-worker sitting here this morning when I arrived. But Marie's ok."

My heart went bumpty-bumpty-bump.

As soon as Melanie clicked off my phone, I rang the agency. They confirmed police were called to Marie. I asked why nobody had contacted me. The agency manager couldn't apologise enough. I told him I felt too numb to talk and would ring him when I arrived home. I threw my things in the car, got some petrol, and drove home. I was there in forty minutes.

The scene I was met with gave no indication of the drama that had unfolded whilst I was away. There was Marie sitting quietly at the dining table with her colouring book and pencils, and poor Melanie, involved in yet another of our dramas, gave me an "I just cannot believe it" look.

Melanie told me that Agency Girl had called her just after eight, that morning, telling her she'd better get to our house quick because she (Agency Girl) was no longer at the house with Marie. With a justified sense of alarm, Melanie called a taxi, dropped her children off early at the nursery, and went to my house. On arrival, the front door was wide open, and a stranger was sitting with Marie. The woman told Melanie the police had been at the house when she arrived at half past midnight to relieve Agency Girl of her shift. Agency Girl had been asked to remain at the house all night to make it easier for both new staff member and Marie but had refused and had wanted to go home.

I picked up the phone and rang the agency.

I was told that when Agency Girl put Marie to bed just after ten o' clock, Marie started screeching because she hadn't wanted to go to bed. Agency Girl then rang the on call agency staff manager, and told him Marie was being difficult, and she (Agency Girl) did not want to stay on the shift. The on call agency staff manager told Agency Girl to explain to Marie that she had to go to bed. If Agency Girl had any more concerns about Marie's behaviour she was told to ring the on-call back. Agency Girl rang the on-call staff member back ten minutes later. She told him she was afraid Marie was going to hurt her. The on call staff member told Agency Girl if she felt Marie was a threat, to dial 999. And that's what she did.

The police went straight to the house, more than likely expecting an altercation with some strapping middle-aged woman, only to find 5-foot Marie sitting on the sofa unaware of the developing situation. The police sat with Agency Girl (to protect her from Marie) for one-and-a-half hours until a staff replacement could be found and then they drove Agency Girl home. Yes, that's what I said—the police drove Agency Girl home.

After the weekend, I went with Marie to the Police Station to ask for a copy of the incident report. The police woman behind the desk said that due to data protection they were not allowed to discuss the incident with me. Even though police had been in my house, they had been there to protect Agency Girl.

"From her?" I asked the policewoman, indicating Marie sitting quietly in her wheelchair. The officer opened her mouth in surprise and told me to wait whilst she tried to get some information. She returned a minute later and said that no police report had been made because when the police arrived at my house Marie hadn't appeared to be a threat.

Here We Go Again

It was goodbye to another agency and back to the drawing board. What are parents supposed to do when they find themselves in these predicaments? It would be too easy (and cruel) to say, oh, this isn't working, she needs to go into care. But why should she? It was the support services I found difficult to cope with, not Marie. Why should Marie be deprived from living at home because of a failure in the support system? And why on earth hadn't the agency staff contacted me after the police had been called? It just didn't make any sense. My thoughts turned to people in 'independent living' with no family to speak up for them. How does anybody know what goes on?

The only thing I could do to try and resolve the matter was to ring the Care Quality Commission (CQC) to discuss my concerns. I explained the situation to the lady who took my call and she told me she would pass on my details to an inspector who would ring me within the next couple of days. Two weeks went by and no call from them. I rang again on the third week to remind them. Two days later an inspector phoned me. The caller ID was a local number and I asked if she had an office nearby but she told me she worked from home. (What a great job!) I asked her why it had taken her so long to ring me and she said she'd thought the complaint had been dealt with satisfactorily. (Hey? Did I just hear right?) She said after speaking with the Agency she had come to the conclusion that Marie's disturbing outburst had been the result of having to share her bedroom with Agency Girl. She said the poor thing (Marie) must have been embarrassed and resentful at the lack of privacy with someone else sleeping in her bedroom.

Yeah, right, now why didn't I think of that?

45

Getting the Balance Right

Despite the problems I had finding suitable overnight respite cover, Marie had great support workers during the day. They clearly enjoy spending time with Marie because, unlike some of their clients whom they collect at their front doors, if the weather is cold, they can support Marie at home. However, I was beginning to hear stories from support workers about how when they met up with their clients they had nowhere to go, often whiling away the hours in a café or pub to avoid walking around in the cold. I found these reports quite upsetting and wrote to Jo Anderson at Liverpool City Council, asking if it would be possible for people who opted for Direct Payments to still have access to day care centres. It made sense to me since the social services were always complaining how underused the day centres are. I told Mr Anderson that disabled people, like my daughter, needed a base and somewhere to go with their support worker for a hot drink and a warm during the long winter months. I am happy to say my request was granted and Marie now accesses the local adult day centre as a drop-in, for three afternoons a week, accompanied by her support worker.

Positives and Negatives

Marie has been at home for almost five years, and, after much trial and error, I think we finally have the balance right. So, life is happy and peaceful and hard. Like all special needs families, as we adapt to the constant assessments and changing categorisations of our sons and daughters, we grasp at support when times get tough at home. For us, as for most, there are no more Dr. Kidd's to consult when we're struggling to cope with a certain aspect of challenging behaviour. We just whistle in the dark and hope for the best.

We no longer have allocated social workers, and gone are the secure long-term placements where parents could rest with the knowledge that their son or daughter would be cared for in a safe and appropriate environment for the rest of their lives. Today, parents are now doing what they never imagined they'd have to do after their son or daughter has left home for so called "independent" living—due to poor staff training and standards—they are bringing them back home.

With the respite support now reduced to 21 days a year, and for some, no longer entitled to any respite, because they do not fall into the 'substantial' or 'critical' category, it's the family carers that are going to suffer ill health. I believe that within two years there will be an influx of severely disabled people requiring emergency (long term) care because the family carers, who've saved the government thousands, have bled their last drop of blood and have no more to give. What then? Unless there is some forward planning for the construction of community based sheltered apartments where people with a severe learning disability can live with maximum support to cater for their complex needs, there's going to be a huge crisis.

There is Much to be Done

Back in 1988, when we heard the local learning disability hospital was to close, my son, Patrick sat at the dining table with Anna and wrote a letter to the local newspaper which resulted in the following article:

The Lincolnshire Echo

Friday, November 4, 1988

Harmston Hall Hospital—the mentally handicapped unit due to close next year—has received a touching tribute from the seven-year-old brother of a temporary patient.

In a letter to the Echo, young Patrick Daly describes the unit as "The best hospital in the world" and he adds: "I will build a hospital one day when I'm grown up and I will try and find the nurses to help me run it".

Patrick, whose 23-year-old sister Marie has cerebral palsy and a severe mental handicap, is acutely aware of the difference in the hospital, which will close as patients are moved into the community. In his letter he says: "We used to see groups of handicapped people going to the small hospital cafe. Now we don't see anybody because they're all being moved out.

"When my sister goes into the hospital Dr Garry and the nurses understand her best".

Patrick's mum, Michelle Daly, said both he and her five-year-old daughter Anna were aware of the change in the hospital.

"They see people in there on one visit and then they don't see them again. They have noticed how some of the patients are sad", she said.

"At one time there was a big community in the hospital but now people are on their own and looking lost—there is no laughter anymore".

Marie goes into Harmston Hall for short periods of stay, mainly to give her family a holiday break.

"She is living at home with us because of the support we get from Harmston Hall.

"We have used the hospital for 10 years and the nurses understand Marie and know her well.

"I can ring up the hospital in an emergency or when I need a break and Marie goes in for a while. There is that kind of support there. I doubt I could that in an emergency in the community", she said.

"There is the kind of understanding where they will just take Marie in and she enjoys going there for short periods. She knows the nurses and the patients— although they are leaving now.

"When the hospital closes it will be pretty bleak really.

"If the people are trained the way the nurses are—

when looking after people with complex needs, then
Marie will be all right.

"But I feel the people in the community units don't
have that experience. I haven't got the same kind of
confidence in the community scheme", she said.'

I never believed a hospital could meet the needs of children on a permanent basis, but lots of adults enjoyed the community life they provided despite the assumption that living in such an environment robbed people of their dignity and self respect.

Today I wonder why the government allowed hospitals like Stoke Park, in Bristol to get so run down leaving no alternative but to close them. Some of us sighed with relief believing the loss of our family support system on the wards was only temporary. We were conned into believing patients would be moving on to pastures greener—and families would be afforded the same support system in the community that hospitals had provided. We were promised 'community care' but where is the community care and the specialist services we needed? They are practically non-existent.

In Rosa Monckton's BBC Documentary, *When Love is Not Enough* Rosa exposed the battles that families face to get the basic care for their children. We saw how isolated they are, how little help they get, and how exhausted they become in fighting to get what should be given to their children as an absolute right. Rosa says, "There is a lack of commonsense, an absence of compassion and a labyrinthine bureaucracy which is almost impossible to navigate. Initiatives spew out of Whitehall, but none of the money, or the services seem to reach the families who are most in need. There is much to be done".

46

Above and Beyond

So here I am at the end of our story. I hope it's helped other parents and family carers to realise they are not alone. I've been as honest as I can be by talking about the ups and downs of our lives. If I said my life was all sweetness and light I would be doing a disservice to other families who are struggling to get through each day.

Families rely so much on the kindness and integrity of support workers who quite often go above and beyond the call of duty and some of Marie's certainly deserve a mention. Carley Flynn came and sat with Marie one evening so I could go and see Leonard Cohen at the Liverpool Echo Arena. Sandra Harrison came over one Sunday on her day off when my obstinate computer would not let me install a new printer and stayed until she had it up and running. Melanie Seddon took Marie to Asda in a taxi and arrived home with a huge cake with the image of my book, I Love Charlotte Brontë, iced on the top. Ann Rimmer arrived at my house at 8 o'clock on a Sunday morning so I could go down to Radio Merseyside to be interviewed by Maureen Walsh. She also looked after Marie until one o'clock in the morning, when I did a few more guest slots on Linda McDermott's BBC radio Merseyside programme. I used to worry about arriving home too late and didn't want to take advantage of Ann, but one night when I was going out of the front door she called after me: "Don't dare go running out of there at midnight like Cinderella. I'm fine here; you stay out and enjoy yourself." And so I did!

After the disastrous respite trials at home I started to look at the holiday homes for people with severe learning difficulties and found a small home about thirty miles away. First, Marie had the daily visits then the overnight stays, (with her own bedding!) then the weekends and after that, a two-week stay. Marie's challenging behaviour and unsettled nights require a one-to-one round the clock staff. Finding this facility has given me great peace of mind.

I can see that I've always been a square peg trying to fit into a round hole. It must have been difficult at times for my children to have such a rebellious mother; trying to find their way in a world I had tried so desperately to protect them from. Being a parent is difficult. I adored my children and there can't be any doubt in their minds how loved they are but I've made many mistakes from doing what I felt was the best decision at the time. There's no right or wrong, is there? We just have to go with our gut feeling. Sometimes I wish I'd been more conventional and they could have had a more ordinary life. Had a mother who was accepting of everything instead of challenging everything I disagreed with! Yet there's one thing I will never regret and that's bringing them up with Marie; their problem was the mother they had, not the sister they had.

When Anna first returned to England in 2000, I was invited to give a talk to the students in her English class about my book, *Marie's Voice*. The tutor asked Anna what it was like growing up with a disabled sister, and Anna, bless her, replied that when she was little she hadn't known there was anything wrong with Marie; she just thought she had two mothers. I am proud of both my children who've grown into kind caring human beings despite their unconventional life and not because of it. A couple of years ago Anna was featured in the *'Positive Living In the North West' Body Positive magazine*, where she worked as a volunteer with HIV sufferers. This is the piece she wrote.

My Story So Far

Anna Daly

'*I*'m a support worker for women who hear voices and I've done this job for two and a half years. My role is varied and very rewarding. A part of my job is to listen to my clients and empower them. I deal with a lot of distress and challenges. My clients are very important to me and I am grateful to each and every one of them for everything they have taught me.*

I have studied counselling for several years and I'm currently about to finish the first year of my diploma. People have always confided in me and I have never felt the need to repeat what they have said. I have a great interest in human rights and I believe in freedom!

I am honoured to be a part of Body Positive and I admire the work that is achieved there. I chose Body Positive because I think HIV is a very important illness and I know it's difficult to come to terms with. I am grateful to my clients to let me be a part of their experience. I have a lot of empathy for people living with HIV and I'm dedicated to learning more about this subject.

*Although HIV is life changing, the future can be positive. There is a
lot of support available for people living with HIV. I do not judge and
I welcome individuals from all walks of life to come and talk to me in
confidence. I want people to know that support is out there and they
can come to Body Positive for a confidential chat.*

Don't suffer in silence.'

That was certainly true of Anna; you can tell her anything and she
won't repeat a word. She has since obtained her counselling diploma
and continues her volunteering work.

I believe God gave me the strength to look after Marie.
When people pulled the feet from under me, it was He who offered
his outstretched hand and stood me back on the ground again. And
just as each of us is chosen to do a certain task, I am glad I was given
this job. I'm sure when God brought us together he must have had a
twinkle in his eye—and certainly a sense of humour to put two such
strong-willed characters side by side.

Some years ago my visit to Liverpool had coincided with the
Grand National. Driving through the busy traffic on that hot
sunny afternoon, I approached the Picton Clock in Wavertree. I
looked around me nostalgically. The road to the left led to where
my grandmother, Annie had first lived when she came across to
Liverpool from County Mayo.

Across the road to the right was the 'big hospital.' As I neared those
high walls that shout out the world I knew I couldn't drive past it.

I turned down the side road towards the gates and drove on
apprehensively. I didn't know why I kept punishing myself and
returning to this gloomy place. When I approached the entrance I was
shocked at the sight that met my eyes—it had all been pulled to the
ground.

'If stones could speak what stories they'd tell,' I thought sadly.

I looked across to the crumpled remains of what was once the
hospital lodge. I could almost hear the stifled giggles from Liz, John
and Peter when, so many years before, they had marched behind me
through those hospital gates with their collection of old toys tucked
under their arms, passing the porter on the lodge, noses in the air as
if they knew where they were going. They had followed my trail into

the wards for our first tour of inspection!

And months later, having satisfied myself with the conditions, Liz and I had pushed Marie through those same hospital gates in Sara's squeaky old red pram. Feeling like a lamb going to the slaughter I had gone to meet Dr. Rogerson for the first time.

Looking over to where the ward once stood I remembered the day of Alison's case conference a few years later when the 'professionals' had almost fought each other to have their ideas put into practice, even at the risk of the little blind girl's welfare. Shivers ran through me as I once again pictured the knitting nurse wheeling a frail child through the hospital grounds in the snow when she had only been dressed for a summer's day. My heart felt heavy. Memories, memories, so many memories. But now it was gone forever; just a piece of history.

I think of all the people who've helped us over the years. I never saw Sister Henry after the convent closed down, yet I will always be grateful for the day she came onto our nursery floor like a breath of fresh air and gave Marie the freedom she so desperately needed. Then there was Matron at Taunton who offered me a job, and Sister Green who, despite her 'difficult' reputation showed me nothing but kindness: Dr. Prentice, who took the time to help me have Marie transferred, and Dr. Rogerson who took a chance and trusted me by accepting Marie in a hospital hundreds of miles from her home. Marie's mother who took the selfless step of entrusting her daughter into my care and Dr. Kidd who was always there to recharge my batteries whenever they started to go flat; the nurses at Aras Attracta, for all they did for Marie, and my friend Sam, whose love, friendship and generosity enriched both of our lives.

I feel blessed to have shared my life with such a special person and hope I fulfilled the promise I made to Marie to provide her with a loving home where her voice has always been heard loud and clear.

It doesn't seem that long ago when she first pulled me to the floor by my hair. I can still feel her grip on my hand as she dragged her little feet across the polished floors in an effort to walk. Today, as I look back over time, it makes me wonder—had I really taken Marie's hand all those years ago or had she taken mine?

Learning Disability Nursing—now what's that all about?
'Moving towards tomorrow together!'

Over the last 100 hundred years the history of learning disability nursing has been littered with rumour, myth and prejudice:

- There's no future in it
- You are not real nurses; you don't need to be very clever to do it
- You don't need nurses to care for people with a learning disability
- It only happens behind high walls and closed doors
- It's only about 'warehousing' people
- It doesn't take a nurse to care for someone with a learning disability; anyone can do it.

So, what is a learning disability nurse?

He or she is an individual with a passion to ensure people with a learning disability get what you and I take for granted – and that's just an equal chance at life! The learning disability nurse is a highly-skilled individual who has undertaken a university programme leading to both an academic qualification and professional qualification to nurse the individual who has a learning disability.

What do learning disability nurses do?

They work in a range of settings across a lifetime continuum to facilitate lifestyle choices for individuals, their families and significant others. Those settings could be in a large general hospital to ensure a smooth pathway for someone through the scary world of health care (health facilitators). They could be school nurses ensuring the health needs of your child are met effectively in the school day and beyond. They could work in specialist assessment and treatment centres where individuals with a learning disability receive intensive care at a crisis point in their life.

Learning disability nurses work in nursing homes, residential homes and supported living, facilitating a valued lifestyle for the individual that promotes inclusion, rights, choice, and fun.

Learning disability nurses have a unique skill set that if utilised effectively not only bring about real positive change for an individual and their family but upholds the value base of a right to a meaningful fully participative life, not just a service.

Many of you will have come across a learning disability nurse employed in a community nursing team. These teams have different focuses dependent on the county in which you live in, but are there to help with the good and not so good times in the lives of people with a learning disability; their intervention could be at transition, or through a particularly stressful life event.

What don't learning disability nurses do?

They take part in every conceivable aspect of the life of an individual that promotes inclusion.

What do I do?

I began my training as a learning disability nurse in 1979. It was not fashionable to undertake such a programme and at the time was actively discouraged from doing so by the education system.

If I was 18 today I would still make the same career choices. Working with and for people who have a learning disability is a bit like an itch for me; something I'm always reaching to identify; there isn't a week goes by when something doesn't flick my switches about the "how, why, or what" of learning disability nursing!

I moved into nurse education because I needed a bigger audience with which to share my enthusiasm and make a broader impact into the development of services.

At the time of writing, there are 16 universities across the 5 nations who offer learning disability nursing as a separate branch within their menu of opportunities.

Check out: www.positivechoices.org.uk.

Look at some of the celebrations student nurses in learning disability nursing take part in.

~ *Helen Laverty*
Health Lecturer
School of nursing, midwifery & physiotherapy
University of Nottingham

Catherine
Julia Donal

"From nowhere the screams of my 11 year-old son, Tony, pierced the bright sunny afternoon. I turned and he was running toward me, arms outstretched, eyes bulging with terror.

"Mum, Mum, come quick, our Cathy's been run over"

My heart was racing—pounding, as Tony and I ran frantically toward the road where a crowd of people were already gathered. I pushed my way through and couldn't believe what I saw. My little girl—my beautiful little girl, was lying in the middle of the road with blood coming out of her nose and ear. Her leg was bent halfway up her back and her eyes were tightly shut. I thought she was dead.

That terrible feeling of foreboding that I had had all that day had come to light. My nightmare had begun!"

Julia tells the heart-wrenching story of life with Catherine, and how the tragic road accident in 1972, left her 6 year-old daughter with brain damage.

What I Wished I'd Known About Raising a Child With Autism

A Mom and a Psychologist Offer Heartfelt Guidance for the First Five Years

Bobbi Sheahan and Kathy DeOrnellas, PH.D. [Paperback]

I am here to tell you the truth about autism. It isn't always pretty, but sometimes it's beautiful. My name is Bobbi Sheahan. My husband, Ben, and I have four children. From the beginning, Grace, our second-born, was different. Her behaviour ranged from quirky to baffling—and sometimes frightening. When Grace was three, we received confirmation of what we had already figured out through trial and error: Grace has autism. It was because of the three years of "trial and error" that I teamed up with Grace's psychologist, Kathy DeOrnellas, Ph.D., to write "What I Wish I'd Known About Raising a Child With Autism: A Mom and a Psychologist Offer Heartfelt Advice for the First Five Years" (Future Horizons, April 2011). We hope to spare other parents some of the pain, discouragement, and confusion that can accompany the early years of parenting a child who has or may have autism.

I am a lawyer who transitioned to full-time motherhood in my thirties. We wanted a big family, and our first two children, Lucy and Grace, are barely a year apart. When Grace was an infant, she was quiet. So quiet that we began to notice that she didn't babble or make many sounds at all. She didn't cry when you'd expect a baby to cry: not when she got her shots, and not even when she was hurt. Not ever. Not even stitches-to-the-face hurt (twice). She didn't nap, and, as time went by, she made no moves towards speaking or potty training. Frightened by Grace's fearlessness, her ability to defeat childproofing, and her propensity to injure herself, more than one babysitter refused to come back.

Around the age of three, Grace began to speak in precocious bursts: the entire script of a cartoon, complete with voices; her favourite book; all twelve days of Christmas; the whole 23rd Psalm. She didn't make eye contact, and she patrolled the perimeter of the playground instead of playing with other kids. She loved the swings, and she seemed not to understand when she injured other people. Her senses seemed to be completely miscalibrated; her hearing was acute, yet she took an inordinate amount of time to process the speech of others who spoke to her. The not-feeling-pain thing persisted too; I still cringe at the story of the time that Grace grabbed a hot light bulb and didn't respond to the burn, but did cry and cover her ears at my shriek as I pulled her hand from the lamp. Believe it or not, that wasn't the worst light bulb incident; when she was three, Grace ate a light bulb. Well, part of a light bulb. She began eating other things, too, including my anniversary roses.

"Of course it isn't autism," I would say. "She's affectionate. Plus, she's a girl—what are the odds?" (More than 80 percent of those diagnosed with autism are male.) A near-tragedy finally moved us to discover Grace's autism. As I read everything that I could get my hands on, I was shocked to realize that a book like "What I Wish I'd Known About Raising a Child With Autism" didn't already exist. I suggested to Dr. DeOrnellas that we write this book to spare other parents some agony, some confusion, and perhaps some lost time and resources.

What I Wish I'd Known About Raising a Child With Autism is my third book. My first two books, published by Texas Lawyer Press (a division of American Lawyer Media), are reference books for attorneys. When I left my law practice to turn my full attention to my family and my writing, little did I know where that path would lead. For two decades, I used my writing to persuade courts and educate lawyers, but it was in becoming a mother that I truly found my voice, my inspiration, and my life's work. This book is not only the story of my family's journey of discovery, but my love letter to my daughter and my message of hope for parents.

Bobbi Sheahan and Kathy DeOrnellas, Ph.D. are available for interview. Contact Morgan Whatley or Bobbi Sheahan:

media@bobbisheahan.com

Bringing Up a Challenging Child at Home: When Love is Not Enough

Jane Gregory [Paperback]

Chrissy is the oldest of Jane Gregory's three children. She is an engaging, vivacious young woman, with a great sense of fun, and a much-loved sister and daughter. The flip side is that she sometimes exhibits behaviour that other people find very challenging.

It was apparent from an early age that Chrissy had a learning disability but no one could explain what had caused her problems. Then, when she was 22, researchers at Oxford University analysed her DNA using ground-breaking new genetic testing experiments, and found that she had a rare chromosome disorder. She was subsequently diagnosed with autism too.

In her book, *Bringing Up a Challenging Child at Home*, Jane describes life with Chrissy candidly and pragmatically - from the slow, chilling realisation that something was wrong with her 'perfect' baby, to the profound effects on her family. She relates her struggles to cope with Chrissy's bizarre behaviours and her long search for answers to understand the reasons behind her severe unpredictable mood swings. Offering practical advice to other parents, Jane explains how she got effective support and treatment for Chrissy, and how her experiences altered her own perspectives on life. Her story provides professionals as well as parents with a unique insight into what it is like to bring up a complex and challenging child.

'Two years after my book was published, Chrissy left school and moved into a residential care home near us where the staff were good and understood how to communicate with her,' says Jane.

'But things began to deteriorate. The service moved to a different location—the new place was too small for Chrissy and the three other ladies she shared with. Around the same time Chrissy had to change medication. After this and another placement broke down due to inadequate medical support, it was suggested she go into an assessment and treatment unit. We were supportive of this—we just wanted her to be safe. The commissioners wanted to send her to a unit 64 miles away but we used a solicitor to fight for her to go into one nearer her home. She was in a terrible state when she arrived at the unit – she had bald patches from pulling her hair out and was covered in bruises and abrasions from self-inflicted wounds.

It's very distressing to see her when she's like this, but when she does get the right care and support, things can be very different.

Now, Chrissy is more stable and enjoying a much better quality of life, but she is still in the unit after over three years, as there were long delays starting medication changes. The commissioners are doing little to plan her future placement because of a four-year dispute over which area will fund Chrissy's package of care when she leaves.

Despite the involvement of a solicitor, and Local Government and NHS Ombudsmen, the funding dispute is still not resolved, and Commissioners are doing the bare minimum to case manage Chrissy's care.

I've had to involve a solicitor four times now because of problems getting the right care for Chrissy. This isn't how it should be.'

21241753R00169

Printed in Great Britain
by Amazon